THE NEOLIBERAL STATE, RECOGNITION AND INDIGENOUS RIGHTS

NEW PATERNALISM TO NEW IMAGININGS

THE NEOLIBERAL STATE, RECOGNITION AND INDIGENOUS RIGHTS

NEW PATERNALISM TO NEW IMAGININGS

Edited by Deirdre Howard-Wagner, Maria Bargh
and Isabel Altamirano-Jiménez

Australian National University

PRESS

Centre for Aboriginal Economic Policy Research
College of Arts and Social Sciences
The Australian National University, Canberra

RESEARCH MONOGRAPH NO. 40
2018

ANU PRESS

Published by ANU Press
The Australian National University
Acton ACT 2601, Australia
Email: anupress@anu.edu.au

Available to download for free at press.anu.edu.au

ISBN (print): 9781760462208
ISBN (online): 9781760462215

WorldCat (print): 1045423229
WorldCat (online): 1045423071

DOI: 10.22459/CAEPR40.07.2018

Cover design and layout by ANU Press. Cover image: *Gulach* (2006) by Terry Ngamandara Wilson.

Contents

Part 1: The connection between the act of governing, policy and neoliberalism

Part 2: Pendulums and contradictions in neoliberalism governing everything from Indigenous disadvantage to Indigenous economic development in Australia

List of figures

List of tables

List of abbreviations

ABA	Aboriginals Benefit Account
ACE	annual catch entitlement
ACT	Australian Capital Territory
AFN	Assembly of First Nations
AGM	Annual General Meeting
ANU	The Australian National University
APY	Anangu Pitjantjatjara Yankunytjatjara [Lands]
ATSIC	Aboriginal and Torres Strait Islander Commission
BERL	Business and Economic Research Ltd
CAEPR	Centre for Aboriginal Economic Policy Research
CATSI Act	*Corporations (Aboriginal and Torres Strait Islander) Act 2006*
CDC	cashless debit card
CDEP	Community Development Employment Projects
CE	Chief Executive
CEO	chief executive officer
CHIP	Community Housing Infrastructure Program
DCT Act	*Social Security Legislation Amendment (Debit Card Trial) Act 2015* (Cwth)
DSP	Disability Support Pension
FAO	Food and Agriculture Organization
FHRMIRA	*Family Homes on Reserves and Matrimonial Interests or Rights Act 2013* (Canada)
FNPOA	*First Nations Property Ownership Act 2012* (Canada)
FOMA	Federation of Māori Authorities

FPIC	free, prior and informed consent
HRC	Human Rights Committee
HREOC	Human Rights and Equal Opportunity Commission
IAS	Indigenous Advancement Strategy
ICHO	Indigenous Community Housing Organisation
ILO	International Labor Organization
ISQ	Iwi Settlement Quota
ITQ	individual transferable quota
MIO	Mandated Iwi Organisation
MMP	mixed-member proportional
MP	member of parliament
NAFTA	North American Free Trade Agreement
NCA	National Commission of Audit
NDIS	National Disability Insurance Scheme
NGO	non-government organisation
NPARIH	National Partnership Agreement on Remote Indigenous Housing
NPM	new public management
NSW	New South Wales
NT	Northern Territory
NTER	Northern Territory Emergency Response
NWAC	Native Women's Association of Canada
NZIER	New Zealand Institute of Economic Research
OECD	Organisation for Economic Co-operation and Development
OTS	Office of Treaty Settlements
PMC	Australian Government Department of the Prime Minister and Cabinet
Qld	Queensland
QMS	Quota Management System
RFSC report	*Resilient families, strong communities: A roadmap for regional and remote Aboriginal communities* report

RTA legislation	*Residential Tenancies Act 1997* legislation
SA	South Australia
SIHIP	Strategic Indigenous Housing and Infrastructure Program
TAC	total allowable catch
UK	United Kingdom
UN	United Nations
UNDRIP	United Nations Declaration on the Rights of Indigenous Peoples
USA	United States of America
WA	Western Australia
Yawuru RNTBC	Yawuru Native Title Holders Aboriginal Corporation

Contributors

Isabel Altamirano-Jiménez is Zapotec from the Tehuantepec Isthmus, Oaxaca, Mexico. She is an Associate Professor of Political Science and Canada Research Chair in Comparative Indigenous Feminist Studies at the University of Alberta, Canada. Her research explores how the impact of resource extraction is embodied and how the reclamation and revitalisation of indigenous women's knowledge and people's fundamental human rights over their bodies intersect with present-day economic and environmental challenges. Among her recent books are *Indigenous encounters with neoliberalism: Place, women, and the environment in Canada and Mexico* (2013, UBC Press) and *Living on the land: Indigenous women's understandings of place*, edited with Nathalie Kermoal (2016, AU Press).

Maria Bargh is from the Te Arawa/Ngāti Awa tribes and is Head of School and Senior Lecturer in Te Kawa a Māui/School of Māori Studies, Victoria University of Wellington. Her research interests focus on Māori politics, including constitutional change and Māori representation, voting in local and general elections, and the Māori economy including hidden and diverse economies. She also researches on matters related to Māori resources, such as freshwater, mining and renewable energy.

Avril Bell is an Associate Professor in Sociology at the University of Auckland, New Zealand. Her research is focused particularly on Aotearoa/New Zealand and centres on issues of settler colonialism, indigenous–settler relations and possibilities for decolonisation. She is the author of *Relating Indigenous and settler identities: Beyond domination* (2014, Palgrave Macmillan) and many journal articles and book chapters on these topics.

Shelley Bielefeld is the Inaugural Braithwaite Research Fellow at the RegNet School of Regulation and Global Governance at The Australian National University (ANU). Her research concerns social justice issues affecting Australia's First Peoples, including problems arising from the Northern Territory Intervention begun in 2007, the Stronger Futures framework begun in 2012, and scrutiny of welfare reform measures. Her work on Indigenous law and policy law is influenced by the concerns expressed by people subject to those strictures. Dr Bielefeld recently commenced an appointment as an Australian Research Council Discovery Early Career Researcher Award (ARC DECRA) Fellow at the School of Law at Griffith University.

Cathryn Eatock is a Gayiri/Badtjala woman, with ancestral connections to the lands of central Queensland, Australia. Cathryn is a PhD Candidate within the Department of Sociology and Social Policy at the University of Sydney, following her completion of a Master in Human Rights. Cathryn is also the Chairperson of the Indigenous Peoples Organisation, a coalition of Aboriginal and Torres Strait Islander organisations and individuals in Australia that advocates for Indigenous rights, nationally and at the United Nations.

Daphne Habibis is an Associate Professor of Sociology in the School of Social Sciences, and former Deputy Director of the Institute for the Study of Social Change at the University of Tasmania. The common thread throughout her career has been a concern with social inequality, with the last decade focusing on social housing and Indigenous issues, including race relations and remote Indigenous housing. She has over 60 publications and is co-author of *Social inequality in Australia: Discourses, realities and futures* (2009, Oxford Unversity Press), as well as Australia's best-selling sociology textbook *Sociology* (2016, 6th edition, Pearson). Daphne combines theoretical, scholarly work with applied policy analysis. Her recent work examined how housing provision to remote communities is at the intersection between Aboriginal aspirations for self-determination and the state's agenda of active citizenship for Aboriginal people. Earlier work included developing a research agenda on kindness as an ethical emotion that extends beyond the interpersonal to institutional domains. Current projects include an Australian Housing and Urban Research Institute study on how housing is implicated in improving outcomes for women and children in situations of family violence, and an ARC Linkage grant that asks Aboriginal people for their views on settler Australian people and culture.

Deirdre Howard-Wagner is sociologist and socio-legal scholar and Fellow in the Centre for Aboriginal Economic Policy Research (CAEPR). She was formerly an ARC DECRA Fellow in the Department of Sociology and Social Policy at the University of Sydney. Her research on neoliberalism, state governmentality and Aboriginal rights is having great impact both internationally and nationally. Her publications are historical and comparative in nature. Her ARC DECRA project, titled 'Indigenous success in addressing Indigenous disadvantage and improving Indigenous wellbeing', built on this work but took it in new directions. Her current research has an urban focus. She currently holds a three-year ANU Futures Scheme Award to develop urban Indigenous-driven development as a major area of research at ANU and an ARC Discovery titled, 'Reconfiguring new public management to recognise the distinctive role of Aboriginal organisations and rights of Indigenous peoples in social service delivery'.

Louise Humpage is an Associate Professor in Sociology at the University of Auckland, New Zealand. She has written widely in the areas of indigenous affairs policy and welfare reform in both New Zealand and Australia. She has further research interests in refugee policy/adaptation and public attitudes to the welfare state, with the latter culminating in *Policy change, public attitudes and social citizenship: Does neoliberalism matter?* (2015, Policy Press).

Fiona McCormack is a senior lecturer and convenor of the Anthropology program at the University of Waikato, New Zealand. Her research interests include economic and environmental anthropology, marine social science, indigeneity and treaty claims. Her field sites include Aotearoa/New Zealand, Hawai'i, Iceland and Ireland. Some of her recent publications include: *Private oceans: The enclosure and marketisation of the seas* (2017, Pluto Press); 'Indigenous claims: Hearings, settlements, and neoliberal silencing' (*PoLAR: Political and Legal Anthropology Review*, 39(2):226–43, 2017); and 'Sustainability in New Zealand's quota management system: A convenient story' (*Marine Policy*, 80:35–46, 2017).

Dominic O'Sullivan is Associate Professor of Political Science at Charles Sturt University. He is a member of the Te Rarawa and Ngāti Kahu *iwi* of New Zealand. He has more than 55 publications including six books. His most recent, *Indigeneity: A politics of potential: Australia, Fiji and New Zealand*, was published by Policy Press in 2017.

Alexander Page is a non-Indigenous researcher and PhD Candidate in Sociology at the University of Sydney, located on lands of the Gadigal clan of the Eora Nation. His thesis, titled 'Indigenous agency, service delivery, and settler colonial governance in the advancement era', involves working with multiple Aboriginal community organisations in Greater Western Sydney to explore the resistance and negotiation of Indigenous sector employees to various levels of Australian Government following the introduction of the Commonwealth's Indigenous Advancement Strategy policy (2014 to present).

Will Sanders has been analysing aspects of Australian Indigenous affairs since the 1980s. He has been on staff at the ANU CAEPR since 1993, in which capacity he related closely to Aboriginal and Torres Strait Islander Commission staff and elected members until 2004–05.

Karen Soldatic is an ARC DECRA Fellow (2016–19) at the Institute for Culture and Society, Western Sydney University. This fellowship, 'Disability income reform and regional Australia: The Indigenous experience', draws on Karen's extensive research and policy expertise on global welfare regimes and the impact of state regimes on the lived experience of disability.

Patrick Sullivan is a political anthropologist whose work for Aboriginal organisations since the early 1980s has involved practical research and advice on issues of land use and distribution, community control of community development, and governance institutions at the local and regional levels. For two separate periods, he was the Senior Anthropologist for the Kimberley Land Council, formulating anthropological and policy advice on local, national and international projects, as well as native title cases. From 2002 to 2012, he was a Research Fellow, and Senior Research Fellow, in Indigenous Regional Organisation, Governance and Public Policy at the Australian Institute of Aboriginal and Torres Strait Islander Studies. He concentrated his research on public policy approaches to Indigenous affairs. He is the author of numerous scholarly articles and practical reports, and the book *Belonging together: Dealing with the politics of disenchantment in Australian Indigenous policy* (2011, Aboriginal Studies Press). He is currently an Adjunct Professor at the National Centre for Indigenous Studies (ANU), and Professor at Nulungu Research Institute, University of Notre Dame Australia, Broome. He leads the ARC-funded project 'Reciprocal accountability and public value in Aboriginal organisations'.

Mandy Yap is a Research Fellow at the Crawford School of Public Policy at ANU. Prior to that, Mandy worked at CAEPR and the National Centre for Social and Economic Modelling. Since 2013, Mandy has worked in partnership with the Yawuru community in Broome to develop culturally relevant indicators of Indigenous wellbeing. Mandy has collaborated with researchers nationally and internationally on projects such as 'Data sovereignty for Indigenous peoples' and 'Indigenous peoples, sustainable development and the capability approach'. Mandy is also an Australian Endeavour Fellow and is working on a co-authored book, *Indigenous peoples and the capability approach* to be published in 2018 by Routledge. Mandy has an interest in the area of composite measures of quality of life with a particular focus on methodologies surrounding selection and weighting of composite measures of wellbeing.

Eunice Yu is a Yawuru woman from Broome, Western Australia. She has extensive experience and active involvement across community for the past 25 years, working to facilitate change through strategic research and innovative policy development. She has lengthy administrative and managerial experience gained while working for the Australian Government for over 20 years. Eunice is a former councillor with the Shire of Broome. She serves as a board member of the Kimberley Development Commission, sits on the round table for Aboriginal and Torres Strait Islander Statistics with the Australian Bureau of Statistics and on the Ipsos Aboriginal and Torres Strait Islander Advisory Group.

Preface

The retreat of nation states from recognition of indigenous peoples' rights in the 21st century has been experienced within a broader ascent of politics, which has been framed within the rubric of neoliberalism.

In November 2016, an international group of scholars from Aotearoa/ New Zealand, Australia and Canada gathered in Canberra to participate in a small, by-invitation symposium titled, 'Indigenous Rights, Recognition and the State in the Neoliberal Age'. The symposium was funded by the Centre for Aboriginal Economic Policy Research (CAEPR) and the Research School of Social Sciences at The Australian National University (ANU). The purpose of the symposium was to bring together a small group of sociologists, political scientists, political economists, anthropologists, law and society scholars and political philosophers to critically explore the theoretical, social, racial and political-economic dynamics underwriting indigenous policy in the neoliberal age—an age in which laws and policies with respect to indigenous peoples are being reformed and remade. Participants were invited to share innovative, practical and provocative ideas with respect to indigenous rights, recognition and the state in the neoliberal age. This book is the first edited collection to engage with the topic of indigenous rights, recognition and the state in the neoliberal age, drawing on most, but not all papers presented over the two-day symposium.

Speakers who made an important contribution to our discussions and ideas that culminated in this collection, but did not contribute a formal chapter, include Associate Professor Stephanie Gilbert (Wollotuka, University of Newcastle), Dr Kirsty Gover (Law, Melbourne University), Mary Spiers Williams (Law, ANU), Annie Te One (National Centre for Indigenous Studies, ANU), Sarah Ciftci (Socio-Legal Studies, University of Sydney) and Dr Katherine Curchin (CAEPR, ANU).

1

From new paternalism to new imaginings of possibilities in Australia, Canada and Aotearoa/ New Zealand: Indigenous rights and recognition and the state in the neoliberal age

Deirdre Howard-Wagner, Maria Bargh
and Isabel Altamirano-Jiménez

Introduction

The election of Evo Morales as the first indigenous President of Bolivia in 2005 is widely credited to the Cochamba Water War (Spronk 2007: 8). The Cochamba Water War progressed from an indigenous movement and a specific issue to the creation of an indigenous political party and election of the first indigenous President. The Bolivian water war, the Puebla Panama Plan in Mexico, the Mackenzie Valley pipeline in Canada (Altamirano-Jiménez 2004) and Māori resistance to the neoliberal agenda from 1984 onwards (Bargh 2007: 26) inspired much theorising about indigenous people successfully contesting neoliberalism (Altamirano-Jiménez 2004, Bargh 2007, Spronk 2007: 8, Postero 2007). Bargh and others, for example, documented not only 'overt Māori resistance to neoliberal policies, but also more subtle stories of activities, which implicitly challenge neoliberal practices and assumptions by their support for other ways of living' (Bargh 2007: 1). Scholars make visible the persistence of the colonial in the concrete and material conditions of everyday neoliberal governance and life (Howard-Wagner & Kelly 2011: 103). As Bargh (2007), Altamirano-Jiménez (2013), Howard-Wagner (2010b, 2015) and others note, indigenous categorisations of neoliberal practices as a form of colonisation relate to a concern that neoliberalism in its multiple forms poses a threat to indigenous ways of life. This scholarship also critically reflects on the reshaping of the relationship between the state and indigenous peoples under neoliberalism (Altamirano-Jiménez 2004, Bargh 2007, Howard-Wagner 2009). For example, it draws attention to the increasing intervention in the lives of indigenous peoples (Howard-Wagner 2007, 2009, 2010a, 2010b) and the dispossession of indigenous people through privatisation (Wolfe 2006, Howard-Wagner 2012, Altamirano-Jiménez 2013, Coulthard 2014). It does not, however, preclude agency, resistance and decolonisation.

Interpretive micro-studies about indigenous peoples' engagement with neoliberalism provide particular value. They tell us about actually existing neoliberalism in the context of intervention in the everyday lives of indigenous peoples, contests over rights, contests over policy and the complex decisions indigenous people are making about how to protect their rights and navigate diverse economies involving neoliberal policies and practices.

Ngāti Tūwharetoa and the Mighty River Power

The area of water management in New Zealand is an example of these complex decisions.

Successive New Zealand governments have argued that 'no one owns water'; however, in the agriculture sector farmers can trade water permits and water bottling companies make significant profits based on water's zero cost (Young 2012). The Waitangi Tribunal has acknowledged Māori arguments that they continue to have customary rights to water and has stated that Māori have proprietary rights in water (Waitangi Tribunal 2012).

One tribe in the central North Island, represented by the Tūwharetoa Māori Trust Board, has signed a commercial arrangement with partially state-owned enterprise Mighty River Power (Bradley 2014). The Tūwharetoa Māori Trust Board has the legal right to charge commercial users of Lake Taupō for water. Their legal right stems from their customary rights and was reaffirmed in 1992 and 2007 (New Zealand Government 2007). On the face of it, the commercial arrangement looks like an adoption of the commodification of water. However, there are several elements that complicate this oversimplified assessment. One is that the Tūwharetoa Māori Trust Board only proposed the commercial arrangement after the government partially sold the shares in Mighty River Power in order to generate government revenue. Prior to that, the Trust Board allowed for the drawing of water for the public good of generating electricity. In addition, despite the commercial arrangement, the Trust Board is focused on improving water quality and remains intent on protecting the water as a treasure, 'for the benefit of our future generations' (Tūwharetoa Māori Trust Board 2017).

'Actually existing neoliberalism'

How neoliberalism manifests in different contexts is where discussions about the enabling and constraining aspects of neoliberal governance in the context of indigenous peoples become extremely useful. This is one of the objectives of this edited collection and what sets it apart. It draws out policy coherence in three liberal settler states, Australia, Canada and New Zealand, but also exposes the idiosyncratic operational dynamics of neoliberal governance within and between these countries. Individually, the empirically grounded, interpretive micro-studies thus provide particular value. Read together, however, this collection broadens the debate and the analysis of contemporary government policy. This collection also gets away from the standard focus on resource development and land rights and into intense and complex matters of social policy, disability policy and the like.

Thus, one of the objectives of this collection as a whole is to reveal both the particularities of historical-geographical-legal situations, or the forms of 'actually existing neoliberalism' that are 'variegated' by historical, geographical and legal contexts and complex state arrangements (Brenner et al. 2010). At the same time, it presents examples of a more nuanced agential, bottom-up indigenous governmentality in which indigenous actors engage in trying to govern various fields of activity, both by acting on the conduct and contexts of everyday neoliberal life, and by acting on the conduct of state and corporate actors as well (Barnett 2005: 10).

Further, this collection aims to reveal the highly variegated features, impacts and outcomes of neoliberalism (Fine & Saad-Filho 2017: 695). It does so in an original way, by juxtaposing broader global dynamics through a variety of comparative interpretative perspectives. Importantly, read together, the collection reveals the different features and outcomes of neoliberalism in Australia, New Zealand and Canada, but also how neoliberalism redefines the relationship between the economy, the state, society and indigenous people in different social policy contexts within these nation states; that is, how it gives rise to the (variegated) neoliberalisation of everyday life (Fine & Saad-Filho 2017: 697). It does so by drawing together disparate national and disciplinary perspectives, providing valuable insights into hitherto little-known areas of public policy and indigenous activism, and offering a sustained and coordinated critique of the status quo.

Together, the essays reveal levels of contingency and context-specific variation. The collection thus leans towards a Foucauldian approach as it 'is more attuned to the contingency and unanticipated consequences of neoliberal agendas' (Barnett 2005: 8). Importantly, when you put a collection of disparate, short essays together, the definitional context can often be missing. This introduction does a lot of the groundwork for the collection, providing much of the context and definitional background that is needed, as well as teasing out the constraining and enabling aspects of neoliberal governance in different contexts. It pulls the collection together, giving the reader important background knowledge so that the reader can gain more from the collection as a whole. The objective of Chapter One is to explain the approach adopted, then draw out some of the key themes from the chapters within this collection, contributing to the overarching purpose or thesis of the book. This is followed by an outline of the organisation of the book. First though, we briefly revisit the debates about the value of neoliberalism as an analytic tool: a point also taken up by various authors within this collection, such as Will Sanders, Patrick Sullivan and Dominic O'Sullivan.

Neoliberalism and the deep contests over its value as an analytic tool

We are mindful of the expansive literature on neoliberalism, its usefulness as a concept, and an equally prominent debate around the best understanding of contemporary indigenous politics in the neoliberal age. Our aim is to present both sides of the coin, bringing into consideration a more agential turn (Bargh 2007, Howard-Wagner 2006, 2012).

With regard to the deep contests over neoliberalism's value as an analytical tool, challenges to the use of the term neoliberalism concern its application as a concept of universal relevance: the idea that neoliberalism, if it is to be worthy, needs to be shown as applicable universally. Such a challenge suggests that 'neoliberalism is everywhere, but at the same time, nowhere' (Venugopal 2015: 165). The purpose of this argument is that it serves as the death knell for neoliberalism, watering down its analytical potency. This argument emerges from the tendency to equate neoliberalism with laissez faire and 'assume that a strong and direct correlation exists between the normative prescriptions of neoliberal theory, and neoliberalism in practice' (Cahill 2010: 305). The economic project of the state in the neoliberal age is conceptualised as essentially non-interventionist, involving less government, and as laissez faire.[1] Importantly, what scholars such as Damien Cahill, and others (e.g. Brenner et al. 2010), have done is to distinguish between neoliberalism in theory and practice, turning their attention to 'actually existing neoliberalism' (Cahill 2010: 305). The point that Cahill is making is that 'for actually existing neoliberalism to come to an end would require an end to, or the undermining of, one or more of the following processes: deregulation, privatisation or marketisation' (Cahill 2010: 309). It would, for example, as Cahill also notes 'require limits placed upon the freedoms of capital gained under neoliberalism … and social protections that quarantine individuals from market dependence, and … a shift in the balance of class forces in favour of labour (Cahill 2010: 309).

---

1   Social scientists first engaged with neoliberalism as a liberal project aimed at economic freedom. Thus, many also argued that neoliberalism had at its centre a critique of the state, particularly the 'excesses, inefficiencies and injustices of the extended State, and the alternatives posed in terms of the construction of a "free market" and a "civil society" in which a plurality of groups, organizations and individuals interact in liberty' (Rose and Miller 1991).

So, why do we refer to the neoliberal state?

Social scientists have long been concerned with an over-valuing of the problem of the state in the context of 'actually existing neoliberalism', turning their intention instead to the action of governing. Increasingly too, social scientists turn to analysing neoliberal projects or solutions as not simply economic projects, but also social projects that produce specific outcomes, particularly in the context of the reforming of the social state systems and social strategies of the state (e.g. Brown 2003, Harvey 2006, Wacquant 2009, 2010). As Cahill notes, 'it has been demonstrated that the state has maintained a pervasive presence in the regulation of economic and social life during the last three decades, thus contravening a key normative prescription of neoliberal theory' (Cahill 2010: 305). In practice then, while the role of the state has changed from the direct deliverer of services, the regulatory apparatuses of the state have not been diminished (Cahill 2010: 305).

What we are talking about then is the predilection for neoliberal solutions (Cahill 2010: 309) in everything from wicked social problems to water management. What is more, we are interested in revealing the complexities of how indigenous people engage with 'actually existing neoliberalism'. For example, how indigenous people protect their rights and navigate this predilection for neoliberal solutions.

Alongside this, there is growing body of scholarship that examines the racialised effects of neoliberalism (Goldberg 2002, 2009, Winant 2004, Razack 2008, Soss et al. 2011), particularly in the context of indigenous peoples (Howard-Wagner 2006, 2010b, 2012, 2017, Moreton-Robinson 2009). This is also taken up by authors within this collection, such as Shelley Bielefeld and Alex Page.

The '(variegated) neoliberalisation of everyday [Indigenous] life'

While the broad aim was to stimulate thinking about indigenous policy in the neoliberal age, the contributors to this volume vary in their engagement with the theme of indigenous rights, recognition and the state in the neoliberal age. This collection represents how ad hoc rationalisations and different political projects of neoliberalism can manifest as contradictory (Larner et al. 2007). The impact of neoliberalism in specific communities is shaped by different geographies, histories and material circumstances.

The reorganisation of the state and its functions has been welcomed by some indigenous communities. For others, its highly interventionist and devastating effects have entailed a radical erosion of recognition of status and rights.

Neoliberalism as shaping and constraining forms of recognition on offer

Many of the authors within this collection explain how 'actually existing neoliberalism' has shaped and constrained the forms of recognition on offer from the state (in the case of Australia and Canada) and the Crown in (Aotearoa/New Zealand).[2] Avril Bell, for example, reminds us that:

> At its Hegelian roots, recognition theory is about the struggle to achieve a relationship of equals between two subjects. To recognise subjectivity of another is to recognise their equal and autonomous status as self-determining people worthy of respect (Bell this volume, Chapter 4).

What predominates is what Jakeet Singh calls 'recognition from above' whereby 'the state is the arbiter of just and unjust claims for recognition from subordinate groups' (Singh 2014: 47, Williams 2014: 8). Besides being the arbiter of recognition, the state also defines the terms of recognition. For example, although the state has legally recognised indigenous identity and rights, identity and rights are essentialised in ways that facilitate the economic interests of the state in the neoliberal

---

2   The Crown is used in New Zealand broadly to mean the state as a whole. There is no precise definition in New Zealand law, although it is defined in the *Crown Proceedings Act 1950* and the *Public Finance Act 1989*. The interpretation in the *Crown Proceedings Act 1950* states: 'The Sovereign or the Crown means the Sovereign in right of his or her government in New Zealand'. The *Public Finance Act* states that the 'Crown or the Sovereign – a) means the Sovereign in right of New Zealand; and b) includes all Ministers of the Crown and all departments'. The definition goes on to exclude a number of entities including an Office of Parliament, a Crown entity and a state enterprise.

For many Māori, the term 'the Crown' invokes reference to the partnership between the English and Māori in the Treaty of Waitangi 1840. Contestation over the definition occurs for Māori therefore when trying to argue where Treaty of Waitangi obligations lie. As Bell's chapter illustrates, the question of whether local government in New Zealand is part of 'the Crown' and has legal obligations to Māori continues to be debated. There are other legal debates within New Zealand about which branches and mechanisms of the state might be considered agents of the Crown for the purposes of describing breaches of the Treaty of Waitangi in the Settlements process (see Williams 1999: 234–5 and Shore & Kawharu 2014).

age. Moreover, while indigenous identity is recognised, the complex articulation of indigenous peoples' inclusion in the neoliberal economy attempts to foreclose other alternatives.

Chapters within this collection also examine how local arrangements in which indigenous peoples are the agents of recognition (Coulthard 2007: 456), and thereby have greater control over the redistributive impact of revenues and expenditures to address indigenous peoples' social exclusion, can promote indigenous peoples' social inclusion and address disadvantage. That is, how 'recognition from below' occurs 'when people in dominated social positions turn away from institutionalised power hierarchies, shaping their own social orders without approval or permission of any authority beyond themselves' (Williams 2014: 10). As Williams notes, 'These processes of self-constituting power, realised (inter alia) through acts of resistance or through prefigurative political movements, also entail struggles for recognition, but the agents of recognition are [Indigenous peoples]' (ibid.). Thus, what Glen Coulthard defines as 'recognition from below' is an important consideration. Coulthard defines this as the:

> practices of 'self-recognition' through which dominated or colonised subjects 'critically revalu[e], reconstruct … and redeploy … culture and tradition' and, in the process, radically transform their own self-consciousness as political agents (2007: 456, cited in Williams 2014: 10).

Importantly, many of the authors within this collection examine the complex trajectories of neoliberalism, highlighting how it contains and constrains different political, economic and social possibilities, while also explaining and understanding the alternative political, economic and social possibilities the neoliberal age offers.

They also consider how neoliberal governance often entails a shift in state recognition, considering this shift and what is needed to create contexts in which recognition from below is possible. For example, in this collection Will Sanders argues—in the context of Australia, but applicable to New Zealand and Canada—that '[w]hat is needed in contemporary Australian Indigenous policy is some re-recognition of the attempt at decolonisation and the contribution that a peoples approach can make'. Sanders gives more detailed consideration to this proposition in relation to the 10 years of federal Indigenous affairs in Australia after the abolition of the Aboriginal and Torres Strait Islander Commission (ATSIC). Rather than neoliberalism, the broad sociological term Sanders finds most helpful in Australian Indigenous affairs is decolonisation. As Sanders writes, he 'resist[s] the term neoliberalism as it seems to foreclose, rather than open, possibilities'. Sanders argues, '[w]hile there is no denying the rise of market liberalism in ideas about government since the 1980s, other ideas have also still had a presence, such as decolonisation and a "peoples" approach'. He goes on to propose that '[f]raming and labelling are important, and it may be that insisting that this is still the age of decolonisation, as well as neoliberalism, is a way to keep alive ideas about the recognition of Indigenous rights'.

This too concerns the state and changing game plans, but also the nuances and complexities of changing game plans, in relation to indigenous rights and recognition in the neoliberal age (Bargh 2006).

The neoliberal state and the United Nations Declaration on the Rights of Indigenous People

It is important to situate the constraints of the neoliberal age in the context of formal international recognition of indigenous rights. Recent developments in international law indicate that states and international institutions have finally become responsive to indigenous peoples' demands. The ratification of the United Nations Declaration on the Rights of Indigenous Peoples (UNDRIP) in 2007 constitutes a landmark, setting the standards for the treatment of indigenous peoples by the state.[3] Although UNDRIP can be understood as a counter balance to state power, the duties of states and other actors are embedded in neoliberal governance rationalities (Lindroth 2014: 342). The provisions in UNDRIP are both liberal and anti-colonial in that they advance indigenous peoples' freedom to pursue economic, social and cultural development. From this point of view, the right to culture simultaneously pushes the human rights paradigm, by explicitly centring self-determination, and reproduces individual civil and political rights.

The right to indigenous self-determination has been considered to be the main tenet and symbol of the indigenous movement (Daes 2003: 303). However, the meaning of indigenous self-determination is not only

---

3   For the full text of the United Nations Declaration of the Rights of Indigenous Peoples, see www.un.org/development/desa/indigenouspeoples/declaration-on-the-rights-of-indigenous-peoples.html.

contested but resisted by many states. Although UNDRIP seems to push the envelope in articulating indigenous self-determination, it limits this right to the extent and format that the international community of states has supported. As far as the indigenous peoples' claim to self-determination is concerned, Article 3 of UNDRIP states: 'Indigenous peoples have the right to self-determination. By virtue of that right they freely determine their political status and freely pursue their economic, social and cultural development'. In responding to governments' objection to this right, Article 46(1) notes:

> nothing in this Declaration may be interpreted as implying for any State, people, group or person any right to engage in any activity or to perform any act contrary to the Charter of the United Nations or constructed as authorising or encouraging any action which could dismember or impair totally or in part, the territorial integrity of political unity of sovereign and independent States.

This means that indigenous self-determination is qualified as a 'domestic or internal' right that can only be exercised within the boundaries of the state.

Disagreements over the meaning of self-determination and the attempts to bracket it resulted in the failure of states and indigenous peoples to agree on a text for the document. These disagreements were central to Australia, Canada and New Zealand's failure to ratify the Declaration in 2007. These countries noted that UNDRIP was not a suitable basis for developing a binding agreement because it did not reflect customary international law.

Two years later, in 2009, the Australian Government endorsed UNDRIP, followed by New Zealand and by Canada in 2010. Canada's endorsement emphasised the fact that UNDRIP is 'aspirational' and that this country would interpret this document in a manner consistent with its national laws. Similarly, Australia noted that, while UNDRIP was non-binding, it remained a set of important principles for states to aspire to. Whereas New Zealand stated that its endorsement was limited by its legal and constitutional frameworks. In reversing their initial rejection, these states 'selectively endorsed' (Lightfoot 2012) UNDRIP, reflecting their willingness to support cultural rights but not indigenous self-determination as it connected to land and natural resources. Moreover, it reflects states' interest in engaging in intergovernmental relations and negotiations with indigenous peoples outside the sphere of rights. What has been termed the 'implementation era' (Gover 2015) is characterised by how agreements and settlements between settler governments and indigenous peoples are operationalised within the legal frameworks of the state. This era started in the early 1990s, in the context of neoliberal restructuring, and has dealt with matters of property and jurisdictions. In this context, the delegation of services delivery has been instrumental to the creation of partnerships with the private sector. As several of the contributors show, these processes of service delivery brought indigenous people and organisations into the neoliberal market.

Influenced by the Truth and Reconciliation Commission of Canada's Calls for Action explicitly calling upon the government to fully endorse UNDRIP, in 2016 newly elected Prime Minister Justin Trudeau eliminated Canada's objections to the Declaration. However, indigenous organisations and advocates have criticised the Trudeau Government for not implementing UNDRIP. Cree MP Romeo Saganash introduced a Bill to harmonise Canadian laws with UNDRIP. Parliament has not voted on this Bill and Prime Minister Trudeau has not fully supported the Bill, arguing UNDRIP could not be supported word by word (Barrera 2017).

Although UNDRIP sets minimum standards for the treatment of indigenous peoples and enhances the significance of human rights norms, another central theme that deserves consideration is the contradictory coexistence of both recognition of status and rights and economic development. On the one hand, UNDRIP has legitimated human rights as the predominant language for making social justice claims. On the other, it conceives of freedom and the realisation of self-determination primarily through the market economy. Because of the exceptional status of indigenous people, international law is founded on a specific understanding of their cultural survival attached to land and traditions. The acknowledgement of the impact of colonialism becomes about the elimination of impediments to the right to economic development. This apparent contradiction is productive. It simultaneously produces the neoliberal indigenous subject and an indigenous identity that looks back, framing indigenous peoples as always in need of intervention (Howard-Wagner 2006, 2009, Altamirano-Jiménez, 2014). As Clarke notes, when neoliberalism produces cultural difference, it does so by fragmenting existing meanings and enabling new possibilities for the state (Clarke 2004). By privileging specific types of knowledge, language, cartographic representations and legal traditions, the language of rights has produced indigenous peoples as a distinctive category that requires particular kinds of measures (Altamirano-Jiménez 2014, Lindroth 2014). Moreover, because the state is the grantor of rights, one way its power is manifested is in deciding who qualifies for rights and who meets the standards to be recognised as indigenous. In this context, while the law requires indigenous peoples to meet certain standards, failure of indigenous peoples to fully participate in the market is conceived of as an anomaly that can be changed. Indeed, interventions are justified in the name of rights and 'improving' people's lives (Li 2010: 388). As peoples in disadvantage and under threat, indigenous communities require special measures, justifying states' intervention in their lives. The chapters in this collection show interventions are prompted by the social, economic and cultural conditions of indigenous peoples. As Yap and Yu note in their chapter, such conditions are measured in relation to a good market in which having a job, living a healthy lifestyle and being able to consume become markers of success. Similarly, Isabel Altamirano-Jiménez demonstrates that, while the introduction of matrimonial property rights on reserves in Canada is represented as a way to exercise the right to development, indigenous people are blamed for their circumstances and the 'backwardness' of their cultures.

Rethinking and revaluing indigenous economies vs winding back indigenous rights

Maria Bargh, and many of the authors within this collection, call for a rethinking and revaluing of indigenous economies, especially the economy of indigenous rights, including how indigenous people act as economic actors; the multiple economic, social and cultural activities that indigenous people engage in as economic actors; and the public value that indigenous people, organisations and communities contribute to the economy and society. This approach creates new imaginings of possibilities.

This is not to say that indigenous rights cannot exist within the context of the market—a point taken up in a number of the chapters within this collection. Historically excluded, indigenous peoples are encouraged to integrate into the global economy and realise their newly recognised rights to development via the market and self-government, which fit well with the reduction of the state and the transfer of administrative responsibilities.

Although recognition of indigenous self-government is observed in Canada and New Zealand, recognition in relation to land and economic development has been far more fraught in Australia. Even so, in New Zealand, the neoliberal age has seen the state (or the Crown, as it is commonly referred to in reference to its role and obligations stemming from the Treaty of Waitangi) deal with Māori in ways that are reminiscent of more longstanding colonial practices of civilising indigenous peoples through market training (Bargh 2007). Since 1984, when the first neoliberal policies were introduced in New Zealand, successive governments have become more firmly supportive of Māori economic development and have rearticulated the Treaty settlements process— which aims to rectify Crown breaches of the Treaty of Waitangi—to be rather narrowly about the economic development of assets repatriated to Māori. By characterising the Treaty settlement process in this way, and celebrating Māori economic identities and economic success, the Crown channels Māori aspirations for self-determination into a neoliberal market framework. Accompanying this process is one where Māori are treated as simply one type of actor among many others in the private sector, all with allegedly equal rights to tender for contracts to deliver services or to enter joint ventures with government agencies, such as in forestry. Wider government policies in the areas of housing, social welfare or health continue to treat Māori as subjects that are not entirely capable of governing their own affairs and therefore require training and intervention in their lives. Similar rationalities and dynamics have emerged in Australia and Canada.

Canada also underwent a period of changes and cuts in the 1980s, which were detrimental to the welfare state. Marked by the economic crisis and the political discontent produced by the patriation of the Canadian Constitution in 1982, social policy-making was reoriented towards the goals of economic integration and privatisation, which were seen as the key to domestic wellbeing (Banting 1996, McKeen & Porter 2003: 125). The neoliberal transformation undermined universality in favour of major reductions in social programs and the transfer of social welfare responsibilities from the federal government to the provinces. Moreover, there was a shift from viewing social support as an entitlement of citizenship to developing policies that emphasise individual responsibility and economic independence regardless of people's status in society (Bashevkin 2003). Although Canadian citizenship has been undermined by neoliberalism, for some indigenous people the recognition of their rights in the Constitution and devolution of responsibilities were welcomed, as the welfare state had also been the most interventionist for their communities.

While the state–society relation was being reconfigured, the Canadian Government embarked on the negotiation of North American Free Trade Agreement (NAFTA). To facilitate economic integration, major barriers to resource extraction were lifted. The Canadian Government introduced privatisation of state assets, services, land and resources, with the purpose of creating the conditions for economic integration. Indigenous peoples were encouraged to integrate into the global economy and realise their newly recognised collective rights via the market and self-government, which fit well with the reduction of the state and the transfer of administrative responsibilities. NAFTA paved the way to deepen resource extraction during the Harper administration and the speeding of environmental assessments, and, in turn, indigenous discontent with the scale of resource extraction.

Australia too has gone through many of the shifts and changes experienced in New Zealand and Canada. However, in Australia, the neoliberal age has entailed the winding back of Indigenous rights (Howard-Wagner 2008). What began as former prime minister Howard's assertions in 1996 that the pendulum had swung too far in favour of Indigenous rights, particularly in relation to native title rights and to symbolic gestures and special measures (Howard-Wagner 2006), developed into a complex hybridisation of neoliberal strategies that today target every dimension of Aboriginal life, from social security payments and school attendance to the way that Aboriginal organisations do business. Importantly, in the Australian context, the abolition of ATSIC, the Northern Territory Emergency Response, income management (e.g. the cashless welfare card), the announced closure of Aboriginal homelands in the Northern Territory and later Western Australia, the Indigenous Advancement Strategy, the new mainstreaming, market training and the overall heightened state governmentality in the name of Indigenous improvement can be understood as actions of government in the neoliberal age. Authors refer to such political moments in the governing of Indigenous affairs in Australia in the first and second sections of the collection.

Contradictorily then, rather than less government, the turn towards individual indigenous wellbeing and poverty governance in the neoliberal age has entailed a turn away from self-governance and freedom of the rights/

welfare state era and return to government intervention and intrusion into private lives of indigenous people and the affairs of indigenous people in all three countries. This is one of the major contradictions of neoliberalism. That is, as Nadesan notes in citing the work of Mitchell Dean (2002: 129), while purporting to govern through individual freedom, neoliberal governance:

> employs diverse and heterogeneous forms of power to establish and preserve 'a comprehensive normalisation of social, economic and cultural existence' and thus the state 'attempts to govern as much through "domination"—a word that covers a myriad of conditions—as it does through freedom' (Nadesan 2008: 35).

Drawing too on the work of Mitchell Dean, Nadesan goes on to note that 'normalisation … does not necessarily entail therapeutic adjustment but rather, containment and extrication of risk … Concerns for "responsibility" and "obligation" outweigh freedom and rehabilitation' (Nadesan 2008: 35).

At the same time, the assumption that indigenous communities' dysfunction can be solved by participating in the economy continues to undermine other possibilities. Authors in this collection draw attention to the ways that neoliberal governance in Australia, Canada and New Zealand colonises the indigenous domain. For example, Louise Humpage and Fiona McCormack illustrate how, increasingly, Māori are recognised as economic actors and as 'private sector', but at the same time Māori risk erosion of culture by participating in neoliberal policies. Maria Bargh, Louise Humpage and Dominic O'Sullivan illustrate how neoliberalism has simultaneously provided opportunities and inhibited Māori rights. Louise Humpage also explains how compromises made by Māori for specific and discrete gains may further embed neoliberalism.

Land, privatisation and territorial reorganisation

There are also authors within this collection, such as Isabel Altamirano-Jiménez and Cathy Eatock, who contribute in critical ways to our understandings of the role of Western conceptualisations of property and land to create 'governable' indigenous spaces under neoliberalism.

So, although the negotiation of land claim agreements opened the space for contemporary political arrangements of self-administration, indigenous communities have struggled, to different degrees, to use such framework to build their own economic capacity. Then again, indigenous participation in the economy and economic development is also commonly misread as neoliberal co-option. Importantly, as many of the authors in this collection remind its readers, indigenous economic aspirations did not suddenly arise in the neoliberal age. The chapters within this collection highlight such complexities.

In Canada, privatisation has been central to territorial reorganisation and the devolution of risk and responsibilities to indigenous communities. Government policies actively encourage private–public partnerships with industry, assuming indigenous communities and industry are equal. Because these partnerships are considered private, they lack accountability. As Altamirano-Jiménez shows in this collection, the combination of private property and indigenous women's rights has become a technology of governance that not only delegates both risks and responsibilities onto indigenous peoples, but also attempts to contain their resistance to such policies. Privatisation is not only reconfiguring indigenous territories and producing different regimes of resource management, but also exacerbating the trend of land and resource appropriation (Altamirano-Jiménez 2013, Pasternack 2015). As Altamirano-Jiménez further demonstrates, discourses of responsibility and efficiency to impose private property conceal past and current processes of land dispossession and territorial reorganisation.

In the Australian context, the territorial reconfiguration of land usage and tenure in Australia's Northern Territory facilitated Western conceptualisation of entrepreneurial initiatives, through the move away from community-based approaches to land management and ownership to a model of individual housing/leasehold tenure (Howard-Wagner 2012: 234). This was one of the key features of the Northern Territory Emergency Response laws. That is, the Australian Government changed and introduced various laws in relation to access to Aboriginal land in Australia's Northern Territory through a provision known as a 'whole of [Aboriginal] township lease' to 'attract investment, increase access to home ownership and help local business to prosper' (Australian Government 2011). The whole-of-township lease has also been aimed at increasing business and economic development in Indigenous townships. The Housing Precinct leases established under the joint AU$672 million

Strategic Indigenous Housing and Infrastructure Program (SIHIP) in 2009 by the federal and Northern Territory governments, for example, set up a framework for individual private property ownership through building houses and introducing market-based rents and normal tenancy agreements (Howard-Wagner 2012: 234). In this collection, Cathy Eatock illustrates how employment and home ownership objectives are also imposed at the expense of cultural survival in the context of recent policy changes in the Australian state of Western Australia, under the *Resilient families, strong communities: A roadmap for regional and remote communities* report, which could potentially result in the closure of around 120 smaller remote communities in Western Australia.

Neoliberal governance, welfare responsibilities and domestic wellbeing

We can establish certain patterns associated with neoliberal governance, such as markets regulating economic activity, welfare responsibilities being transformed into commodity forms that are regulated according to market principles, economic entrepreneurship replacing old forms of regulation and active individual entrepreneurship replacing the passivity and dependency of responsible solidarity (Rose & Miller 1991: 198). Over time, social policy-making reoriented towards the goals of economic integration and privatisation, which were seen as the key to domestic wellbeing (Banting 1996, McKeen & Porter 2003: 125). This also entailed a restructuring of welfare and social services through a form of market managerialism.

Importantly, at the same time, a shift has occurred from viewing social support as an entitlement of citizenship to developing policies that emphasise individual responsibility and economic independence, regardless of peoples' status in society (Bashevkin 2003, Brodie 2008). In Australia, New Zealand and Canada, the social contract of the modern welfare state has been undermined by neoliberalism. Furthermore, for some social groups, such as indigenous people, the neoliberal state has been highly interventionist.

Neoliberalism and paternalism

The intersectionality between neoliberalism and paternalism, associated with the disciplinary turn embodied in the processes and practices of governing through neoliberal paternalism, is pointed to in several chapters in this collection (Howard-Wagner 2017). In making this argument, authors in this collection demonstrate how neoliberal technologies are deployed to govern the lives of indigenous peoples. In this regard, we see how neoliberal concepts like normalisation, mainstreaming, mutual obligation and conditionality come into play in the governing of indigenous communities, organisations and individuals in the neoliberal age.

This is very much a significant characteristic of the social projects of neoliberalism in Australia, Canada and New Zealand, and elsewhere. While governments still provide government benefits and pensions and social services, they have, for example, provided incentives for, and encouraged, citizens to rely on superannuation funds and private health funds, rather than 'old age pensions' or 'medicare'. Accessibility to and eligibility for government benefits and pensions has also changed around issues of universality and entitlement. This is a point taken up by Karen Soldatic and Shelley Bielefeld in this collection. A key government objective is to move people from welfare to work, and in order to target the employment gap among disadvantaged groups, introducing stronger conditionality is a prominent government strategy. Soldatic draws our attention to the effect that this has had on those Aboriginal and Torres Strait Islander people with disabilities who live in regional parts of Australia.

It is passive welfare populations, also known as the poor and disadvantaged, who are the target of neoliberal social projects (Howard-Wagner 2017). The socio-economic conditions of the poor/disadvantaged individual are the target of intervention (i.e. lack of education, training and employment, lack of parenting skills). The multitude of interventions span from parenting programs that aim to train indigenous parents to be 'good parents' to those that require senior managers of indigenous organisations to undertake governance and leadership training to acquire 'good governance'. It also entails the increased use of nudge policy or behavioural economics that steer the choices that individuals make; or, even worse, the paternalistic forms of conditionality, such as conditional cash transfers, that regulate individual behaviour, and, if necessary, manage an individual's income, tying support to certain conditions of appropriate behaviour. Government funding to the frontline social service sector, too, explicitly targets individuals through highly prescribed eligibility criteria.

A number of the authors within this collection describe how individuals rather than structural inequalities are framed as the problem, including Shelley Bielefeld, Louise Humpage, Dominic O'Sullivan and Maria Bargh. In the Australian context, for example, governing through Indigenous disadvantage has not only permitted the neoliberal state to reduce Aboriginal and Torres Strait Islander peoples to a socio-economically disadvantaged group or sub-population ('the Indigenous population') within the wider Australian population, but has also enabled the neoliberal state to reconfigure the way it recognises the rights of Aboriginal and Torres Strait Islander peoples. This has limited the possibility of Indigenous intervention, dispossessing Aboriginal and Torres Strait Islander peoples of their rights, and ignoring different social histories and divergent social locations, and past and present effects of discriminatory treatment (Howard-Wagner 2017). Mandy Yap and Eunice Yu take this up in their chapter in the context of indigenous wellbeing, noting that this idealised vision measures and evaluates all domains of society according to 'good market' indicators: a good job, healthy lifestyle and consumer rationality. This relationship—between the governing of poverty, passivity and dependency on welfare in terms of defining poverty or disadvantage and wellbeing, managing eligibility, and managing the poor more generally—is thus an important theme running through this collection.

From precarity to poverty governance in the neoliberal age

Several authors within this collection also highlight the precarious experience of indigenous people in the neoliberal age. Karen Soldatic and Shelley Bielefeld draw our attention to precarity associated with accessibility to government benefits, while Daphne Habibis, Patrick Sullivan, Deirdre Howard-Wagner and Alexander Page draw our attention to precarity associated with insecure funding arrangements and competitive processes for Aboriginal organisations.

This examination moves beyond precarity to investigate how new forms of mutual obligation introduce new forms of subjectification, different from those estalished by welfare state policy, and how this relates to a preoccupation with poverty governance in the neoliberal age (Howard-Wagner 2006, 2017). Mutual obligation is based on the precepts of extending and disseminating market values to social institutions; its objective is to empower the individual to govern themselves as a rational entrepreneurial actor (Brown 2003: 4). Its target is 'passive welfare'. Mead (1997: 1) describes mutual obligation—a hybrid model of neoliberalism and service provisioning in which welfare recipients who are party to this form of agreement are bound by certain conditions relating to behavioural change—as neo-paternalism because of the intervention and 'close supervision of the poor'. Green also argues that mutual obligation, for example, is a mix of neoliberalism and social interventionism (Green 2002: 33). Behavioural economics that steer the choices made by recipients of government funding (such as Aboriginal communities) or social security, or the paternalistic forms of conditionality, such as conditional cash transfers, that regulate individual behaviour (and if necessary manage an individual's income, tying support to certain conditions of appropriate behaviour) are taken up in Shelley Bielefeld's chapter. Bielefeld shows how the targeting of 'passive welfare' has led to the linking of benefits to outcomes, imposing conditions on the recipients of welfare benefits, and also how this has affected Indigenous welfare recipients—particularly with the rolling out of the Healthy Welfare Card in communities with large numbers of Indigenous welfare recipients such as Ceduna, Kununurra and Wyndham.

Poverty governance in the neoliberal age has manifested as a complex, overt racial project in which indigenous peoples are invented, constituted and assimilated into the neoliberal body politic through the positive paternalistic governing of their disadvantage (Howard-Wagner 2017). Paternalistic poverty governance goes beyond a lack of consent on indigenous peoples' part to being governed in this way (Wilson 2015); it harks back to moments in Australia's colonial past when the Indigenous peoples of Australia were treated as childlike, simple-minded and 'incapable of dealing with financial matters' (Bielefeld 2012: 528). The paternalistic neoliberal state not only assumes the right to interfere in the lives of indigenous peoples, violating their rights and autonomy, but takes a directive and supervisory role in their lives. This is where authors within this collection draw on what Mead (1997) first termed the 'new paternalism' to denote the directive and supervisory approach to governing indigenous poverty/disadvantage in the neoliberal age. Paternalism is being reproduced as the very basis of policy formation, which functions as an act of tutelage in the logic of the colonial civilising mission, reinforcing paternalism and, in this case, racial hierarchy (Howard-Wagner 2017). Yet, this is not simply the endless repetition of hierarchical colonial relations. It is a colonising moment in and of itself. The authors within this collection contribute to our understanding of neoliberal interventionism in the context of poverty governance and the racialised effects for indigenous people (Howard-Wagner 2017).

Game changes and 'actual existing neoliberalism'

Many of the authors draw our attention to how the rules of the social policy game have changed in the neoliberal age. One way that authors draw our attention to the changing rules is through an analysis of the economics of social policy in the neoliberal age, in which markets rather than basic rights forefront social policy agendas. Karen Soldatic examines how disability has shifted from the fringes to the centre of policy in most OECD countries. This is due to a concern about the economic costs of disability to society, which in turn means that the governance of disability is concerned with disability costs; thus, attention turns to disability as welfare and cutting access to (in Australia) the Disability Support Pension (DSP). She examines the new rules of the game in which people with disabilities are now assessed according to work capacity, forcing many off the DSP and onto Newstart Allowance (an Australian government income support payment). She notes how the Commonwealth Ombudsman found that Aboriginal and Torres Strait Islander peoples are significantly disadvantaged under the eligibility rules and criteria. She also highlights the spatial experience of Aboriginal and Torres Strait Islander people with disabilities residing in regional Australia, pointing out how the interstice of disability and regionality creates uneven and differentiated outcomes through heightened exposure to economic insecurity, which is exacerbated through diminished access to the DSP.

Daphne Habibis discusses how changes to Aboriginal housing policy have created markets where markets did not previously exist. She discusses the roles mainstreaming, normalisation and coercion play in the Aboriginal housing policy space. She argues for a hybrid housing model to replace the one-size-fits-all approach, one that allows for improvements in remote housing, but also allows for self-determination and innovation. In making this argument, Habibis highlights the partial success of these neoliberal strategies of governance, but she also points to the agency and resistance and determination of Aboriginal people to retain their hard-won land rights and resist the closure of communities.

Social services have also been transformed through the inculcation of enterprising values and market-like relations. That is, governments have restructured the delivery of social services to enable and promote economic competition. Governments have again created markets where markets did not formerly exist (Dean 2004: 161), and have thus extended the market to the social. This is a point taken up by contributors to this collection, such as Avril Bell, Daphne Habibis (as discussed), Deirdre Howard-Wagner, Louise Humpage and Patrick Sullivan. Authors apply this lens to understand the 'quiet revolution in the way government does business with Indigenous organisations' (Vanstone 2005) in Australia compared with New Zealand.

Yet the marketisation of social service delivery, known as new public management (NPM), or 'neoliberal public management' as Patrick Sullivan in this collection calls it, has had different effects in New Zealand and Australia. In New Zealand, focus on contracts and neoliberal distrust of the state's abilities also led to the creation of numerous public–private partnerships with unexpected consequences for Māori groups, many of whom were perceived as 'private' actors. Mason Durie (2004) and Avril Bell (this volume, Chapter 4) make this point in relation Māori service provision. Bell notes, '[d]evolution, contracting social service provision to private providers, enabled the development of Māori providers contracted to delivery services to their own communities'. In New Zealand, therefore, the Māori rhetoric of self-determination at times had resonance with the neoliberal agenda to outsource government services. Nonetheless, government agencies responsible for Māori development and policy adopted business plans that meant goals and outputs were contracted and purchased. This form of contracting regime resulted in mainly outputs that aligned with, and embedded, neoliberal policies (Kelsey 2005: 83).

Game changes are associated too with standardisation. As Will Sanders notes, the new mainstreaming at a government department level has seen very different Indigenous-specific programs inherited from ATSIC turned into much more standardised versions of general government programs. This new mainstreaming also entails the standardisation of Aboriginal service delivery and Indigenous-specific programs into one-size-fits-all programs; so much so that specialised Indigenous organisations become redundant and what becomes important is value for money. This is where mainstreaming meets market rationality. The new mainstreaming differs in that it is not about mainstream services operating alongside Aboriginal services as a form of supplementary service delivery, which was the case in the ATSIC years, but that the new mainstreaming is an apparatus or a technology of neoliberal entrepreneurial governance (Hall 2003: 1). Deirdre Howard-Wagner elaborates on this definition of new mainstreaming, explaining how Indigenous organisations in the Australian city of Newcastle now compete for access to government funding within the mainstream social service market. The new mainstreaming therefore also entails the promotion of competition between Aboriginal and mainstream service providers for funding to deliver services to disadvantaged Aboriginal and Torres Strait Islander peoples. Patrick Sullivan and Deirdre Howard-Wagner propose that this is a consequence of a major game change in Indigenous affairs in Australia associated with standardisation and mainstreaming in the era of NPM.

State modernisation and NPM

NPM is an international phenomenon, but its generic intent has different local manifestations and it has wide-ranging historical geographies (Peck 2004). Generally, in the 21st century it has come to be known as more than economic liberalisation and privatisation. It is seen as an agenda of administrative reform and state modernisation in the neoliberal age. NPM has been critical to neoliberal governance of social order, particularly reorganisation of the welfare state and poverty governance.

While in Canada and New Zealand there are emerging signs of co-production of government policy, creative and community-centric approaches to public administration, and a growing acceptance of indigenous autonomy (Coates 2016), the NPM era has had a far grimmer effect on Indigenous organisations in Australia. In the Australian state of New South Wales, apart from the OCHRE Local Decision-Making approach, which has as its unrealised vision co-production and greater autonomy among Indigenous organisations at a regional level, there is no co-production of government policy and no creative and community-centric approaches to public administration. This could potentially shift with the Australian Prime Minister Turnbull announcing in early 2017 that he would be shifting from transactional government to enablement (Turnbull 2017: 1, Howard-Wagner, in press).

This shift is critical given the adverse effect of NPM on indigenous organisations (see Sullivan in this volume). For example, it has had negative consequences for autonomous Indigenous organisations in Australia: a point explored in different ways by Patrick Sullivan, Deirdre Howard-Wagner, Alexander Page and Will Sanders. Sanders, for example, illustrates how this is part and parcel of the 'new mainstreaming', which follows the abolition of ATSIC.

This turns our attention to another important thread running through a number of the papers within this collection: the severing of ties with the state in the neoliberal age or, to quote Cathy Eatock in this collection, 'look[ing] beyond the hegemony of the nation state', which turns our attention to both recognition and to the issue of indigenous–state relations as a relationship of dependency.

Indigenous economic development as a pathway to self-determination in the neoliberal age

Within the collection, the theme of severing ties with the state is taken up in relation to indigenous self-determination. There are two important arguments running through this collection. The first concerns what self-determination fundamentally means to indigenous peoples. The second concerns the pathways that indigenous people pursue to achieve self-determination in the neoliberal age. This turns our attention to the relationship between economic development and self-determination in the neoliberal age. Government agendas in relation to indigenous economic development are suddenly promoting indigenous economic development. On the one hand, Bell nails the problem in this in one sentence: 'Māori economic development is expected to lessen the Māori welfare "burden"'. On the other hand, it happens that this approach fits, to a degree, with indigenous desires for sovereignty/autonomy. Yet McCormack, Bell and Humpage all express reservations about the ways that Māori are attempting to work with neoliberal practices.

A number of authors within this collection engage with such considerations. For example, Fiona McCormack argues that 'indigeneity may be just as likely to appropriate neoliberalism for its own ends as the other way around'. However, she also notes that, while a space has opened up for indigenous economic development, 'the spaces opened for indigeneity under neoliberalism reflect market rather than democratic rationality' (McCormack 2011: 283). Furthermore, McCormack notes that the '"opening of spaces", incongruously, may strengthen the capacity of the state to shape and neutralise opposition'. Avril Bell adds that it does not reflect a distinctly indigenous rationality or value base. McCormack also makes a critical point in relation to how dispossession occurs through the market, quoting Fairhead et al. who argue that 'those who have valuable assets, but are earning incomes too low to permit social reproduction, inevitably have to sell them' (Fairhead et al., 2012: 243, cited in McCormack this volume). Deirdre Howard-Wagner makes this point too, in relation to Aboriginal organisations in Newcastle.

Patrick Sullivan brings a further consideration, attempting to open up wider discussion in relation to Aboriginal organisations and their role in society, arguing that 'the concept of public value remains a form of contemporary nomenclature that offers an opportunity to make visible the full value of Aboriginal organisations to their publics in a manner intelligible to government'.

So, while dispossession occurs through the market, it also provides a mechanism for achieving self-determination in the neoliberal age. Many of the authors illustrate how indigenous economic development and enterprise offers greater access to self-determination, changing the relationship indigenous peoples have with the state. While Deirdre Howard-Wagner illustrates how the pathway to autonomy and self-determination for urban Aboriginal organisations in the Australian city of Newcastle has long been pursued through external partnerships and associations and/or flexible and innovative entrepreneurial solutions (such as social enterprise, asset-building and Indigenous-driven economic development), she argues that economic development offers a way of ending what has become a disciplinary relationship of dependency in which Indigenous organisations now do business in a highly regulatory and disciplinary regime of NPM. The pursuit of economic development comes from a growing indigenous anti-statism in the context of funding dependency, in which Aboriginal organisations, who are distinctly apathetical to the capacity of the state to deliver on Indigenous rights, and highly dependent on prescriptive government funding, pursue market strategies to achieve self-determination. Economic development is a means to an end: it provides a pathway to financial sustainability. However, the pursuit of economic development agendas has not fundamentally changed the objectives of Aboriginal organisations in relation to their distinctive role in society in relation to Aboriginal peoples and their rights to self-determination and community development.

So the temporary alignment between neoliberal and indigenous political projects serves certain ends. For example, economic development is a means to which indigenous peoples can become significant economic actors. Bell points to the case of Waikato-Tanui and Ngāi Tahu. Howard-Wagner points to similar motivation in the case of the economic agendas of the Darkinjung Local Aboriginal Land Council and Awabakal Ltd.

In Chapter 16, Maria Bargh progresses this argument in relation to indigenous entrepreneurship and economic development, bringing to the fore critical considerations. As Bargh notes, this is not simply a case of 'a group of elite Māori recognised by the Crown as economic actors, indoctrinated in neoliberal thought and a marginalised underclass of Māori resistance'. Moving beyond the binary or conceptualisations of Māori enterprise and Māori as 'only either champions or victims of neoliberal policies and practices', Bargh explores the 'areas of a diverse economy that are forging other alternative neoliberal or non-neoliberal worlds'. It is more instructive to consider what Māori want from economic and political activity and the ways in which they are agents in managing neoliberalism's constraints and pursuing its possibilities (Bargh, this volume, Chapter 16). For example, Māori agency is evident in the non-market opportunities that Bargh shows them as pursuing, as well as in the ascription of 'legal personhood' to a mountain as part of the Tūhoe Treaty settlement.

Organisation of the book

This collection is divided into three sections. The first teases out nuances in relation to indigenous rights and recognition in the neoliberal age. The contributors to the first section of the book also focus on the connection between governing, policy and neoliberalism, and illustrate the technologies mobilised to produce indigenous subjects capable of adjusting to increasingly changing and uncertain circumstances.

In Chapter 2, Isabel Altamirano-Jiménez shows how the introduction of matrimonial property rights on reserves in Canada not only functions to support the economic structure of the settler liberal state but also blames indigenous people for their circumstances and the 'backwardness' of their cultures.

Similarly, in Chapter 3, Cathy Eatock illustrates how resilience is used to terminate services in smaller remote Aboriginal communities in Australia and to impose private property for the purposes of fighting poverty. Building on Moreton-Robinson (2009), Eatock contends that resilience becomes a means to discipline Indigenous welfare recipients to take responsibilities for themselves while the state moves away from recognition.

In Chapter 4, Avril Bell focuses on the nature of the recognition of Māori by local government. Bell argues that neoliberal politics has shaped and constrained the recognition that is on offer. She introduces a number of important considerations taken up in more detail throughout the collection. Like O'Sullivan, she notes that devolution has led to Māori delivering services previously delivered by the state. Like McCormack, she suggests that the spaces opened up for Māori reflect market rationalities. She sees significant problems with the combining of neoliberalism and indigenous political projects because of the constraints it places on Māori governance models and the failure of those models to gain greater political power. Local government is for Bell emblematic of the failure of the Crown to adequately recognise Māori as partners to the Treaty of Waitangi.

In this chapter, neoliberalism comes to be more clearly identified as cooperative with recognition rather than opposed to it.

In Chapter 5, Mandy Yap and Eunice Yu note that, in Australia, policies aimed at improving Indigenous wellbeing have attempted to measure Indigenous performance according to hegemonic ideals and values that fail to consider Indigenous peoples' historical experiences of colonisation. The authors offer a broader perspective of Indigenous self-determination through working with the Yawuru community in Broome to model co-production of knowledge from the ground up.

Importantly, Yap and Yu draw on important empirical research to show that child welfare policy is determined by neoliberal values, but that Indigenous self-determination and wellbeing derives from different principles. This is an important contribution to this collection, by clearly including a discussion of Indigenous values as an alternative to neoliberal values. Although the chapter as a whole does not directly consider neoliberalism, it is a key part of this volume, which aims to cover the issue of neoliberalism and indigenous rights in the contemporary world. Considering this question only from the perspective of the state and non-indigenous frameworks would be limiting.

While a number of the authors in the second section, 'Pendulums and contradictions in neoliberalism governing everything from Indigenous disadvantage to Indigenous economic development in Australia', have contributed to our understanding of changes to Indigenous rights and recognition in Australia over the past decade or so, the chapters in this section provide a more in-depth understanding of the Indigenous policy in Australia in the present moment, giving more detailed consideration to this moment in the context of the neoliberal age.

In Chapter 6, Will Sanders draws attention to the demise of Indigenous representation in the Australian public policy space, as well as the narrowing administrative location of Indigenous-specific programs, following the abolition of ATSIC. In doing so, he revisits some of his arguments about how the former ATSIC and Indigenous organisations could together be thought of as moving 'towards an Indigenous order of Australian government' (Sanders 2002). He points to the importance of a strong Indigenous presence within Australian political institutions, arguing that Australia needs a strong Indigenous representative body within its political institutions for the very simple reason that some law and governmental authority in Australia *must* flow from Indigenous peoples and their precolonial history. He also explains how Australian public policy is still trying to recover from the abolition of ATSIC, over a decade on.

Sanders' deeply knowledgeable account of the end of ATSIC and the various new arrangements that have succeeded is a discussion of the profound changes in policy and Indigenous representation. He adopts a slightly different approach from some researchers, including in his rejection of the framing of neoliberalism as an immoveable force. While monolithic accounts of neoliberalism do foreclose possibilities for change, recent moves towards representation continue to show the importance of decolonising peoples' ideas in the contemporary world and how this challenges conventional framings of neoliberalism as opposed to such moves.

In Chapter 7, Karen Soldatic explores the effects of significant policy change in national disability income support, with particular reference to the impact of neoliberal restructuring of welfare regimes on Aboriginal and Torres Strait Islander people with disabilities in regional centres across Australia. Commonly referred to as welfare-to-work measures, there has been ample research globally on their implications for non-disabled income benefit recipients, though research on their impact on people with disabilities is minimal, and almost non-existent in terms of the effects on indigenous people living with disabilities. Income support measures have been critically important for regional towns experiencing ongoing economic change. Yet, we do not know how regional communities respond to these policy changes, nor do we understand how national disability income support policy impacts upon the wellbeing of Aboriginal and Torres Strait Islander people with disabilities living in regional Australia. Soldatic maps some of the issues that emerged out of interviews with disability service providers and advocacy groups responding to the changes on the ground.

In Chapter 8, Shelley Bielefeld explains the reduction of Indigenous peoples' rights in the context of cashless welfare transfers as a neoliberal intervention in the lives of Indigenous welfare recipients, tracking the introduction of the federal government trial of a Healthy Welfare Card following the Forrest Review in 2014. She examines the neoliberal rationalities underlying the intent of the Review and the legislation that saw the Healthy Welfare Care trialled in communities with significant numbers of Indigenous welfare recipients: Ceduna, Kununurra and Wyndham. She explains how Indigenous welfare recipients are tasked with 'responsibilisation'. However, Bielefeld also presents an alternative approach, or what she refers to as a reparations framework for Australia's First Peoples, funded by a kind of integrity tax, arguing that a new 'politics of distribution' (Ferguson 2015: 10) is long overdue.

In every policy field, there are some well-worn truths about how some of the stubborn features of policy areas are generated by characteristics that arise from aspects of neoliberal governance. This is especially true of Aboriginal housing in Australia where the way state and federal governments address problems of Aboriginal homelessness, high levels of crowding and poor-quality housing is seen to contribute to and perpetuate them. State recognition of Indigenous housing rights is characterised by tensions, contradictions and policy turnarounds in which the imposition of neoliberal ideologies of normalisation come up against the realities of culture and place. The result is policy instability and problematic outcomes for Aboriginal individuals and communities. In Chapter 9, Daphne Habibis analyses how these dynamics have played out in efforts to improve remote Aboriginal housing over the last three decades. She explains how, following the demise of ATSIC, Indigenous housing policy in Australia swung away from local provision by Aboriginal organisations towards the mainstreaming of housing delivery. In remote communities, this culminated in the National Partnership Agreement on Remote Indigenous Housing (NPARIH). Drawing on an investigation into the NPARIH reforms, Habibis suggests that in the closing years of NPARIH, policy is now swinging away from state to community provision. She reflects on how this policy roundabout impacts on Aboriginal communities and what can be done to address this.

In Chapter 10, Alex Page turns his attention to a more detailed consideration of the racialised effects of the IAS on Aboriginal organisations. His chapter points to the precarious or 'fragile' position of the Indigenous sector with minimal accountability of, and increased control by, the Australian Government at the federal level. He also points to how the IAS contributes to the undermining of the Indigenous sector's important role and achievements as an expression of Indigenous self-determination.

Along with many of the authors in this collection, Patrick Sullivan turns his attention to the intensification of techniques of control beyond traditional bureaucratic practice into every facet of social life under new or neoliberal public management, and how these impact upon previously relatively autonomous and largely self-governing organisations, such as Indigenous corporations. However, in Chapter 11, Sullivan not only draws on a case study of the effects of neoliberal public management, showing its importance, he equally demonstrates the importance of critically analysing contemporary public management as a coercive extension of the state, as well as considering alternatives. In his chapter, Sullivan aims to do so broadly, while tying this analysis to the position of Indigenous civil organisations in the Australian polity as a whole.

Going in a slightly different direction to Sullivan, in the next chapter Deirdre Howard-Wagner tracks the history of urban Aboriginal organisations, and explains the distinctive role they play in society in relation to urban Aboriginal peoples and their rights to self-determination and community development. In Chapter 12, Howard-Wagner explains how Aboriginal people in Newcastle had found organisational mechanisms for exercising their rights to self-determination and autonomy in matters relating to their internal and local affairs. She argues that urban Aboriginal organisations in this locality have proven essential to advocacy, the maintenance of community development and the creation of new social infrastructure, with their success resulting in both economic and social outcomes. She then goes on to explain how NPM reforms to social service delivery at the federal and state level, alongside changes in Indigenous policy over the last 12 years—including the new mainstreaming of Aboriginal service delivery after the abolition of ATSIC in 2005 and the Community Development Employment Projects (CDEP) program shortly after, and, more recently, the Indigenous Advancement Strategy (IAS)—has affected the capacity of urban Aboriginal organisations in Newcastle to perform these roles. She draws on a case study of these organisations in Newcastle to explain how new agendas to pursue economic development and become financially sustainable are a means to an end in terms of pursuing self-determination in the neoliberal age.

The final section in this collection is titled 'The dynamic relationship Māori have had with simultaneously resisting, manipulating and working with neoliberalism in New Zealand', and the authors of these chapters examine this relationship from a range of perspectives.

In Chapter 13, Dominic O'Sullivan argues that neoliberal reforms in New Zealand have had a significant but inconsistent influence on Māori legal, political, economic and cultural opportunities. He suggests that, despite a range of negative impacts for Māori (e.g. in the area of unemployment rates), the policy measures used to reduce the size of the state-created opportunities for some Māori to increase their collective wealth. He suggests that Māori delivery of public services has produced enhanced self-determination. He outlines the relationship between Tūhoe and the state as evidence of the creation of new relationships, which, O'Sullivan argues, were not previously possible on a significant scale.

O'Sullivan provides an excellent discussion of the many complex issues surrounding the possibilities and challenges created by Māori interaction with neoliberal regimes. His chapter concerns a different context with very different dynamics. The questions of agency and opportunity are very different to the coercive paternalistic form that Australian neoliberalism has taken. Its conclusions are obviously contested by others in the volume, but it is clearly in conversation with the other chapters. O'Sullivan's argument that '[t]he possibilities for Māori self-determination are broad and multifaceted. They exist beyond the neoliberal paradigm, as much as they exist within it' makes an important contribution to the perspectives in this volume.

In Chapter 14, Louise Humpage argues that the Māori political party has begun to achieve its goals in social policy for supporting Māori, but the political constraints it faces ultimately undermine the party's ability to hinder the broader running of neoliberalism. Humpage provides a detailed analysis of the Māori Party's social policy initiative, 'Whānau Ora', and argues that while the initiative has challenged aspects of neoliberalism, it has also extended neoliberalism. She concludes that compromising political relationships, like that between the Māori Party and the National Party, ultimately makes it less likely that some indigenous peoples will challenge neoliberal principles and policies in the future.

In Chapter 15, Fiona McCormack explores the case of fisheries management in New Zealand and in particular the introduction of the Quota Management System in 1986 as an example of market environmentalism. The individual transferable quota within the system, McCormack argues, is based on a neoliberal understanding that private property rights are superior to other forms of rights. She highlights how wealth, or a least money, can be generated from trading in quota rather than actual fish and can encourage these forms of market behaviours. McCormack argues that new class distinctions are therefore created among Māori, with some involved in trading quota and others trying to maintain fishing livelihoods. She concludes with a note of hope—that alongside the new class distinctions there are examples of Māori efforts to 'Māorify the economy', making the rolling out of neoliberalism an incomplete and contested process.

In her chapter, Maria Bargh argues there has been increasing recognition of Māori enterprises and of the Māori economy in a neoliberal age, which has been supported by some levels of political recognition particularly facilitated by the Māori Party. This recognition has led to criticisms of the emergence of a Māori neoliberal elite. In Chapter 16, Bargh argues however that this dichotomy of Māori neoliberal elite versus victims/resistors does not provide a full picture, and many of those people and entities labelled neoliberal are involved in numerous non-neoliberal activities. Highlighting these diverse activities, Bargh encourages an awareness and attentiveness to the many possibilities already existing outside of neoliberalism.

References

Altamirano-Jiménez I (2004). North American first peoples: Slipping up into market citizenship? *Citizenship Studies*, 8(4):349–65, doi.org/10.1080/1362 102052000316963.

Altamirano-Jiménez I (2013). *Indigenous encounters with neoliberalism: Place, women, and the environment in Canada and Mexico*, UBC Press.

Altamirano-Jiménez I (2014). Indigeneity, law and performance in the atlantic coast of Nicaragua. In Gilbert H & Gleghorn C (eds), *Recasting commodity and spectacle in indigenous America*, Institute for Advanced Studies, University of London Press, London.

Australian Government (2011). *The benefits of township leasing in the Northern Territory*, Fact Sheet, www.fahcsia.gov.au/sa/indigenous/progserv/ land/township_leasing/Pages/factsheet_3.aspx.

Banting K (1996). Social policy. In Doern, GB, Pal L & Tomlin B (eds), *Border crossings: The internationalization of Canadian policy*, Oxford University Press, Toronto.

Bargh M (2006). Changing the game plan: The Foreshore and Seabed Act and constitutional change. *Kōtuitui: New Zealand Journal of Social Sciences Online*, 1(1):13–24, doi.org/10.1080/1177083X.2006.9522408.

Bargh M (2007). Māori development. In Bargh M (ed.), *Resistance: An indigenous response to neoliberalism*, Huia, Wellington.

Barnett C (2005). The consolations of 'neoliberalism'. *Geoforum*, 36(1):7–12.

Barrera J (2017). Email reveals Trudeau Liberals playing games with UDRIP. *APTN National News*, 11 May, aptnnews.ca/2017/05/11/email-reveals-trudeau-liberals-playing-double-game-on-undrip-saganash/.

Bashevkin S (2003). Do urban governance changes affect women's representation? A preliminary look at Toronto and London. *Canadian Issues*, February:23–5.

Bielefeld S (2012). Compulsory income management and Indigenous Australians, *UNSW Law Review*, 35(2):522–60.

Bradley G (2014). Mighty River signs secret Lake Taupo deal with Māori Trust. *New Zealand Herald*, 22 December, www.nzherald.co.nz/business/news/ article.cfm?c_id=3&objectid=11377982.

Brenner N, Peck J & Theodore N (2010). Variegated neoliberalization: geographies, modalities, pathways. *Global Networks*, 10(2):182–222, doi.org/10.1111/j.1471-0374.2009.00277.x.

Brodie J (2008). We are all equal now: Contemporary gender politics in Canada. *Feminist Theory*, 9(2):145–64.

Brown W (2003). Neoliberalism and the end of liberal democracy, *Theory and Event*, 7(1), doi.org/10.1353/tae.2003.0020.

Cahill D (2010). 'Actually existing neoliberalism' and the global economic crisis. *Labour & Industry: a journal of the social and economic relations of work*, 20(3):298–316.

Clarke J (2004). Dissolving the public realm: The logics and limits of neoliberalism. *Journal of Social Policy*, 33(1):27–48, doi.org/10.1017/S0047279403007244.

Coates K (2016). Indigenous support for development is being heard. *Inside Policy*, MacDonald Laurier Institute, June, www.macdonaldlaurier.ca/indigenous-support-for-development-is-being-heard-ken-coates-in-inside-policy/.

Coulthard G (2007). Subjects of empire: Indigenous peoples and the 'politics of recognition' in Canada. *Contemporary Political Theory*, 6(4):437–60, doi.org/10.1057/palgrave.cpt.9300307.

Coulthard G (2014). *Red skin, white masks: Rejecting the colonial politics of recognition*, University of Minnesota Press, doi.org/10.5749/minnesota/9780816679645.001.0001.

Daes EI (2003). Article 3 of the Draft UN Declaration on the Rights of Indigenous Peoples: Obstacles and consensus. Paper presented at the Rights and Democracy Seminar of Experts on the Right to Self-Determination of Indigenous Peoples, New York.

Dean M (2002). Powers of life and death beyond governmentality. *Cultural Values* 6(1–2):119–38, doi.org/10.1080/1362517022019775.

Dean M (2004). *Governmentality: Power and rule in modern society*. SAGE Publications, London.

Durie M (2004). *Public sector reform, indigeneity, and the goals of the Māori development*, Commonwealth Advanced Seminar.

Fairhead J, Leach M & Scoones I (2012). Green grabbing: A new appropriation of nature? *Journal of Peasant Studies* 39(2):237–61, doi.org/10.1080/03066150.2012.671770.

Ferguson J (2015). *Give a man a fish: Reflections on the new politics of distribution*, Duke University Press, Durham & London, doi.org/10.1215/9780822375524.

Fine B & Saad-Filho A (2017). Thirteen things you need to know about neoliberalism. *Critical Sociology* 43(4–5):685–706.

Goldberg DT (2002). *The racial state*, Blackwell, Massachusetts.

Goldberg DT (2009). *The threat of race: Reflections on racial neoliberalism*, Blackwell, Massachusetts.

Gover, K (2015). Settler state theory, 'CANZUS' and the United Nations Declaration of the Rights of Indigenous Peoples. *European Journal of International Law* 26(1):345–73.

Green K (2002). Welfare reform in Australia and the United States: Tracing the emergence and critiques of the new paternalism and mutual obligation. *The Drawing Board: An Australian Review of Public Affairs* 3(1):15–32.

Hall S (2003). New Labour has picked up where Thatcherism left off: Blair's project has been to absorb social democracy into neoliberalism. *The Guardian*, 6 August:1.

Harvey D (2006). Neo-Liberalism as creative destruction. *Geografiska Annaler: Series B, Human Geography* 88(2):145–58, doi.org/10.1111/j.0435-3684.2006.00211.x.

Howard-Wagner D (2006). Post Indigenous rights: the political rationalities and technologies governing Federal Indigenous Affairs in Australia in the contemporary period. PhD thesis, University of Newcastle, Australia.

Howard-Wagner D (2007). Restoring social order through tackling passive welfare: The statutory intent of the *Northern Territory National Emergency Response Act 2007* (Cth) and *Social Security and Other Legislation Amendment (Welfare Payment Reform) Act 2007* (Cth). *Current Issues in Criminal Justice*, 19:243.

Howard-Wagner, D (2008). Legislating away indigenous rights. *Law Text Culture* 12:45.

Howard-Wagner D (2009). Whiteness, power relations, resistance and the practical recognition of Indigenous rights in Newcastle. *Theory in Action*, 2(1):40–65, doi.org/10.3798/tia.1937-0237.08028.

Howard-Wagner D (2010a). The state's Intervention in Indigenous affairs in the Northern Territory: Governing the Indigenous population through violence, abuse and neglect. In Browne C & McGill J (eds), *Violence in France and Australia: Disorder the postcolonial welfare state*, Sydney University Press, Australia.

Howard-Wagner D (2010b). From denial to emergency: Governing Indigenous communities in Australia. In Fassin D & Pandolfi M (eds), *Contemporary States of Emergency: The Politics of Military and Humanitarian Interventions*, Zone Books.

Howard-Wagner D (2012). Reclaiming the northern territory as a settler-colonial space. *Arena Journal*, 37/38:220.

Howard-Wagner D (2015). Child wellbeing and protection as a regulatory system in the neoliberal age: Forms of aboriginal agency and resistance engaged to confront the challenges for aboriginal people and community-based aboriginal organisations. *Australian Indigenous Law Review* 19(1):88–102.

Howard-Wagner D (2017). Governance of indigenous policy in the neoliberal age: Indigenous disadvantage and the intersecting of paternalism and neoliberalism as a racial project. *Ethnic and Racial Studies* 41(7):1332–51, doi.org/10.1080/01419870.2017.1287415.

Howard-Wagner D (in press). 'Moving from transactional government to enablement' in Indigenous service delivery. *Australian Journal of Social Issues*.

Howard-Wagner D & Kelly B (2011). Containing Aboriginal mobility in the Northern Territory: From protectionism to interventionism. *Law Text Culture* 15:102.

Kelsey J (2005). Māori, Te Tiriti, and globalisation: The invisible hand of the colonial state. In Belgrave M, Kawharu M & Williams D (eds), *Waitangi revisited*, Oxford University Press, Oxford.

Larner W, Heron RL, & Lewis N (2007). Co-constituting 'after neoliberalism': Political projects and globalizing governmentalities in Aotearoa/New Zealand. In England K & Ward K (eds), *Neoliberalization: States, networks, peoples*, Blackwell, Oxford, doi.org/10.1002/9780470712801.ch9.

Li T (2010). Indigeneity, capitalism and the management of dispossession. *Current Anthropology*, 51(3):385–400, doi.org/10.1086/651942.

Lightfoot S (2012). Selective endorsement without intent to implement: Indigenous rights and the anglosphere. *The International Journal of Human Rights*, 16(1):100–22. doi.org/10.1080/13642987.2012.622139.

Lindroth M (2014). Indigenous rights as tactics of neoliberal governance. Practices of expertise at the United Nations, *Social and Legal Studies* 23(3):341–61, doi.org/10.1177/0964663914524265.

McCormack F (2011). Levels of indigeneity: The Maori and neoliberalism. *Journal of the Royal Anthropological Institute*, 17(2):281–300.

McKeen W & Porter A (2003). Politics and transformation: Welfare state restructuring in Canada. In Clement W & Vosko S (eds), *Changing Canada: Political economy as transformation*, McGill-Queen's University Press.

Mead LM (1997). The rise of paternalism. In Mead LM (ed.), *The new paternalism: Supervisory approaches to poverty*, The Brookings Institution, Washington.

Moreton-Robinson A (2009). Imagining the good indigenous citizen: Race war and the pathology of patriarchal white sovereignty. *Cultural Studies Review*, 15(2):61–79, doi.org/10.5130/csr.v15i2.2038.

Nadesan M (2008). *Governmentality, biopower and everyday life*, Taylor and Francis, New York.

New Zealand Government (2007). *Ngāti Tūwharetoa*, www.govt.nz/treaty-settlement-documents/ngati-tuwharetoa/.

Pasternack S (2015). How will capitalism save colonialism: The privatization of reserve lands in Canada. *Antipode* 47(1):179–96, doi.org/10.1111/anti.12094.

Peck E (2004). Modernisation: The ten commitments of New Labour's approach to public management? *International Public Management Journal* 7(1):1.

Postero N (2007). *Now we are citizens: Indigenous politics in postmulticultural Bolivia*, Stanford University Press.

Razack S (2008). *Casting out: The eviction of muslims from western law and politics*, University of Toronto Press, Toronto.

Rose N & Miller P (1991). Political power beyond the state: Problematics of government. *British Journal of Sociology* 43(2):173–205, doi.org/10.2307/591464.

Sanders W (2002). *Towards an Indigenous order of Australian Government: Rethinking self-determination as Indigenous affairs policy*, Discussion Paper 230, Centre for Aboriginal Economic Policy Research, The Australian National University, Canberra.

Shore C & Kawharu M (2014). The Crown in New Zealand. *Sites* 11(1):17–38, doi.org/10.11157/sites-vol11iss1id267.

Singh J (2014). Recognition and self-determination approaches from above and below. In Eisenberg A, Webber J, Coulthard G & Boiselle A (eds), *Recognition vs self-determination: Dilemmas of emancipatory politics*, UBC Press, Toronto, Vancouver.

Soss J, Fording R & Schram S (2011). *Disciplining the poor: Neoliberal paternalism and the persistent power of race*, Chicago University Press, Chicago, doi.org/10.7208/chicago/9780226768786.001.0001.

Spronk S (2007). Roots of resistance to urban water privatization in Bolivia: The 'new working class', the crisis of neoliberalism, and public services. *International Labor and Working-Class History* 71(1):8–28, doi.org/10.1017/S0147547907000312.

Turnbull M (2017). Speech to Parliament on the 2017 Closing the Gap Report, 14 February 2017, www.pm.gov.au/media/closing-gap-report-statement-parliament.

Tūwharetoa Māori Trust Board (2017). *Tūwharetoa Māori Trust Board stands by water interests*, media release, 5 July 2017, www.tuwharetoa.co.nz/media-statement-tuwharetoa-maori-trust-board-stands-by-water-interests/.

Vanstone A (2005). Address to National Press Club, 23 February, Canberra.

Venugopal R (2015). Neoliberalism as concept. *Economy and Society* 44(2):165–87.

Wacquant L (2009). *Punishing the poor: The neoliberal government of social insecurity*, Duke University Press, doi.org/10.1215/9780822392255.

Wacquant L (2010). Crafting the neoliberal state: Workfare, prisonfare, and social insecurity. *Sociological Forum* 25(2):197–220.

Waitangi Tribunal (2012). *National freshwater and geothermal inquiry*, Government Print, 2012, forms.justice.govt.nz/search/Documents/WT/wt_DOC_59941926/Wai2358W.pdf.

Williams D (1999). *Te Kooti Tango Whenua: The Native Land Court 1864–1909*, Huia Publishers, Wellington.

Williams M (2014). On the use and abuse of recognition in politics. In Eisenberg A, Webber J, Coulthard G & Boiselle A (eds), *Recognition vs self-determination: dilemmas of emancipatory politics*, UBC Press, Toronto, Vancouver.

Wilson J (2015). Why it's time to stop worrying about paternalism in health policy. In Schramme T (ed.), *New perspectives on paternalism and health care*, Springer, Switzerland, doi.org/10.1007/978-3-319-17960-5_13.

Winant H (2004). *The new politics of race: Globalism, difference, justice*, University of Minnesota Press, Minneapolis.

Wolfe P (2006). Settler colonialism and the elimination of the native. *Journal of Genocide Research* 8(4):387–409, doi.org/10.1080/14623520601056240.

Young A (2012). Key on water: no one owns water. *NZ Herald*, 7 February, www.nzherald.co.nz/nz/news/article.cfm?c_id=1&objectid=10783913.

PART 1

The connection between the act of
governing, policy and neoliberalism

2

Privatisation and dispossession in the name of indigenous women's rights

Isabel Altamirano-Jiménez

Introduction

The restructuring of the neoliberal state has had important effects on indigenous communities. One the one hand, it has opened up the space for the recognition of indigenous rights. On the other, recognition has reinforced the authority of the state and produced zones of legal dissonance. Although the recognition of indigenous rights at the national and international law levels has been unprecedented, continued intervention in indigenous life calls attention to the strategies used by the state to blame indigenous peoples for their 'backwardness' while intervening to improve their lives.

In this chapter, I consider how the simultaneous recognition of indigenous 'culture' as a set of practices for asserting land rights and the representation of indigenous 'customs' as 'inconsistent' with state laws and international human rights shapes how the neoliberal state relates to indigenous peoples. Focusing on the Family Homes and Matrimonial Interests Act in Canada and the Indigenous Electoral Reform 2014 in Mexico, I analyse how indigenous women's rights are contentiously mobilised by the respective states in order to intervene in indigenous communities. While the first example is concerned with the introduction of private property on reserve land, the second one focuses on using indigenous women's rights to further limit indigenous self-government. In both examples, the vulnerability of indigenous women is conceived of as an inherently indigenous cultural problem that is remedied by introducing changes that 'improve' their lives. This chapter argues that, as a strategy of governance, 'culturalising' problems depoliticises patriarchy and histories of dispossession and demands that indigenous peoples take responsibilities for increasing risks. From this perspective, the indigenous neoliberal subject is vulnerable and resilient: vulnerable to 'improvement', yet resilient to risks.

Governance, privatisation and the neoliberal state

Theorisations of neoliberalism have often treated it exclusively as an economic project involving deregulation, regulation, privatisation, individualisation and transformation of state–citizen relationships. Similarly important are theorisations of neoliberalism as a governance process that is not primarily focused on the economy but rather on desired political, social, cultural and environmental effects (Brown 2001). The concept of neoliberal governance assemblage captures how the economy, society and the environment are governed by networked interactions between states, financial institutions, non-governmental organisations, political elites and communities, producing specific outcomes. Larner warns that although hegemonic, neoliberalism is not a unified entity and requires that we pay attention to its variance and to the contradictory nature of its policies (2003: 510). Others (Peck 2004, Howitt 2009) have noted that although local contexts determine outcomes, it is important to identify the commonalities within the apparent differences.

Despite the importance of these contributions, often scholars have failed to consider how neoliberalism interacts with colonialism. As has been argued elsewhere, neoliberal policies emerge from and are rooted in specific colonial, social, political, cultural and economic contexts, shaping their locally contingent form (Altamirano-Jiménez 2013). A limited body of scholarship has focused on the reshaping of the relationship between the state and indigenous peoples under neoliberalism in North America (Altamirano-Jiménez 2004, 2013, Macdonald 2011, Pasternack 2015).

More recently, a critical body of scholarship has drawn attention to how dispossession has continued under historically changing capitalist forms of accumulation (Altamirano-Jiménez 2004, 2013, Coulthard 2014, Pasternack 2015).

In settler contexts, neoliberalism has been considered part of the same structure of domination (Strakosch 2015) that drives indigenous dispossession. Although historically colonial states have systematically dismantled indigenous nationhood, neoliberal state policies blame indigenous peoples for their conditions of life. In other words, neoliberal state policies not only blame indigenous peoples for surviving colonisation, but also force them to be responsible for the effects of colonisation. By conceiving of colonialism and neoliberalism as separate yet articulated processes, it is possible to track the forms dispossession takes and the current ways through which dispossession is managed.

In Canada, indigenous peoples have been resisting dispossession and privatisation of their lands since the mid-19th century, with the Enfranchisement and Assimilation Acts and later the White Paper 1969. While indigenous rights have been recognised, indigenous peoples have been granted a form of precarious citizenship that is tested every day. Individualisation, self-caring and pathologising discourses have served to rationalise indigenous communities' precarious living conditions as a product of dysfunctional cultural traditions and lifestyles and not as a result of dispossession (Howard-Wagner 2012, Altamirano-Jiménez 2013, Strakosch 2015). The promotion of private property on reserve to combat poverty and extent matrimonial property rights to First Nations women not only erases the history of land dispossession but also legitimises the state as the grantor and distributor of property rights.

In Mexico, on the other hand, while indigenous land has been alienated, the recognition of indigenous 'normative systems' as an extension of indigenous peoples' rights to political autonomy has created legal dissonances. Moreover, the characterisations of indigenous laws as backward, illiberal, 'customary' practices that discriminate against indigenous women has justified state intervention in indigenous communities affairs to contain indigenous self-government.

The Family Homes and Matrimonial Interests Act

In a 30-year span, the Canadian state created government commissions and legislation to advance women's rights. However, the Canadian Government began to eliminate funding for women's organisations in the late 1990s with the intention of reducing its deficit. When the Harper Conservative government was first elected in 2006, it continued to undermine human rights and the status of women under the assumption that gender equality has long been achieved in Canada (Brodie & Bakker 2008, Altamirano-Jiménez 2009). These assumptions are not only at odds with the reality of women's lives, but also disregard those, such as indigenous women, whose rights were never fully realised. Indigenous women are the most marginalised and impoverished in Canadian society: they have borne a gendered burden because of the Indian Act. The Indian Act defined who was an 'Indian', created the reserve system and transformed indigenous peoples into wards of the state. In defining who was and was not 'Indian', the government took away the self-determination from indigenous nations, and inflicted racist and sexist consequences on affected First Nations women and their children. Gendered colonial policies created differences between indigenous men and women and between Indian and non-indigenous women, positioned indigenous women's rights as being in conflict with the inherent and constitutional rights of First Nations to self-determined citizenship, and have important implications for other policies regarding traditional marital practices, housing and justice (Green 2007, Green & Peach 2007).

In 1986, the Supreme Court of Canada ruled that provincial and territorial laws on matrimonial real property do not apply on reserve land, which falls under the federal government jurisdiction. This decision created a gap in the law between First Nation men and women, and between indigenous and non-indigenous women. Lack of matrimonial property rights on reserve has resulted in the women having little recourse in cases of domestic violence. If colonial laws and policy changed communities' forms of social organisation and the boundaries of inclusion and exclusion within indigenous communities, neoliberal policies bring indigenous lands into the market while claiming to extend human rights to property for women.

When prime minister Stephen Harper came to power in 2006, he implemented a new Aboriginal policy whose main focus was to alleviate indigenous poverty. He rejected the Kelowna Accords signed by premiers and indigenous leaders to close the gap between indigenous and non-indigenous Canadians. Harper noted that the Kelowna emphasis on reserves did not reflect the fact that the majority of the indigenous population lives in cities (Carlson 2011). His indigenous policy focused instead on strategies to alleviate poverty and programs based on supposed common sense and the acceptance of everyone's responsibility. The then Minister of Indian Affairs suggested that the federal government would never be able to meet the housing needs of First Nations people unless they took responsibility for themselves and utilised an inactive asset: their land (Department of Indian and Northern Affairs Canada 2010).

Unlike previous governments, the Harper Government dismissed the need to establish a new relationship with indigenous peoples, noting all that was needed was to make the existing relationship work (Altamirano-Jiménez 2011: 116). The government's commitment to indigenous peoples focused on empowering those indigenous citizens who were 'ready' to assume their place in the economy, while protecting the vulnerable (Carlson 2011). At the core of this major policy was the creation of new legal mechanisms to title and privatise property land on reserve. With the support of prominent indigenous leaders, Bill C-63, the First Nations Property Ownership Act (FNPOA), was introduced in the House of Commons on 10 December, 2009 'to enable participating First Nations communities to request that the Government of Canada make regulations respecting the establishment and operation of a system for the registration of interests and rights in reserve lands'.[1]

This Bill was represented as an opportunity for First Nations to finally become property owners and entrepreneurial subjects: a gesture of inclusion that is only possible when erasing the history of land dispossession (Pasternack 2015: 184). The production of ideas concerning the privatisation of reserve land resulted from a powerful alliance among think tanks, indigenous leaders, politicians and some academics like Thomas Flanagan, adviser to prime minister Harper. Flanagan and Alcantara (2002, see also Alcantara 2005) rationalised privatisation as an opportunity to alleviate poverty and allow First Nations people to

---

1   For the full text of the Bill, see www.lop.parl.gc.ca/Content/LOP/LegislativeSummaries/40/2/c63-e.pdf.

become more productive members of Canadian economy. Inspired by 'successful' experiences of privatisation in countries of the global south, including Mexico, and by the World Bank's recommendations on land administration and poverty reduction (1994), these authors advanced the idea that while there are advantages to customary property rights, the disadvantages are many, including the lack of legal recognition (Flanagan & Alcantara 2002: 4). The authors argued that customary land tenure was subject to political management and did not provide tenure security, leaving individuals little incentive to pursue economic development projects on reserves. Flanagan and Alcantatra argue that customary land holding and other 'cultural' practices such as relying on kin relations and in-kind contributions were fuelling unemployment and consequently poor housing conditions that exist on many reserves (2002: 9). In their view, capitalising on land is encouraged, not as a way to honour treaties, but rather because property makes land more productive (Pasternack 2015: 180). In 2011, Conservative members of parliament proposed changing the reserve system and advocated for private property. The FNPOA became the site of convergence among state and non-state actors, and some indigenous leaders, supporting privatisation on reserves. Others, in contrast, opposed, seeing the Bill as a version of the White Paper 1969.

While privatisation on reserve was being debated, the Harper Government's concern with 'protecting' the vulnerable was translated into Bill S-2, Family Homes on Reserves and Matrimonial Interests or Rights Act (FHRMIRA). The Bill aimed to increase protection for the spouse who was not named in a certificate of possession. In pushing for the Bill, the Minister of Aboriginal Affairs and Northern Development (as the ministry was then known), Bernard Valcourt, noted: 'It is unacceptable that in this day and age people living on reserve are not afforded the same rights as those living off reserves' (Parliament of Canada 2013). The Conservative Government in power relied on female MPs to advance the Bill, which they represented as a basic issue of gender equality. The Bill provisions prevented the person entitled to the allotment (i.e. named on the certificate of possession) from selling the land without permission and from evicting their spouse from the family home. If the introduction of private property on reserve was cast as a way to empower indigenous communities who are ready to be part of the economy, Bill S-2 was justified as a way to extend rights to First Nations women. In this case, the right to property is granted to First Nations women to rectify civil and political rights violations. However, this construction conceals the violence of imposing private property on reserve de facto.

The Native Women's Association of Canada (NWAC) consultation showed that First Nation women do indeed experience greater disadvantages and are allocated less property certificates than men. NWAC's study showed that a greater percentage of women live off-reserve and that the differences between on- and off-reserve suggest that matrimonial real property has an uneven impact on where a child resides. While the report acknowledged that matrimonial property rights would greatly benefit women, the report recommended the adoption of a more holistic approach based on indigenous peoples' traditions and that accommodates human rights, and acknowledges the leading traditional role of First Nations women in their communities (NWAC 2008).

The FHRMIRA ultimately received Royal Assent in June 2013. In the end, NWAC did not support the Bill. The Assembly of First Nations (AFN) also rejected the Bill, arguing it was a unilateral decision that interfered with First Nations' land title and treaty rights (AFN 2014). Both NWAC and AFN alleged that the government consultation process had not been comprehensive and that many of their recommendations had not been adopted. The organisations claimed the government had omitted two important recommendations. One, the limited access to courts and lawyers in remote communities and two, the need for resources to help First Nations develop their own codes and dispute resolution (AFN 2014).

FHRMIRA allows bands to enact their own matrimonial property codes. It states that when a relationship ends, each partner is entitled to half of the value of the interest in the family home. I have noticed elsewhere (Altamirano-Jiménez 2012) that FHRMIRA also has substantial problems. For example, in order for FHRMIRA to apply, applicants must have access to lawyers and the court systems, which is difficult in remote rural communities. Further, it operates with the assumption that the family homes are occupied by a nuclear family, ignoring the fact that a 'family home' may be occupied by multiple family members, who may not have the ability to actually pay mortgage or rent. A 2006 census conducted by Canada Mortgage and Housing Corporation found that 53 per cent of indigenous people on reserves live in homes that needed major repairs or were overcrowded, or both (Canada Mortgage and Housing Corporation 2011).

Moreover, FHRMIRA does little to mitigate the potential homelessness of either of the parties involved in a marriage breakdown. Although the extension of matrimonial property rights to indigenous women on reserve was justified as the inclusion of indigenous women in the enjoyment of citizenship rights, FHRMIRA does not address the current housing and shelter shortages that complicate the division of property. MacTaggart points out that the application of FHRMIRA will likely produce gender discriminatory outcomes as a result of the historical gender disparities and current housing shortages (2015: 2). As a fundamental pillar of colonialism, property is a modality through which Canada continues to be produced as a white settler society. Dispossession of indigenous lands was central in creating property in Canada, the extension of property rights to indigenous people is crucial for the neoliberal state to delegate its fiduciary obligations and responsibilities to First Nations communities.

Recognising indigenous law, alienating land

While in settler societies private property is entwined with colonial practices of land dispossession, the privatisation of collectively held indigenous and peasant lands while the North American Free Trade Agreement (NAFTA) was being negotiated in Mexico provides some insights about one of the cases Flanagan and Alcantara consider a 'success story' in advancing private property on reserve in Canada. In the early 1990s, the Salinas Government introduced a series of neoliberal changes aimed at liberalising indigenous and peasant control over their lands and other resources. Following Igoe and Brockington (2007), the concept of 're-regulation' is used here to illustrate how the Mexican state transformed previously untradeable entities such as the *ejidos* (plots of land that could not be sold or bought, granted by the state to indigenous people and peasants who had been dispossessed) and communal fishing grounds into tradeable commodities through privatisation. While the recognition of property was represented as a way of protecting indigenous landholdings, transferable property also allows capital to access different types of resources. As NAFTA was being negotiated, a reform package aimed at liberalising different types of resources was passed. Article 27 of the Mexican Constitution not only liberalised indigenous peoples' and peasants' control of their lands but also made it possible to buy fishing grounds and coastal land for aquaculture purposes. With this change, indigenous and peasant communities were no longer considered impoverished and egalitarian communities in need of government's help, but instead were seen as entrepreneurial petty producers who needed to use their resources more efficiently (Leslie 2000: 41). Indeed, narratives of old, backward and unsustainable livelihoods justified 'trade not aid' and promoted neoliberal policies as the salvation strategy in rural areas (World Bank 1990). Moreover, while land plots were previously granted mainly to males, women had historically participated in agricultural activities and accessed resources informally (Altamirano-Jiménez 2013: 83). Privatisation effectively excluded women from having access to the resources they used and from the customary inheritance rights they enjoyed before the counter reforms (Deere & León 2000).

Besides Article 27, Article 4 of the Constitution (now Article 2) was also changed to recognise the 'pluricultural' nature of the Mexican state and the right of indigenous peoples to self-determination and to exercise their customary laws in the internal regulation of their communities, while protecting individual rights, human rights and particularly indigenous women's rights. The ratification of the International Labor Organization Convention 169 (the Indigenous and Tribal Peoples Convention) by the Mexican Government in 1989 was central to defining the ways in which indigenous internal normative systems were recognised. According to Article 1 of Convention 169:

> tribal peoples in independent countries are those whose social, cultural, and economic conditions distinguish them from other sections of the national community, and whose status is ruled wholly or partially by their own customs and traditions or by special laws or regulations.[2]

Article 8(2) states that tribal and indigenous peoples 'have the right to retain their customs and institutions, where these are not incompatible with fundamental human rights defined by the national law and with internationally recognized human rights'.

Although the Mexican national constitution recognised indigenous peoples' rights in 1992, states were given the option to implement these rights on an individual basis. Oaxaca became the first state to change its internal constitution. In 1995, it recognised indigenous normative systems, a longstanding claim of the indigenous movement; later, in 1998, it recognised the collective right to indigenous autonomy. Oaxaca is located in southwestern Mexico, next to the states of Puebla, Chiapas, Guerrero and Veracruz. Oaxaca is Mexico's most culturally diverse state and has the largest indigenous population. According to official data

---

2   For the full text of the Indigenous and Tribal Peoples Convention 1989, see www.ilo.org/dyn/normlex/en/f?p=NORMLEXPUB:12100:0::NO::P12100_ILO_CODE:C169.

(Instituto Nacional de Estadistica y Geografia 2016), 48.8 per cent of the population belongs to one of the 16 indigenous peoples inhabiting this state. Oaxaca has 570 municipalities, more than any other state in the country. Historically, the creation of municipalities has been one way for indigenous communities to maintain their territorial and political autonomy, as they constitute a third level of government in Mexico (Velásquez Cepeda 1998: 15–114, Recondo 2001).

State recognition of indigenous customary law fostered a heated debate on the nature of the rights granted to indigenous peoples. While indigenous opposition to the privatisation of indigenous land was ignored, the recognition of indigenous customary law became the site of contestation over the status of indigenous communities. In this polarised discussion, supporters of indigenous customary law tended to idealise the indigenous past and communities' harmonious norms and practices, while opponents reproduced colonial discourses portraying indigenous communities as residues of primitive cultures. In this debate, violence and discrimination against indigenous women became the ultimate measurement of the 'backwardness' of indigenous cultures. Stories of women being sold into marriage, discriminated against and exploited justified questioning the ability of indigenous peoples to govern themselves in light of such illiberal practices (Newdick 2005: 74). Although certain practices that discriminate against indigenous women have been justified as being 'customary', the assumption that national and international law are neutral conceals the ways in which the limited recognition of indigenous rights frees state financial resources while restructuring indigenous communities. Moreover, the characterisation of indigenous customary practices as being incompatible with human rights, specifically the rights of indigenous women, has been used by political elites to oppose and limit indigenous autonomy (Sierra 2009: 4, Kuokkanen 2012: 44). By mobilising this definition of 'customary', states and international organisations have attempted to justify gender inequalities as inherent to indigenous cultures and not as a result of colonialism or of structural power relations.

The economic restructuring of the country was marked by the elimination of tariffs and import permits for agricultural goods, the end of subsidies and the dismantling of state-run agricultural institutions. The consequent contraction of domestic market prices, along with cuts in the state's support for agriculture, made traditional rural livelihoods extremely challenging, fuelling massive international and urban migration as families struggled to make ends meet. Although the introduction of private property was to homogenise relations to property and to create a land market, indigenous *ejido* holders have responded differently. Some maintain indigenous principles of collective land holding, others conceive of land in economic and exclusive terms, exacerbating conflict (Torres-Mazuera 2016: 60). Moreover, the simultaneous privatisation of *ejido* lands and the recognition of indigenous normative systems created a situation where the territorial jurisdiction of indigenous peoples and that of self-government become legally dissonant as a result of coexisting legal systems. Furthermore, indigenous legal principles have become blurred as a result of the contestation of rights, and individuals drawing on different interacting legal regimes. This blurring, I argue, is used productively by the state to regulate its relationship with indigenous peoples. Constitutionalism and recourse to law have been essential to the reconfiguration of the neoliberal state and indigenous peoples' resources. As Povinelli has noted, rather than taking away resources from the national colonial state, the primary purpose of recognising indigenous customary law has been 'to provide the symbolic and affective conditions necessary to garner financial investment in the global economy' (2002: 42). I would add that by recognising indigenous customary law, the state has downloaded the risk of land dispossession onto self-regulated indigenous communities, which are under constant state surveillance.

The notion of autonomous internal regulation represents the state as a neutral entity fostering good governance and the community as a space of relationships—instead of a geographical or political space—where the behaviour of its members needs to be regulated according to its own values (Li 2011: 101). The notion of internal self-regulation is thus central to how indigenous traditional normative systems are recognised and can be measured according to various indicators, including universal human rights. Therefore, indigenous normative systems are seen as 'naturally present yet potentially deficient' (Li 2011: 105), requiring constant intervention from the state. Poole notes that the perceived deficiency of indigenous traditional normative systems is in fact productive (2006). Legal recognition in Oaxaca created a grey area in which the legitimacy of indigenous customary law is always in question (Velásquez Cepeda 1998: 150). Unlike the liberal state that sought to expand its power and control over the national territory, the neoliberal state seems to seek to create zones of illegibility where marginalised populations take responsibility for themselves under the constant threat of being misrecognised by the state (Poole 2006: 19). Both the colonial and the neoliberal state strategies, however, constitute attempts to legitimise authority through the distribution of inclusion and exclusion.

While property rights were not extended to indigenous women as part of the neoliberal land reforms, the Oaxaca Indigenous Law included an article on the rights of indigenous women without clearly specifying them. Article 46 affirms that the state government will promote, within the framework of indigenous traditional norms, the recognition of women in their communities and their full participation in activities not defined by tradition. The way indigenous women's rights and tradition were articulated in this article reinforces the idea that indigenous traditions are inherently illiberal. From this perspective, indigenous women's experiences of domestic violence, poverty and discrimination are understood as exclusively cultural problems hindering women's ability to exercise agency. By deploying a static and essentialised definition of 'customs' and 'tradition', the state attempts to situate gender inequalities as a product of indigenous cultures (Merry 2003).

By constructing indigenous law as illiberal and national law as objective, neutral and protecting rights, the state has become the arbiter of what practices are acceptable, while moving away from issues of distribution and social programs. The linking of self-regulated communities, development and indigenous women's rights have constructed a field of governance that enables the state and its experts to intervene in indigenous peoples' everyday lives. While the law attempts to create the perception that the state is absent from the sphere of indigenous normative systems, it is very much part of it (De Marinis 2011: 482–3). The law also conceals how processes of state formation and market involvement have already produced specific constellations of governance practices in specific places (Li 2001: 159).

Conclusion

In this chapter, I have explored the role of private property in reorganising indigenous communities under neoliberalism. Specifically, I have shown how indigenous women's rights are mobilised by the state as a technology of inclusion with the purpose of containing self-government and indigenous resistance to changes in property rights. I argued that this technology of inclusion operates in new flexible ways, moving away from categorical recognition and instead focusing on the indigenous neoliberal subjects' capacities to behave in expected ways.

Property is a modality through which Canada has been and continues to be produced as a white settler society. If dispossession of indigenous lands was central in creating property, the extension of property rights to indigenous people is crucial for the neoliberal state to delegate its responsibilities and potentially its fiduciary obligations to First Nations communities. Moreover, the extension of matrimonial property rights to indigenous women living on reserve has de facto introduced private property on reserve. In Mexico, on the other hand, the privatisation of *ejido* lands became a mechanism for reorganising and transforming indigenous communities into petty producers who needed to utilise their resources more efficiently. Furthermore, privatisation downloaded the risk of dispossession directly onto indigenous communities. While property was not extended to indigenous women, their rights became a site of intervention in indigenous self-government.

References

AFN (Assembly of First Nations) (2014). *Matrimonial real property on reserves: Our lands, our families, our solutions.* Winnipeg, www.afn.ca/uploads/files/mrp/dec_2014_sca_-_mrp_update_fe.pdf.

Alcantara C (2005). Certificate of possession and First Nations housing: A case study of the Six Nations housing program. *Canadian Journal of Law and Society* 20(2):183–205, doi.org/10.1353/jls.2006.0019.

Altamirano-Jiménez I (2004). North American First Peoples: Slipping up into market citizenship? *Citizenship Studies* 8(4):349–65, doi.org/10.1080/1362 102052000316963.

Altamirano-Jiménez I (2009). Neoliberal and social investment re-constructions of woman and indigeneity. In Dobrowolsky A (ed.), *Women and public policy in Canada today: A study of continuity and change*, Oxford University Press, Toronto.

Altamirano-Jiménez I (2011). Settler colonialism, human rights and indigenous women. *Prairie Forum* 36:105–35.

Altamirano-Jiménez I (2012). Indigeneity and transnational routes and roads in North America. In Castro-Rea J (ed.), *Our North America: From Turtle Island to the security and prosperity partnership*, Ashgate Publishing Ltd, Surrey.

Altamirano-Jiménez I (2013). *Indigenous encounters with neoliberalism: Place, women and the environment in Canada and Mexico*, Vancouver, UBC Press.

Brodie J & Bakker I (2008). *Where are the women?* Canadian Centre for Policy Alternatives, Ottawa.

Brown W (2001). *Politics out of history*, Princeton University Press, Princeton.

Canada Mortgage and Housing Corporation (2011). *2006 Census Housing Series: Issue 13—On Reserve Housing Conditions*, by Jeremiah Prentice in *Research Highlights Socio-Economic Series* 11-007, CMHC (Canada Mortgage and Housing Corporation), Ottawa.

Carlson KB (2011). Stephen Harper's Chiefly practical approach to First Nations' issues. *National Post*, 9 December, nationalpost.com/news/canada/stephen-harpers-chiefly-practical-approach-to-first-nations-issues.

Coulthard, GS (2014). *Red skin, white masks: Rejecting the colonial politics of recognition*, University of Minnesota Press, Minneapolis.

De Marinis N (2011). Breaking the silence: State violence towards Triqui women of Oaxaca, Mexico. *Development* 54(4):480–84, doi.org/10.1057/dev.2011.79.

Deere CD & León M (2000). *Ciudadanía y derechos económicos: la importancia de la tierra para las mujeres latinoamericanas*. Tercer Mundo and Universidad Nacional de Colombia, Bogotá.

Department of Indian and Northern Affairs Canada (2010). *Family Homes on Reserves and Matrimonial Interests or Rights Act*, laws-lois.justice.gc.ca/eng/acts/F-1.2/.

Flanagan T & Alcantara C (2002). *Individual property on Canadian indian reserves*. A Fraser Institute Occasional Paper, The Fraser Institute, Vancouver, www.fraserinstitute.org/sites/default/files/PropertyRightsonIndianReserves.pdf.

Green J (2007). Toward conceptual precision: Citizenship and rights talk for aboriginal Canadians. In Kernerman G & Resnick P (eds), *Insiders and outsiders: Alan Cairns and the reshaping of Canadian citizenship*, UBC Press, Vancouver.

Green J & Peach I (2007). Beyond 'us' and 'them': Prescribing post-colonial politics and policy in Saskatchewan. In Banting K, Courchene TJ & Seidle FL (eds), *Belonging? Diversity, recognition and shared citizenship in Canada*, Institute for Research on Public Policy, Montreal.

Howard-Wagner, D (2012). Reclaiming the northern territory as a settler-colonial space. *Arena Journal* (37/38):220.

Howitt R (2009). Getting the scale right? A relational scale politics of native title in Australia. In Keil R & Mahon R (eds), *Leviathan undone? Towards a political economy of scale*. University of British Columbia Press, Vancouver.

Igoe J & Brockington D (2007). Neoliberal conservation: A brief introduction. *Conservation and Society* 5(4):432.

Instituto Nacional de Estadistica y Geografía (2016). *Datos a propósito del Día Internacional de los Pueblos Indígenas* (*Census data release on International Indigenous Peoples Day*), www.inegi.org.mx/saladeprensa/aproposito/2016/indigenas2016_0.pdf.

Kuokkanen R (2012). Self-determination and indigenous women's rights at the intersection of international human rights, *Human Rights Quarterly* 34, doi.org/10.1353/hrq.2012.0000.

Larner W (2003). Neoliberalism? *Environment and Planning D: Society and Space* 21(5):509–12, doi.org/10.1068/d2105ed.

Leslie K (2000). The privatisation of common-property resources in a Mexican lobster cooperative: Human ecological perspectives. In Durrenberger EP & King TD (eds), *State and community in fisheries management: Power, policy and practice*, Bergin and Garvey, London.

Li T (2001). Boundary work. Community, market and state reconsidered. In Agrawal A & Gibson C (eds), *Communities and the environment: Ethnicity, gender, and the state in community-based conservation*, Rutgers University Press, New Jersey.

Li T (2011). Rendering society technical: Government through community and the ethnographic turn at the world bank in Indonesia. In Mosse D (ed.), *Adventures in aidland: The anthropology of professionals in international development*, Berghahn, Oxford.

Macdonald F (2011). Indigenous peoples and neoliberal 'privatization' in Canada: Opportunities, caution and constraints. *Canadian Journal of Political Science* 44(2):257–73, doi.org/10.1017/S000842391100014X.

MacTaggart SL (2015). Lessons from history: The recent applicability of matrimonial property and human rights legislation on reserve in Canada. *Western Journal of Legal Studies* 6(2), ir.lib.uwo.ca/uwojls/vol6/iss2/3.

Merry S (2003). Human rights law and the demonization of culture (and anthropology along the way). *Political and Legal Anthropology Review* 26(1):55–76, doi.org/10.1525/pol.2003.26.1.55.

Newdick V (2005). The indigenous woman as victim of her culture in neoliberal Mexico. *Cultural Dynamics* 17(1):73–92, doi.org/10.1177/0921374005058027.

NWAC (Native Women's Association of Canada) (2008). *Reclaiming our way of being: Matrimonial real property solutions position paper*, Ottawa. www.nwac. ca/wp-content/uploads/2015/05/2007_NWAC_Reclaiming_Our_Way_of_ Being_Matrimonial_Real_Property_Solutions_Position_Paper.pdf.

Parliament of Canada (2013). Standing Committee on the Status of Women. Evidence presented at meeting 23 April 2003, www.parl.gc.ca/House Publications/Publication.aspx?Language=E&Mode=1&DocId=6097711.

Pasternack S (2015). How will colonialism save capitalism: The privatisation of reserve lands in Canada. *Antipode* 47(1):179–96, doi.org/10.1111/anti.12094.

Peck, J (2004). Geography and public policy: Constructions of neoliberalism. *Progress in Human Geography* 28(3):392–405.

Poole D (2006). Los usos de la costumbre. Hacia una antropología jurídica del estado neoliberal. *Alteridades* 16(31):9–21, alteridades.izt.uam.mx/index. php/Alte/article/view/260/259.

Povinelli E (2002). *The cunning of recognition: Indigenous alterities and the making of Australian multiculturalism*. Duke University Press, Durham and London, doi.org/10.1215/9780822383673.

Recondo D (2001). Usos y costumbres, procesos electorales y autonomía indígena en Oaxaca. In De León Pasquel L (ed.), *Costumbres, leyes y movimiento indio en Oaxaca y Chiapas*. CIESAS and Miguel Ángel Porrúa, Mexico City.

Sierra MT (2009). Las mujeres indígenas ante la justicia comunitaria: Perspectivas desde la interculturalidad y los derechos. *Desacatos* 31(septiembre–diciembre), desacatos.ciesas.edu.mx/index.php/Desacatos/article/view/397.

Strakosch E (2015). *Neoliberal indigenous policy. Settler colonialism and the post-welfare state*. Palgrave Macmillan, London, doi.org/10.1057/978113 7405418.

Torres-Mazuera G (2016). Deregulating the social life of property: Neoliberalism and the proliferation of legal dissonance in Mexico. *The Journal of Legal Pluralism and Unofficial Law* 4(1):58–74, doi.org/10.1080/07329113.2015. 1069060.

Velásquez Cepeda MC (1998). *El nombramiento: Antropología jurídica de los usos y costumbres para la renovación de los ayuntamientos de Oaxaca*. Instituto Estatal Electoral de Oaxaca, Oaxaca.

World Bank (1990). *World development report*. World Bank, Washington DC.

World Bank (1994). *Mexico: Second decentralization and regional development project report*. World Bank, Washington DC.

3

Resisting the ascendancy of an emboldened colonialism

Cathryn Eatock

> We continue to ensure that our land, law, language and culture lives on and continues to be vibrant and long-lasting. We do this by getting back our country, looking after our country and securing our future. (Kimberley Land Council 2016: 3)

Indigenous policy in Australia has undergone a shift over the last two decades, retreating from previous commitments to self-determination, and implementing paternalistic approaches based on an underlying neoliberal ideology that seeks to control and assimilate Aboriginal people to fit within a market model (Altman 2007: 2, Moreton-Robinson 2009: 68, Howard-Wagner 2012: 237). However, the assimilationist intent of these policies and the application of neoliberal approaches to Aboriginal communities ignores the direct causal link between colonialism and Aboriginal poverty and disregards the communal nature of Aboriginal culture. The relationship between neoliberalism and paternalism is explored in a number of chapters within this volume (e.g. Sullivan, Howard-Wagner, Bielefeld, Page). Despite the adoption of the United Nations Declaration on the Rights of Indigenous Peoples (UNDRIP) in 2007, government policies impacting Indigenous peoples in Australia have taken a clearly paternalistic tone, with assimilationist objectives. This chapter considers recent policy changes through the *Resilient families, strong communities: A roadmap for regional and remote communities* report

(RFSC report), which sets out the termination of services to smaller remote Aboriginal communities in Western Australia (WA), as a means to close approximately 120 communities and pressure their community members to move to larger regional and hub towns. This chapter highlights how Indigenous policy is being used to disempower and dispossess Aboriginal communities, as a means to break their unique communal connection to land. The chapter contends that the primacy given to neoliberal objectives by both major political parties has required Indigenous peoples to look beyond the hegemony of the nation state in an attempt to draw on the United Nations (UN) mechanisms and seek engagement with the global community. In leveraging emerging international customary law and associated norms, Aboriginal people strive to pressure the Australian Government to implement its international commitments, to recognise Indigenous rights and to negotiate just outcomes with Australia's Indigenous peoples.

Contemporary colonial dispossession

> Our land is viewed as a common legacy to be handed down to our children and grandchildren—Walter Shaw. (Aboriginal Peak Organisations of the Northern Territory 2015: 32)

The announced closure of up to 150 remote Aboriginal communities by the WA Government, in November 2014, sent fear through the 274 Aboriginal communities in WA. This announcement followed the federal government's decision to transfer responsibility for these communities to the state government. The WA Premier, Colin Barnett, acknowledged 'it will cause great distress to Aboriginal people who will move, it will cause issues in regional towns as Aboriginal people move into them' (Kagi 2014). However, the government justified its decision by claiming these communities were financially unviable and harboured social dysfunction, neglect and child abuse.

The then prime minister, Tony Abbott, further inflamed concerns among remote communities when, in March 2015, he stated 'what we can't do is endlessly subsidise lifestyle choices if those lifestyle choices are not conducive to the kind of full participation in Australian society that everyone should have' (Medhora 2015). This statement highlighted a profound ignorance of the complex cultural connection to country and ties to ancestors, lore and custodial obligations that define remote communities. It also put forward the ideological basis of a policy approach where an individual's worth was premised against their market value as potential employees, and the poverty of Aboriginal communities was seen as an individual and community failure. It also ignored the fact that the wealth of WA's mining and petroleum exports, totalling AU\$98.0 billion in 2012–13 (WA Department of Treasury 2014), had been drawn from the ancestral lands from which Aboriginal people had previously been dispossessed and remained uncompensated. Significantly, it also highlighted an abrogation of the rights of indigenous peoples asserted in the 2007 UNDRIP, which the Australian Government had endorsed in 2009.

The announcement reflected that government policies targeting Aboriginal communities had enacted a neoliberal form of 'managerialism' that disempowers and dispossesses Aboriginal communities, to progress an openly assimilationist intent to break communal connections to land. Neoliberalism, which has prevailed over Western political economies for the last 30 years, refers to a laissez faire form of capitalism that ascribes dominance to the power of market forces (Monbiot 2016). Von Hayek defines neoliberalism as deregulation and fostering of markets, deregulation of labour, reduction of social welfare, privatisation of services, reduction of state regulation and rejection of collective unionism (Von Hayek 1944, cited in Klikauer 2015: 1107). According to Klikauer, 'managerialism' is closely linked with market-oriented reforms, including economic rationalism and neoliberalism, that assert corporate interests as the universal interest of humanity, under the banner of globalisation (Klikauer 2015: 1107, 1113). Neoliberals argue that the welfare state undermines individual responsibility, where welfare recipients become dependent, and see the role of the state as disciplining welfare recipients through punitive measures to discourage long-term welfare dependency (Mendes 2009: 105). When applied to Aboriginal communities, it both ignores that Aboriginal poverty is a direct result of colonialism and that Aboriginal culture is based on a communal rather than an individualistic framework.

These policy approaches reflect a neoliberal conception of modernisation, which seeks to impose assimilationist measures that require viewing Aboriginal communities as 'failed citizens' who need to be compelled to assimilate (Altman 2007: 2). Neoliberal managerialist approaches view cultural difference negatively, as a social determinant that limits opportunity, where, according to Sanders, 'certain people are not adequate judges of their own best interests and must be guided by others, such as government agents' (2014: 1). The imposition of individual land title over communal title and the removal of communities from ancestral lands are promoted as the means to achieve this assimilation.

Following the announced closure of remote communities, the WA Government developed the RFSC report, released in July 2016, noting Aboriginal people are more dependent on welfare than other West Australians, particularly in regional and remote communities, stating '[c] hange will take time and some of it will be hard.' (Government of Western Australia 2016: 3). While the report claims it will consult with Aboriginal communities, the central decisions are laid out, preventing any real input into decision-making. Rather, the RFSC report confirms the WA Government will cut services, including essential fuel subsidies, to remote communities it claimed were not economically viable, even though the fuel is used to power generators that provide critical water pumps and electricity to communities (Government of Western Australia 2016: 16).

The report reflects a policy intent to replace Indigenous social norms with those more aligned with a Western market-based approach. The RFSC report takes a deficit approach that holds Aboriginal communities responsible for the deprivation in their communities, with perceptions of dysfunction used to justify, in part, the closure of remote communities. However, independent reports confirm Aboriginal people have significantly better health and wellbeing outcomes in remote communities compared to Aboriginal people living in larger townships (Amnesty 2011: 3). Improved health outcomes are attributed to increased cultural practice, social and family support, greater physical activity and a healthier diet reliant on more traditional bush foods (Mooney 2009: 17). Remote communities also have fewer social problems and less domestic violence and substance abuse, while providing respite and rehabilitation from substance abuse for Aboriginal youth from towns and cities. These outcomes contrast to those in townships, where people experience higher rates of social dysfunction and disadvantage (Amnesty 2011: 13).

While the RFSC report highlights the low 20 per cent employment rate in remote Aboriginal communities as a justification to close communities, employment levels of only 43 per cent in regional towns (Government of Western Australia 2016: 6) fail to promise employment opportunities. It also disregards the fact that the largest employer in remote communities was the Community Development Employment Projects (CDEP) program, which was abolished in previous reforms. CDEP had provided employment through the topping up welfare payments; though it only provided a minimal wage, it gave community control over the type of services supported, such as childcare, teacher support, community maintenance and elder care, over the 30 years it operated. In the West Kimberley region alone, seven CDEP providers employed 1,600 people, where the CDEP program was considered the lifeblood of communities (CDEP Submission 2011: 3).

Although the RFSC report alleges twice as much spending on Aboriginal people in remote and regional areas compared to non-Aboriginal urban dwellers, citing this as a further justification for the closing of communities, these statistics actually reflect decades of underspending, with communities now chronically overcrowded and many with faulty water and sewage services (Australian Indigenous Health Infonet 2008: 5–6). However, the RFSC report confirms no further funding will be allocated to housing maintenance or additional building in smaller communities, with funding for schools and services to cease. The RFSC instead advocates funding be limited to 10 larger communities that are close to a major source of employment and educational opportunities. The report states new housing will 'preference transitional housing over current models of public and community housing' (Government of Western Australia 2016: 34). To qualify for 'transitional housing', tenants will be required to have one adult in employment and an 85 per cent school attendance rate for children. Transitional housing, the report suggests, is designed to transition tenants to private rental or home ownership. However, while this housing will be released onto the private market, there is no guarantee that the tenants will become owners. Indeed, the high cost of building in remote regions and the low wages of unskilled workers indicates a likely low uptake. In addition, the report commits to change the land tenure of existing housing to remove current communal title (Government of Western Australia 2016: 20).

The RFSC report also argues the distance to markets is an impediment to 'self-determination'. This assertion misrepresents the term's actual meaning, which defines Indigenous decision-making rather than being a reference to employability. In basing policy objectives on a neoliberal market framework, the RFSC report rejects the notion that Aboriginal values and community aspirations may vary from market-based conceptions. Howard-Wagner argues that neoliberal market-driven policies are used to enforce a paternalistic approach, regulating communities and breaking up communal land ownership, which is used to reconstitute a 'neo-settler colonialism' that restructures land tenure away from community ownership to individual housing tenures (Howard-Wagner 2012: 224).

Part of a broader ideological strategy

> This home ownership really upsets me … We own our land and our home is on the land. Our land is where we have ceremony and share culture. We do own our home. Our home is our land. Home is where our grandmothers and grandfathers have been hunting and living. Home is where we belong to, it's our land. The land is our home—Phillip Wilyuka.
> (Aboriginal Peak Organisations of the Northern Territory 2015: 21)

The RFSC report implements recommendations of the *Creating parity* report by Andrew Forrest (the Forrest Review), a WA mining magnate commissioned by the federal government to review Aboriginal employment and training in 2014. The Forrest Review criticises the provision of social housing in remote communities, considering it a disincentive to out-of-region employment, and proposes limiting 'continuing eligibility for public housing for those who take up and retain work for up to 30 months while they transition to the private rental market or home ownership' (Forrest 2014: 46). The review also advocated for the removal of CDEP: though it confirmed people were better off on CDEP, it called for 'equality' with non-Aboriginal people and 'real jobs' in Aboriginal communities (Klein 2014: 4). However, the Forrest Review's flawed assumptions failed to acknowledge the differing cultural values of remote communities that prioritise custodial responsibilities over financial incentives (Klein 2014: 3). The report also argues for the imposition of 'Income Management', a costly and punitive welfare reform that limits access to cash payments (a topic addressed by Bielefeld in this volume, Chapter 8).

Imposing private ownership of lands as a means to overcome poverty was promoted by Hernando De Soto, in the *Mystery of capital*, and embraced by neoliberal market advocates (De Soto 2003). Helen Hughes and Jenness Warin draw on De Soto to argue communal ownership 'impedes the productive use of land, employment creation, and economic development worldwide' (Hughes & Warin 2005: 4), where the poor are marginalised from the global economy because of their incapacity to attract loans and by the potential sale of property. However, Peter van Dijk, South African Micro Finance Council, warns 'if it is simply a swapping of debt, there is no added value' (cited in Tom 2005: 24). Transferring De Soto's theory to remote Aboriginal communities poses additional challenges. At a forum on 'Access to Finance on Aboriginal Lands', bankers raised concerns over low demand, high costs of construction and high-risk profiles of lenders in remote communities, noting resale prices will likely be lower than purchase prices (Tom 2005: 27). They also noted that in communities where mines may contribute to demand, the greater purchasing power may have 'significant implications for the make-up of a remote Aboriginal community' (Tom 2005: 27).

The Australian Government's *Our north, our future: White paper on developing northern Australia* (Australian Government 2015) proposes means of creating economic opportunities through the development of Aboriginal lands and the establishment of simpler land arrangements to support investment, highlighting untapped opportunities for home ownership and leasing arrangements. However, the Australian Human Rights Commission has raised concerns that it 'might have implications for breaking up Aboriginal and Torres Strait Islander communities and diminishing their land ownership' (Australian Human Rights Commission 2015: 76). The White Paper also recommends amendments to the *Aboriginal and Torres Strait Islander Heritage Protection Act 1984* (Cwlth) to simplify cultural heritage regulation, which it suggests is a key barrier to economic development in the north.

David Pick et al., in their review of the impact of neoliberalism on development in WA's Pilbara region, the location of many of the targeted remote Aboriginal communities, suggest neoliberalism has resulted in the weakening of regulation and led to a 'leakage of wealth' from the region (Pick et al. 2008: 518). Pick et al. also confirm development pressures are particularly intense in the Pilbara region, with virtually all of Australia's iron ore, gas and oil extracted from the region (Pick et al. 2008: 519). They argue that neoliberal policies, prioritising economic factors over social needs, had become the norm, where 'the dispossession of Indigenous peoples has led to a number of issues that are proving difficult to resolve' (Pick et al. 2008: 524–5). Significantly, Pick et al. suggest the dependence on mining may prove detrimental in the long term, with no alternatives to the resource industry being developed (Pick et al. 2008: 521).

Western imperialism drew on religious theology and the 'Doctrine of Discovery' to promulgate the superiority of Western civilisation and modernisation as a justification for the exploitation of indigenous lands and decimation of indigenous cultures. Where Aboriginal communities vary from this perception of civility, they are conceived as dysfunctional and are pathologised as a means to subjugate Aboriginal people (Moreton-Robinson 2009: 63, Alfred 2015: 5). The problematising of indigenous peoples deflects the historical and structural causes of indigenous deprivation, as a means for the government to lay responsibility for their impoverishment on individuals, while the ramifications of dispossession and decades of neglect are ignored (Alfred 2015: 5). Aileen Moreton-Robinson argues the denial of the impact of colonisation in producing economic dependency serves to make the ongoing race war against Indigenous peoples invisible (Moreton-Robinson 2009: 70).

The globalisation of neoliberalism has re-energised these colonial assaults in an attempt to erase Indigenous claims, remove connection to place and separate entitlement, completing earlier processes of dispossession (Alfred & Corntassel 2005: 603, Howard-Wagner & Kelly 2011: 121). It is neoliberalism's market-dominated approach that privileges individual rights over communal rights, which, according to Moreton-Robinson, enables 'the impoverished conditions under which Indigenous people live to be rationalised as a product of dysfunctional cultural traditions and individual bad behaviour' (Moreton-Robinson 2009: 68).

Neoliberals assert that the welfare state undermines individual responsibility, where welfare recipients, like addicts, become dependent on welfare. This has led to punitive measures to discourage welfare dependency and assert a work ethic and self-reliance (Mendes 2009: 105). In Aboriginal communities, regulatory and punitive policies are pursued, seeking to assert behavioural change to assimilate these communities into a market-focused framework (Howard-Wagner 2007, Howard-Wagner & Kelly 2011, Bielefeld 2014/2015: 106–7). These policies seek to impose a 'normalisation' on Aboriginal people, through assimilation policies aimed at reproducing lifestyles of the broader Australian community (Howard-Wagner 2007: 246, Sullivan 2011: 3). Will Sanders suggests Indigenous policy approaches have returned to an emphasis on guardianship, particularly in relation to remote and discrete Aboriginal communities that were previously given a degree of autonomy more focused on self-determination and the recognition of land rights as decolonisation strategies (Sanders 2014: 9).

Yet, Aboriginal people living in remote communities assert their right to maintain their cultural values, protect sacred sites and establish alternative economic development initiatives that align with their custodial obligations. Jon Altman argues that remote Aboriginal communities do not fit within a narrow neoliberal market framework. Remote communities' reliance on bush foods, and income derived from environmental management practices and cultural expressions, all contribute to what Altman terms the local 'hybrid economy' that respects traditional lifestyles and values customary decision-making processes (Altman 2011: 4–5). This 'contested notion of economic development' contrasts with policy objectives focused on employment, business and home ownership (Altman 2011: 3). The Indigenous estate, according to Altman, covers 20 per cent of Australia and holds some of the most biodiverse and intact lands in Australia, with untapped potential for carbon emission sequestration and environmental management strategies. Altman challenges government approaches that correlate community development with economic development as a process of modernisation that assesses Aboriginal communities from a deficit perspective (Altman 2011: 4).

Seeking a just footing

> We Aboriginal people have the solutions. We just need [the federal government] to invest in that. I'm travelling around the country talking about treaty, about recognition of our sovereignty. We were here before the British and we need it to be recognized that our law and our system of government is valid—Yingiya Guyula. (Clarke 2016: 2)

With both major political parties asserting a neoliberal agenda, often at the expense of Indigenous rights, Aboriginal people strive to leverage international mechanisms that recognise Indigenous rights to self-determination and 'free, prior and informed consent' (FPIC) as fundamental emerging norms in international law. Although the Universal Declaration on Human Rights and its core treaties initially did not recognise the particular circumstances of indigenous people, James Anaya argues the adoption of the UNDRIP[1] now constitutes international customary law (Anaya 2009: 80). The right to self-determination, Article 3 of the Declaration, is, according to Anaya,

---

1   For the full text of the UNDRIP, see www.un.org/development/desa/indigenouspeoples/declaration-on-the-rights-of-indigenous-peoples.html.

'a foundational right, without which Indigenous Peoples' other human rights, both collective and individual, cannot be fully enjoyed' (Anaya 2010: 15). 'Self-determination' as applied in the Declaration is a process of decolonisation that does not necessitate succession, but rather provides a strategy to assert indigenous rights against state and corporate economic and political interests. For the remote communities in WA, Article 10 specifically states, 'Indigenous peoples shall not be forcibly removed from their lands or territories'. In addition, while WA Aboriginal communities' use of water pumps is threatened by the cessation of fuel subsidies for generators, the UN General Assembly has explicitly recognised the right to water as essential to the realisation of all human rights (United Nations General Assembly 2010).

Though Article 46 of the Declaration was a concession that responded to state concerns that their sovereignty was not contested, the Declaration does confer obligations on colonial states to recognise the pre-existing rights of indigenous peoples. Indigenous people continue to assert that the legitimacy of states remains under question where substantial efforts are not undertaken to address those rights recognised in the Declaration as agreed minimal standards, as a central component of instigating decolonisation processes. In the face of increasing global pressures on indigenous peoples, as neoliberal market forces seek to assert economic interests over indigenous peoples' rights, international law is sought to leverage states' compliance with their obligations to recognise indigenous rights to remain on their lands, to self-determination and to 'free, prior and informed consent'.

While the UN reasserts states' sovereign interests, it remains the only institution where state power may be held to account and its impunity curtailed. The Declaration confirms colonial states have an obligation to recognise the pre-existing and inherent rights of indigenous peoples. The challenge now remains how to translate those commitments broadly endorsed in international law into state approaches that respect and facilitate indigenous decision-making on issues that impact upon them. The contention is to move beyond tokenistic acknowledgement of 'aspirational' rights to honouring those international standards of customary law, cementing the communal rights of indigenous peoples to be self-determining peoples with the capacity and resources to express that autonomy, both locally and globally.

Though the Declaration lacks enforcement mechanisms, it establishes international norms that are broadly accepted as global standards. While states can continue to breach these laws, such breaches may be associated with loss of reputation, international standing and legitimacy (Finnemore & Sikkink 2014: 903). Though many states continue to breach human rights, state desire to maintain perceptions as 'good global citizens' may be used as potential leverage among states with a history of engagement with the UN, such as Australia. Further, the current Australian Government's appointment to the Human Rights Committee (HRC) 2018–20 term may provide additional leverage when highlighting the disconnect between Australia's global commitment and its national policy approach.

Since the adoption of the Declaration, the HRC and other bodies monitoring the implementation of UN treaties have strengthened their responses in relation to indigenous peoples' right to FPIC before undertaking projects or decisions in relation to indigenous lands (Barelli 2012: 6–8). In addition, the HRC has interpreted Article 27 of the International Covenant on Civil and Political Rights, which protects persons belonging to ethnic minorities to enjoy their culture, noting, 'culture manifests itself in many forms, including a particular way of life associated with the use of land resources, especially in the case of Indigenous peoples' (Barelli 2012: 21).

The *Outcome document of the high-level plenary meeting of the General Assembly known as the World Conference on Indigenous Peoples*, adopted by the UN General Assembly in September 2014, reaffirmed the Declaration and rights to FPIC, and committed to developing national action plans to implement the Declaration. In addition, at Article 21, the *Outcome document* also committed to establish nationally 'fair, independent, impartial, open and transparent processes to acknowledge, advance and adjudicate the rights of Indigenous peoples pertaining to lands, territories and resources' (United Nations 2014). Within the UN, it also commits to developing a 'System Wide Action Plan' reviewing the operation of Indigenous mechanisms, treaty bodies and the Universal Periodic Review, and appointed two indigenous experts, alongside two government representatives, to develop indigenous peoples' participation at the UN, including at its General Assembly.

Margaret Keck and Kathryn Sikkink outline the potential to use 'transnational advocacy networks' of civil society to influence more powerful states (Keck & Sikkink 1998: 1). Keck and Sikkink argue that less powerful groups, such as Indigenous peoples, can increase their capacity to influence states through global advocacy and the shifting of international norms, which in turn, through what they term a 'boomerang' effect, can transform practice within state jurisdictions (Keck & Sikkink 1998: 12). According to Keck and Sikkink, the 'boomerang' effect provides a means to influence states when governments violate or refuse to recognise rights, and domestic recourse is limited or the institutions are ineffective. While the concept of Westphalian Sovereignty is accepted as inalienable in international law, where state sovereignty provides protection from external interference on domestic issues, it is no longer sacrosanct, with developments over recent decades acknowledging responsibility among the international community to monitor human rights within nation states (Pitty & Smith 2011: 124). Though the Declaration has been termed an aspirational document rather than a legally binding treaty, it is currently 'used in transnational political advocacy as a source of important international norms' (Pitty & Smith 2011: 126), further asserting its place within emerging international customary law.

Developments in technologies now enable groups to communicate easily and form global alliances over issues that resonate. While incremental policy approaches are less likely to gain traction among a global constituency, issues that highlight stark human rights abuses, such as indigenous dispossession and rights to water, can draw broad global support from divergent groups, as occurred with the North Dakota Pipeline. Though not resolved, it has garnered international support and comment from numerous UN officials (Bearak 2016).

The weight of recrimination

> We want self-determination. We want democracy. We want the power of the people in Arnhem Land and in all Aboriginal communities to be recognised and our rights respected. (Yolngu Nations Assembly 2012)

The attempts to close communities in WA have been perceived as renewed dispossession against remote Aboriginal communities, their rights to self-determination and their ancestral lands. The Aboriginal policy climate of recent years has set the state against Aboriginal people, driven by a neoliberal ideological agenda that promotes powerful corporate interests, while implementing a highly paternalistic and managerial approach that strives to eradicate welfare dependency, denigrating Aboriginal people in remote communities for their deprivation. These policies of removal instigate a renewed phase of colonialism, through the regulation, enforced assimilation and dispossession of remote Aboriginal communities.

In developing the UN, states have defended their claims to colonised territories and their sovereignty, reflected in a lack of enforceable judicial processes for Indigenous complaints to be fairly adjudicated. While these constraints impinge on the effectiveness of international treaties and mechanisms, limiting potential outcomes for indigenous peoples, the UN remains a key means of defence for indigenous peoples. Without external exposure of the immense power disparities between states and indigenous peoples, where hegemonic powers are driven by neoliberal imperatives, state impunity may threaten the very survival of indigenous peoples as they derogate and deny their unique claims as sovereign nations.

This chapter argues that the abuse of Indigenous rights and apparent disregard for Indigenous rights within an Australian policy context requires collaborative international pressure to address intransigent states that fail to comply with international obligations. While internal reviews within the UN consider processes to increase Indigenous capacity through strengthened mechanisms to address this disparity and encourage state compliance, the force of international law is premised on an engaged global public and international expectations for compliance, which can coordinate political campaigns in response to flagrant breaches. It is through the exposure of domestic abuses to broader scrutiny that the domination of the powerful interests of states and corporations may be curbed.

References

Aboriginal Peak Organisations of the Northern Territory (2015). *Aboriginal remote housing forum*, Report prepared by Bisset H, Aboriginal Peak Organisations of the Northern Territory, Darwin.

Alfred T (2015). Cultural strength: Restoring the place of Indigenous knowledge in practice and policy. *Australian Aboriginal Studies* 2015(1):3–11.

Alfred T & Corntassel J (2005). Being Indigenous: Resurgences against contemporary colonialism. *Government and Opposition* 40(4):597–614, doi.org/10.1111/j.1477-7053.2005.00166.x.

Altman JC (2007). *Alleviating poverty in remote Indigenous Australia: The role of the hybrid economy*, Topical Issue 10/2007, Centre for Aboriginal Economic Policy Research, The Australian National University, Canberra.

Altman JC (2011). *The draft indigenous economic development strategy: A critical response*, Topical Issue 3/2011, Centre for Aboriginal Economic Policy Research, The Australian National University, Canberra.

Amnesty (2011). *The land holds us: Aboriginal peoples' right to traditional homelands in the Northern Territory*, Amnesty International.

Anaya J (2009). *International human rights and indigenous peoples*, Aspen Publishers.

Anaya J (2010). *Report by the Special Rapporteur on the situation of human rights and fundamental freedoms of Indigenous People- Situation of Indigenous Peoples in Australia*, Human Rights Council, 4 March.

Australian Government (2011). *Stronger futures in the Northern Territory policy statement*, November, Canberra.

Australian Government (2015). *Our north our future: White paper on developing northern Australia*, June, Canberra.

Australian Human Rights Commission (2015). *Social justice and native title report 2015*, Australian Human Rights Commission, Sydney.

Australian Indigenous Health Infonet (2008). *Review of the impact of housing and health-related infrastructure on Indigenous health*, Australian Indigenous Health Infonet, Mt Lawler.

Barelli M (2012). Free, prior and informed consent in the aftermath of the UN declaration on the rights of indigenous peoples: Developments and challenges ahead. *The International Journal of Human Rights* 16(1):1–24, doi. org/10.1080/13642987.2011.597746.

Bearak M (2016). U.N. officials denounce 'inhuman' treatment of native American pipeline protesters. *Washington Post*, 15 November.

Bielefeld S (2014/2015). Compulsory income management, Indigenous peoples and structural violence—implications for citizenship and autonomy. *Australian Indigenous Law Review* 18(1):99–118.

CDEP Submission (2011). *Reforming CDEP in the West Kimberley, submission to the Employment Services Review Panel*.

Clarke A (2016). Indigenous leaders say they're sick of 'being experimented on'. *Buzzfeed News Australia*, 17 March.

De Soto H (2003). *The mystery of capital: Why capitalism triumphs in the west and fails everywhere else*. Basic Books, New York.

Finnemore M & Sikkink K (2014). International norm dynamics and political change. *International Organisation* 52(4):887–917, doi.org/10.1162/002081898550789.

Forrest A (2014). *Forrest review: Creating parity*. Report to the Commonwealth of Australia, Canberra.

Government of Western Australia (2016). *Resilient families, strong communities: A roadmap for regional and remote communities*, Regional Services Reform Unit, Department of Regional Development, Western Australia.

Howard-Wagner D (2007). Restoring social order through tackling 'passive welfare': The statutory intent of the *Northern Territory National Emergency Response Act 2007* (Cth) and *Social Security and Other Legislation Amendment (Welfare Payment Reform) Act 2007* (Cth). *Current Issues in Criminal Justice* 19(2):243–51.

Howard-Wagner D (2012). Reclaiming the Northern Territory as settler-colonial space. *Arena Journal* 37/38:220–40.

Howard-Wagner D & Kelly B (2011). Containing Aboriginal mobility in the Northern Territory: From 'protectionism' to 'interventionism'. *Law Text Culture* 15:102–34.

Hughes H & Warin J (2005). *A new deal for Aborigines and Torres Strait Islanders in remote communities*. No. 54 *Issues Analysis*, The Centre for Independent Studies, Sydney.

Kagi J (2014). Plan to close more than 100 remote communities would have severe consequences, says WA Premier. *ABC News*, 12 November.

Keck M & Sikkink K (1998). *Activists beyond borders: Advocacy networks in international politics*, Cornell University Press, London.

Kimberley Land Council (2016). *Making rights a reality: The ongoing struggle for land justice in the Kimberley Region, Australia*, Briefing Note, Oxfam International, Oxford.

Klein E (2014). *Academic perspectives on the Forrest review: Creating parity*. Topical Issue 2/2014, Centre for Aboriginal Economic Policy Research, The Australian National University, Canberra.

Klikauer T (2015). What is managerialism? *Critical Sociology* 41(7–8):1103–119, doi.org/10.1177/0896920513501351.

Medhora S (2015). Remote communities are 'lifestyle choices', says Tony Abbott. *Guardian*, 10 March.

Mendes P (2009). Retrenching or renovating the Australian Welfare State: the paradox of the Howard government's neoliberalism. *International Journal of Social Welfare* 18:102–10, doi.org/10.1111/j.1468-2397.2008.00569.x.

Monbiot G (2016). Neoliberalism—the ideology at the root of all our problems. *Guardian*, 15 April:1–7.

Mooney G (2009). *Health and homelands: Good value for money?* Report for The Institute for Cultural Survival, Aboriginal Medical Services Alliance Northern Territory (AMSANT), MITWATJ Health Aboriginal Corporation.

Moreton-Robinson A (2009). Imagining the good indigenous citizen: Race war and the pathology of patriarchal white sovereignty. *Cultural Studies Review* 15(2):61–79, doi.org/10.5130/csr.v15i2.2038.

Pick D, Dayaram K & Butler B (2008). Neoliberalism, risk and regional development in Western Australia: The case of the Pilbara. *International Journal of Sociology and Social Policy* 28(11/12):516–27, doi.org/10.1108/01443330810915224.

Pitty R & Smith S (2011). The Indigenous challenge to westphalian sovereignty. *Australian Journal of Political Science* 46(1):121–39, doi.org/10.1080/10361146.2010.546336.

Sanders W (2014). *Experimental governance in Australian Indigenous affairs: From Coombs to Pearson via Rowse and the completing principles.* Discussion Paper 291/2014, Centre for Aboriginal Economic Policy Research, The Australian National University, Canberra.

Sullivan P (2011). *The policy goal of normalization, the National Indigenous Reform Agreement and Indigenous Partnership Agreements.* Desert Knowledge CRC Working Paper Number 76, Australian Institute of Aboriginal and Torres Strait Islander Studies.

Tom N (2005). Debate the De Soto theory. *African Business*, July(311):23–4.

United Nations (2014). *Outcome document of the high-level plenary meeting of the General Assembly known as the World Conference on Indigenous Peoples.* United Nations.

United Nations General Assembly (2010). Resolution adopted by the Human Rights Council 15/9 Human rights and access to safe drinking water and sanitation. The Human Rights Council, Fifteenth session, Agenda item 3, 6 October.

Von Hayek FA (1944). *The road to serfdom*. Routledge, London.

WA Department of Treasury (2014). *The structure of the Western Australian economy*. Government of Western Australia.

Yolngu Nations Assembly (2012). *Statement from the Second Assembly*, Maningrida, 11–13 October.

4

A flawed Treaty partner: The New Zealand state, local government and the politics of recognition

Avril Bell

Since the establishment of the Waitangi Tribunal in 1975, the key mechanism of recognition for Māori in Aotearoa/New Zealand has been 'Treaty settlements'. These settlements offer some (very limited) compensation for historical injustices, as well as limited recognition of tribes as political partners to the state (see, for example, Belgrave et al. 2005, Bargh 2007a, Mutu 2011, Wheen & Hayward 2012). However, local government entities, while important actors in the lives of *iwi* (tribes) and *hapū* (sub-tribes), are not Treaty partners and have an ambiguous role in the lives of post-settlement[1] Māori communities.

Unlike Australia, Canada or the United States of America, New Zealand's political system is not federal. Government is instead divided between the central state and a range of territorially based local governance bodies, many with overlapping jurisdictions. In simple terms, regional councils govern the environment, their boundaries set by geographical features such

---

1   The idea that Māori–state relations are now largely shaped by the 'post-settlement' era is not to suggest a time after settler colonialism, but to point to the large proportion of *iwi* and *hapū* who have concluded settlements to historical Treaty claims with the Crown. In 2014, the Office of Treaty Settlements (OTS) reported that 72 settlements had been concluded, covering 70 per cent of New Zealand's landmass (OTS 2014). Also see this overview of settlements to mid-2017: www.youtube.com/watch?v=4-IG0owx38U.

as water catchment areas, while city and district councils govern the built infrastructure, with boundaries set around population areas. Then there are unitary authorities, such as Auckland Council, which combine the functions of regional and district/city governance. These arms of the state are hugely important for *iwi*, given the overlapping spaces of governance of *iwi* and local councils.

This chapter explores the current state of local government in Aotearoa/ New Zealand as a partner to Māori tribes seeking recognition for their status as *mana whenua* (holders of territorial authority) and wanting to work in partnership with government as equal and self-determining entities. There is a growing literature on the relationship between local government and Māori, focusing on issues of Māori representation (for example, Waaka 2006, Hayward 2011a, Hayward 2011b, Sullivan & Toki 2012, Bargh 2013) and especially on partnerships between *iwi* and *hapū* and local bodies (for example, Lewis et al. 2009), particularly around environmental co-management and co-governance (for example, Coombes & Hill 2005, Te Aho 2010, Lowry 2012, Muru-Lanning 2012, Forster 2014, Bennett 2015). And as we advance into the post–Treaty settlement era in Aotearoa/New Zealand, the possibilities and problems of this local government relationship are coming more to the fore. Here I explore local government relationships with *iwi* Māori by turning the focus of recognition theory back on the settler state. My argument is that, taking the arms of central and local government together, the New Zealand state is not a fit subject for recognition politics. Particularly at a local government level, the New Zealand state suffers severe historical amnesia, and, more broadly, the New Zealand state can be characterised as an incoherent, shape-shifting subject, enacting partnership in one instance and not the next, and frequently guilty of insincerity, saying one thing while doing another. While the state demands specific modes of governance and behaviour of its *iwi* partners, its own conduct is less than exemplary as a partner in a politics of recognition.

The discussion is divided into three parts. The first part provides an overview of the Treaty settlement process as a politics of recognition within a neoliberal context, which fundamentally shapes the relationships between *iwi* and central government. The second outlines the current state of play in the structural relationships between *iwi* and local government. In the final part of the discussion, I briefly sum up the ways in which the Crown, taking local and central government arms together, fails as a subject of recognition politics.

Central government, neoliberalism and the politics of recognition

At its Hegelian roots, recognition theory is about the struggle to achieve a relationship of equals between two subjects. To recognise the subjectivity of another is to recognise their equal and autonomous status as self-determining people worthy of respect. The language of partnership, which dominates the relationship of the New Zealand state and *iwi* Māori, points towards this understanding; although, in practice, state–*iwi* partnerships fall short of this ideal. Treaty settlements in the New Zealand system provide limited reparation for lost lands and historical injustices. Settlements have three components: an historical account of the Crown's injustices towards the people concerned and an apology for those; forms of cultural redress, which may include renaming of significant places, the return of land and co-governance arrangements over public lands; and forms of financial redress, which may involve a monetary payment and the transfer of property. The aim is to provide a degree of closure on historical injustices and an economic basis for future economic development for *iwi* and *hapū*, succinctly captured in the title of the Office of Treaty Settlements' (OTS 2015) guide to Treaty claims, *Healing the past, building a future*.

As in other jurisdictions, the era of recognition of Māori has coincided with that of neoliberal politics and economics, and neoliberalism has shaped and constrained the forms of recognition on offer. While neoliberal politics differs across time and place, I use this term to capture three fundamental tenets of the ideology: a belief in the supremacy and superiority of market forms and disciplines; a concomitant mistrust of the state as an economic and social actor; and a singular concern with the economic activities and responsibilities of individuals (and collectives), with other spheres of individual and community life deemed private matters, and choices (for brief overviews, see Bargh 2007b, Humpage 2017).[2]

---

2 Some of the variability of successive neoliberal governments in New Zealand is evident in the differing views on 'special rights' for Māori, something the Labour-led governments up until 2004 were broadly in sympathy with. However, in early 2004, the then National Party leader, Don Brash, gave a speech (commonly known as the 'Orewa speech') in which his attack on 'race-based rights' led to a surge in support for his party. Subsequently, whichever party has held political power, the neoliberal dislike for any 'special rights' and provisions has been evident in their policy towards Māori. At the same time, however, this has been held in check by the mixed-member proportional political system and competition between the two main parties for the support of Māori voters (see Humpage this volume, Chapter 14).

The neoliberal preference for market over state provision of services led to policies that opened up spaces for indigenous communities to pursue a degree of self-determination. Devolution, contracting social service provision to private providers, enabled the development of Māori providers contracted to deliver services to their own communities (Bargh 2007c: 36–7, Workman 2017: 180–1). In terms of marketisation, subjecting state activities to market disciplines, the *State Owned Enterprises Act 1986*, which legislated for government entities to operate as commercial businesses (in some cases in preparation for privatisation), created significant opportunities for Māori groups. Section 9 of the Act, which ruled that '[n]othing in this Act shall permit the Crown to act in a manner that is inconsistent with the principles of the Treaty of Waitangi', provided an avenue for Treaty claims and court cases that resulted in the development of Māori broadcasting systems, and in various public lands being set aside for return in subsequent Treaty claims prior to state assets being either privatised or marketised (see Bargh 2007c: 29–30).

The neoliberal ethos is also clear in the emphasis on Māori economic development in Treaty settlements. As Fiona McCormack (2011: 283) argues, 'the spaces opened for indigeneity under neoliberalism reflect market rather than democratic rationality', or, we might add, rather than a distinctly Māori rationality or value base (Kelsey 2005). For the neoliberal state, Māori economic development is in keeping with its primary understanding of citizens as economic and market actors, with the added pay-off that Māori economic development is expected to lessen the Māori welfare 'burden'. To a degree, this emphasis dovetails with indigenous desires for sovereignty/autonomy, providing the opportunity to achieve greater economic self-determination, to be pursued also with the hope that economic power can be leveraged to gain greater political self-determination (Durie 2011: 198–200). Consequently, *iwi* and *hapū*, by and large, have taken up the opportunities on offer. For example, the two *iwi* whose settlements were concluded more than 20 years ago, Waikato-Tainui and Ngāi Tahu, are now significant economic actors both regionally and nationally. Beyond these most prominent examples, there are many cases nationwide where the 'temporary alignment' (Lewis et al. 2009: 181) between neoliberal and *iwi* political projects has enabled *iwi* to pursue their own cultural and social, as well as economic, agendas.

At the same time, however, there are significant problems in combining neoliberal and indigenous political projects. To be recognised as 'post settlement governance entities', *iwi* leadership bodies must adopt corporate forms commensurate with neoliberal governance (Bargh 2007c, Joseph 2012: 161–2). Further, the growing wealth of *iwi* itself, in a situation where neoliberal economics is simultaneously impoverishing Māori individuals and families at the other end of the class spectrum, is seen to cause problematic divisions within the Māori world (Poata-Smith 2004). The Crown's focus on settling with large *iwi* groupings is also seen by many as eroding the power of *hapū*, the more traditional bodies of Māori governance in the precolonial era (for example, McCormack 2012). Thus, in addition to growing class divides, the institution of corporate tribal governance can have the effect of alienating *hapū* from *iwi* governance, and alienating tribal assets from the community itself (for example, McCormack this volume, Chapter 15, Muru-Lanning 2016). More broadly, the political desires of *iwi* and *hapū* for meaningful political power sharing remain largely unrecognised by the Crown (Bargh 2012), so that, overall, a number of critics argue that neoliberal state recognition is purely colonialism in a new guise (for example, see Kelsey 2005, Bargh 2007a, Coulthard 2014).

In her overview of 'the post-settlement world (so far)', Maria Bargh points to the differing expectations of Māori and the Crown regarding Treaty settlement. As she says, Māori want to share political power via structural changes to Aotearoa/New Zealand's governance arrangements in ways that incorporate *tikanga* Māori (Māori law) (Bargh 2012: 166). In contrast, the Crown is interested in Māori economic development and 'restoring the relationship between the claimant group and the Crown' via acknowledgement of, and partial reparation for, historical breaches of the Treaty (OTS n.d., cited in Bargh 2012: 168). But despite the rhetoric of 'restored' relationships (restored to what, we might ask), in many respects the relationship of Crown with *iwi* post-settlement is more of the same and new Treaty breaches continue to occur (for example, the foreshore and seabed debacle in 2004).[3] As Bargh asks, 'How can a relationship be restored when one side of the relationship, such as the Crown … is determining the process and taking limited responsibility for changing their fundamental attitudes, let alone their behaviour?' (2012: 168). This point is echoed by McCormack (this volume, Chapter 15) when she notes that Waitangi Tribunal investigations typically leave unexamined

---

3   There is an extensive literature on the racist and colonial nature of the *Foreshore and Seabed Act 2004* (for example, Charters & Erueti, 2005, 2007).

the political and economic structures that produce and maintain colonial relations. The current form of the politics of recognition then does not really challenge the New Zealand state to reform itself.

Local government and Māori

While the central government's relationships with *iwi* Māori falls short of full partnership, those of local government are even more problematic. The traditional *rohe* (territories) of *hapū* and *iwi* are obviously regionally based. And while the boundaries of local authorities do not exactly coincide with *iwi* boundaries, these government entities are extremely important actors in the lives of *iwi* trying to get on with, in many cases now, their post–Treaty settlement lives. In this context, there are at least two major interconnected problems in the structural foundations of *iwi*–local government relations: the issue of Māori political representation on local councils and the issue of the status of local government as Treaty partners.

The issue of Māori representation has received a lot of attention in the New Zealand media in recent times. At national level, there are currently seven dedicated Māori seats in the parliament of 120 members, with Māori voters having the option every five years to enrol on either the Māori or general electoral roll and the number of Māori seats being adjusted to reflect the proportion of the population on the Māori roll.[4] Since the *Local Electoral Amendment Act 2002*, local government entities have had the option of establishing similar dedicated Māori seats on councils, although only one, The Bay of Plenty Regional Council, has successfully done so, establishing three Māori constituencies alongside four general constituencies, thus ensuring fair representation for the 28 per cent of the local population who are Māori.

While many councils have considered the issue (see Human Rights Commission 2010), very few have tried to implement Māori wards and, to date, no others have been successful. The reasons for this failure are telling. The *Local Electoral Amendment Act 2002* stipulates a number of ways in which local government bodies may modify their systems of representation, but of them all, only the option of establishing Māori wards or constituencies can be overturned by a referendum of voters, this provision effectively acting as a democratic check on the power of

4   See www.elections.org.nz/events/past-events/maori-electoral-option-2013.

councils to enact this change. At least two councils—the Far North District Council and Whakatane District Council—have taken the issue straight to the voters, running polls on their electorates. In both cases, the proposal was voted down. In New Plymouth, the council exercised its right to establish Māori wards, only to have members of the public make use of the provisions of the act to force a referendum on the issue.[5] Pākehā Mayor of New Plymouth Andrew Judd has become a national figure since leading this struggle for improved Māori representation in the city's council, and has since described the provision to establish Māori wards as 'not sincere'.[6]

When the existing local bodies were being amalgamated to form the Auckland 'super-city' in 2010, the issue of Māori representation gained high public profile. The Royal Commission on Auckland Governance, set up to advise on the form of the new council, recommended the establishment of three Māori seats on the council, two elected by voters on the Māori roll and one appointed *mana whenua* representative to represent the interests of local tribes (see Human Rights Commission 2010: 22–7). However, the then Minister of Local Government and neoliberal ACT Party leader Rodney Hide was vehemently opposed to the establishment of Māori seats (an example of undemocratic 'special rights' in his view), and the compromise solution was the establishment of an unelected Independent Māori Statutory Board to advise the council on issues relevant to Māori. Ironically, periodic grumblings now surface about the unelected nature of this board, with the focus being on undemocratic Māori 'privilege' rather than government policy failings.

Māori individuals may of course stand for election to local bodies and some do. Even so, as an ethnic group, Māori are 'chronically underrepresented' in local government, making up only 3.6 per cent of councillors in 2007 for close to 15 per cent of the population at the time (Hayward 2011a: 187, n. 2). In addition, these councillors, elected to general seats, are not mandated to represent Māori per se but the community as a whole, so that arguably Māori issues and interests are even more seriously underrepresented within the local government sector than even these figures suggest.

---

5   Councils must issue a public notice of their intention to establish Māori wards and a petition of at least 5 per cent of the voters in the electorate can force a referendum on the issue.
6   See www.radionz.co.nz/national/programmes/morningreport/audio/201815732/call-for-candidates-to-take-a-stand-on-Māori-representation.

While the issue of Māori representation focuses on the place and role of Māori *within* councils, the issue of Treaty partnerships between councils and *iwi* is one of the relationship *between* Māori and councils. What is the state of the Treaty *partnership* in our society at this level of local government? Reading the settlement deeds the Crown draws up with *iwi* and the apologies the Crown makes, there are many fine words acknowledging the ways the Crown has failed to recognise the *rangatiratanga* (chiefly authority/sovereignty) of *iwi* in the past, acknowledging the historical wrongs that have been committed, and expressing the Crown's desire to now build new Treaty-based relationships with *iwi*. In these apologies, the Crown seeks to set the history of colonial injustice in the past and commits itself to non-colonial relations in the post-settlement era (although with the shortcomings noted in the previous section). But where does local government sit in these new Treaty-based relationships? What are their responsibilities to Te Tiriti? As Janine Hayward (2011b: 79) succinctly puts it, when the Crown devolved *kawanatanga* (governmental) responsibilities to local bodies they completely failed to also devolve the Treaty guarantee to protect *tino rangatiratanga*.[7]

Under the *Local Government Act 2002*, local authorities do not have the status of a Treaty partner. Instead, they have a range of responsibilities to involve Māori in decision-making, to take account of Māori 'culture and traditions with their ancestral land, water, sites, waahi tapu, [sacred sites] valued flora and fauna, and other taonga' and to have processes in place for consultation with Māori. The only references to *iwi* and *hapū* appear in Schedule 3 of the Act, which deals with the process by which councils may seek to amalgamate to create unitary authorities. Tellingly, councils must consult *iwi* and *hapū* if they wish to reorganise the system of governance (although they are not bound to heed their views), but not in their day-to-day operations. While the Crown recognises *iwi* (even if inadequately), they do not oblige local government to do so. From the local government perspective then, *iwi* and *hapū* are just convenient organisations to liaise with to meet their obligations vis-à-vis consulting and involving Māori in decision-making. There is no obligation for local bodies to recognise the territorial authority of *iwi* or their status as Treaty partners. Hence, while

---

7   Article 1 of Te Tiriti o Waitangi (the Māori language version of the Treaty of Waitangi, i.e. the version most Māori leaders signed) grants the right of *kawanatanga* (governance) to the Crown. Article 2 recognises and confirms the ongoing *rangatiratanga* (chiefly authority) of Māori tribal leaders.

most local councils have consultation processes in place with Māori, and some have co-management arrangements over specific resources, these processes fall far short of the governance partnerships that *iwi* are seeking.

This failure to require local authorities to act as Treaty partners is a major flaw in New Zealand's governance arrangements and in the Crown's enactment of its role as Treaty partner. The New Zealand state is effectively split into national entities with the status of Treaty partners and regional entities without, leaving *iwi* caught between the fine rhetoric of partnership in Treaty settlements and the reality of being just another community interest group at home. The only exceptions to this are where the economic power of the local *iwi*, post-settlement, is such that they cannot be ignored—for example, Ngāi Tahu and Waikato-Tainui. In such cases, classic neoliberal privileging of economic power, rather than any commitment to the Treaty, drive the recognition of *iwi* partners (Livesey 2017). As the Constitutional Advisory Panel (2013: 44) very moderately observed:

> Councils are under no imperative to engage with iwi and hapū. Iwi representation, even by the creation of Māori wards, is reliant on individual personalities within each council. It is undesirable that Māori representation in local government continue in this ad hoc manner. Each local authority may determine the mechanisms for fulfilling their obligations to consult iwi. While this approach enables flexibility to find a solution which fits local conditions, it means that there are considerable differences across the country. Such inconsistency can lead to impressions of unfairness and inequality.

If we consider the issue of land, which is at the heart of much of the engagement between *iwi* and councils, we get some sense of the problem this split in the nature of local and central government creates for *iwi*. Historically, local councils have frequently taken Māori reserve land for public works. As academic and Waitangi Tribunal member, Ranginui Walker (2016: 21), notes:

> The pattern of local councils taking land has been so widespread and consistent around the country that it is difficult not to conclude that Māori land was deliberately targeted by local bodies because it was easier and cheaper to access than general land.

But, as Walker goes on to say, given that local authorities are not partners to the Treaty, no Treaty claims can be laid against them. This means that:

> councillors are distanced from the angst of iwi caused by their exploitive behaviour, so they never learn. Nor are they obliged to attend Waitangi Tribunal hearings where iwi air the pain of their grievances and disempowerment *vis-a-vis* local government. Consequently, local bodies are not *au fait* with the Treaty discourse between iwi and the Crown (ibid.).

Overall, the picture of the local government relationship with *iwi* is complex and ineffective. While local councils must consult and take cognisance of Māori interests, their legislative and structural arrangements provide no clear guidance on how this is to be done, and in fact make it difficult, while rendering genuine partnerships impossible.

The Crown as flawed subject of recognition

The overall tenor of the critical literature on the politics of recognition as it relates to indigenous peoples and settler states is that the power imbalance in these relationships sets the settler state up as the recognis*or* with indigenous communities in the role of recognis*ee*, expected to reshape themselves into recognisable forms to receive what limited provisions the settler state is willing to offer (Povinelli 2002, Bell 2014, Coulthard 2014). As McCormack puts it (this volume, Chapter 15), contemporary recognition politics 'incongruously, may strengthen the capacity of the state to shape and neutralise opposition'. The state holds at least most of the cards in the negotiations with *iwi*, and indigenous communities are, to varying degrees depending on the particulars of different systems, required to establish their recognisability. Not only must they provide evidence of their peoplehood, they must also modify their structures and processes to meet the requirements of the neoliberal state. It is here that critical work on recognition by the neoliberal state has pointed to the ways in which indigenous entities have been obliged to take on capitalist and neoliberal forms, values and processes to be 'recognisable' and to receive what benefits and powers the settler state is willing to offer (see Bell 2014: 149–72 for a more detailed overview).

In this final section of the chapter, I turn the lens of judgement on the New Zealand state, and particularly on the differences between central and local government outlined above, to consider whether or not the state is a fit subject for recognition politics. Does the New Zealand state exist in a form that warrants recognition from *iwi* Māori? Is it capable of recognising indigenous partners? Looking back over this brief overview, three crucial flaws are clearly evident in the subjectivity of the New Zealand settler state as Treaty partner: the state is an incoherent, insincere and severely amnesiac subject, unfit for the politics of recognition.

The split structures and responsibilities of the New Zealand state make it a shape-shifting, fragmented or incoherent subject when it comes to relationships with *iwi* Māori. While both central and local arms of the state can breech the Treaty, only central government can be held accountable for such breeches. The arm of the state that *iwi* and *hapū* have the most to do with in the day-to-day enactment of their sovereign and guardian status in their traditional territories is not their partner in this process. Instead, by and large, local government is a hindrance, unable to recognise who they are. This colonial 'business as usual' at local government level is a clear example of Bargh's point (2012: 168) about the limited nature of change on the part of the state.

Further, while central government acknowledges past injustices and speaks fine words of restored relationships, it also handicaps local government relationships with *iwi* Māori. As the *Local Electoral Amendment Act 2002* demonstrates, the gesture made towards Māori representation has proven to be empty and 'insincere', open to the whim of the general electorate where the dislike of anything deemed 'special rights' for Māori almost inevitably results in any move for Māori representation in local government being overturned.

The inability to recognise *iwi* and *hapū* for who they are is compounded by the amnesiac nature of local councils. As Walker (2016) notes, councils are not obliged to hear or even read the histories of Treaty injustices perpetrated in their territories and to which they themselves have frequently been party. This means their memory does not extend beyond the electoral cycle and the lifetimes of the legislation that binds their activities. Councillors in meetings with *iwi* leaders will more often than not know nothing of the history of the land over which they are empowered to exercise governance rights. How then can *iwi* leaders negotiate with such amnesiac subjects as equals?

Finally, these failings of the New Zealand state point to another major gap at the societal level in grappling with *iwi* sovereignty and partnership: the lack of consideration being given to the role of *tangata*

Tiriti/non-Māori New Zealanders as treaty partners. Biculturalism, despite the suggestion in the term of 'two cultures', has largely been about the relationships between Māori and government, with the rest of New Zealand society largely unengaged from the process. The referendums overturning almost all local body attempts to institute Māori wards and constituencies point to this wide societal ignorance of the significance of Māori indigenous status as a major problem New Zealand society has yet to grapple with.

In sum, a focus on the relationship between local government and Māori adds to our understandings of the limitations of the articulation of neoliberalism and the politics of recognition in Aotearoa/New Zealand. Not only does neoliberalism distort recognition politics to privilege economic structures, relations and interests over Māori sovereignty, values and practices, but a focus on local government highlights significant features of the fragmentary and unreliable nature of state engagement as a Treaty partner. Turning the gaze of recognition on the state, to look at central and local government as parts of a whole, allows us to see the ongoing amnesiac, incoherent and shape-shifting character of the state that *iwi* and *hapū* must treat with.

References

Bargh M (ed.) (2007a). *Resistance: An indigenous response to neoliberalism*, Huia Publishers, Wellington.

Bargh M (2007b). Introduction. In Bargh M (ed.), *Resistance: An indigenous response to neoliberalism*, Huia Publishers, Wellington.

Bargh M (2007c). Māori development and neoliberalism. In Bargh M (ed.), *Resistance: An indigenous response to neoliberalism*, Huia Publishers, Wellington.

Bargh M (2012). The post-settlement world (so far): Impacts for Māori. In Wheen NR & Hayward J (eds), *Treaty of Waitangi settlements*, Bridget Williams Books and the New Zealand Law Foundation, Wellington, doi.org/10.7810/9781927131381_12.

Bargh M (2013). Multiple site of Māori political participation. *Australian Journal of Political Science* 48(4):445–55, doi.org/10.1080/10361146.2013.841123.

Belgrave M, Kawharu M & Williams D (eds) (2005). *Waitangi revisited: Perspectives of the Treaty of Waitangi*, Oxford University Press, Melbourne.

Bell A (2014). *Relating indigenous and settler identities: Beyond domination*, Palgrave Macmillan, London, doi.org/10.1057/9781137313560.

Bennett A (2015). The good fight: Power and the indigenous struggle for the Manawatū River. PhD thesis, Massey University, Palmerston North.

Charters C & Erueti A (2005). Report from the inside: the CERD Committee's review of the Foreshore and Seabed Act 2004. *Victoria University of Wellington Law Review* 36(2), www.nzlii.org/nz/journals/VUWLawRw/2005/12.html.

Charters C & Erueti A (eds) (2007). *Māori property rights and the foreshore and seabed: The last frontier.* Victoria University Press, Wellington.

Constitutional Advisory Panel (2013). *New Zealand's constitution: A report on a conversation*, New Zealand Government, Wellington.

Coombes BL & Hill S (2005). 'Na whenua, na Tuhoe, Ko D.O.C. te partner'— prospects for comanagement of Te Urewera National Park. *Society and Natural Resources* 18(2):135–52, doi.org/10.1080/08941920590894516.

Coulthard G (2014). *Red skin, white masks: Rejecting the colonial politics of recognition*, University of Minnesota Press, Minneapolis, doi.org/10.5749/minnesota/9780816679645.001.0001.

Durie M (2011). *Ngā Tini Whetū: Navigating Māori futures*, Huia Publishers, Wellington.

Forster M (2014). Indigeneity and trends in recognizing Māori environmental rights and interests. *Nationalism and Ethnic Politics* 20(1):63–78, doi.org/10.1080/13537113.2014.879765.

Hayward J (2011a). Mandatory Māori wards in local government: Active Crown protection of Māori Treaty rights. *Political Science* 63(2):186–204, doi.org/10.1177/0032318711423908.

Hayward J (2011b). In search of certainty: Local government policy and the Treaty of Waitangi. In Tawhai VMH & Gray-Sharp K (eds), *'Always speaking': The Treaty of Waitangi and public policy*, Huia Publishers, Wellington.

Human Rights Commission (2010). *Māori representation in local government: The continuing challenge*, Wellington.

Humpage L (2017). A land of me and money? New Zealand society under neoliberalism. In Bell A, Elizabeth V, McIntosh T & Wynyard M (eds), *A land of milk and honey? Making sense of Aotearoa New Zealand*, Auckland University Press, Auckland.

Joseph R (2012). Unsettling Treaty settlements: Contemporary Māori identity and representation challenges. In Wheen NR & Hayward J (eds), *Treaty of Waitangi settlements*, Bridget Williams Books and the New Zealand Law Foundation, Wellington, doi.org/10.7810/9781927131381_11.

Kelsey J (2005). Māori, Te Tiriti and globalization: The invisible hand of the colonial state. In Belgrave M, Kawharu M & Williams D (eds), *Waitangi revisited: Perspectives of the Treaty of Waitangi*, Oxford University Press, Melbourne.

Lewis N, Lewis O & Underhill-Semm Y (2009). Filling hollowed out spaces with localized meanings, practices and hopes: Progressive neoliberal spaces in Te Rarawa. *Asia Pacific Viewpoint* 50(2):166–84, doi.org/10.1111/j.1467-8373.2009.01391.x.

Livesey B (2017). Towards Treaty-based management: Treaty discourses and 'everyday work' in planning. In Bell R, Kawharu M, Taylor K, Belgrave M & Meihana P (eds), *The Treaty on the ground: Where are we headed and why it matters*, Massey University Press, Auckland.

Lowry A (2012). Te toi poto, te toi roa: A critical evaluation of Māori-State inclusion in the Ohiwa Harbour strategy, Aotearoa New Zealand. Masters thesis, University of Waikato, Hamilton.

McCormack F (2011). Levels of indigeneity: The Māori and neoliberalism, *Journal of the Royal Anthropological Institute* 17:281–300, doi.org/10.1111/j.1467-9655.2011.01680.x.

McCormack F (2012). Indigeneity as process: Māori claims and neoliberalism, *Social Identities* 18(4):417–34, doi.org/10.1080/13504630.2012.673870.

Muru-Lanning M (2012). The key actors of Waikato River co-governance. *AlterNative: An International Journal of Indigenous Peoples* 8(2):128–36, doi.org/10.1177/117718011200800202.

Muru-Lanning M (2016). *Tupuna awa: People and politics of the Waikato River*, Auckland University Press, Auckland.

Mutu M (2011). *The state of Māori rights*, Huia Publishers, Wellington.

OTS (Office of Treaty Settlements) (2014). *Vote Treaty negotiations: 2014 briefing for the incoming Minister*, Ministry of Justice, Wellington.

OTS (2015). *Ka tika ā muri, ka tika ā mua, healing the past, building a future*, Ministry of Justice, Wellington.

Poata-Smith E (2004). Ka tika ā muri, ka tika ā mua? Māori protest politics and the Waitangi settlement process. In Spoonley P, Macpherson C & Pearson D (eds), *Tangata, Tangata: The changing ethnic contours of New Zealand*, Dunmore, Palmerston North.

Povinelli E (2002). *The cunning of recognition: Indigenous alterities and the making of Australian multiculturalism*, Duke University Press, Durham, doi.org/10.1215/9780822383673.

Sullivan A & Toki V (2012). It's not about race, it's about rights. *Studies in Law, Politics and Society* 57:1–29, doi.org/10.1108/S1059-4337(2012)0000057004.

Te Aho L (2010). Indigenous challenges to enhance freshwater governance and management in Aotearoa New Zealand—the Waikato River settlement. *Journal of Water Law* 20(5):285–92.

Waaka M (2006). Local government. In Mulholland M (ed.), *State of the Māori nation: Twenty-first century issues*, Reed Publishing, Auckland.

Walker, R (2016). Rangatiratanga, kāwanatanga and the constitution, unpublished paper (unpaginated).

Wheen NR & Hayward J (eds) (2012). *Treaty of Waitangi settlements*, Bridget Williams Books and the New Zealand Law Foundation, Wellington, doi.org/10.7810/9781927131381.

Workman K (2017). Unconditional rather than reciprocal: The Treaty and the state sector. In Bell R, Kawharu M, Taylor K, Belgrave M & Meihana P (eds), *The Treaty on the ground: Where are we headed and why it matters*, Massey University Press, Auckland.

5

Expressions of Indigenous rights and self-determination from the ground up: A Yawuru example

Mandy Yap and Eunice Yu

Introduction

While recognition is one way self-determination for indigenous peoples can be enacted, the processes and models of recognition are fraught and complicated (Coulthard 2014). Additionally, the act and process of recognition for indigenous peoples tends to occur within existing dominant Western frameworks and is imbued in power relations; therefore, the extent to which recognition may effectively address the issues of structural injustice remains questionable (Fraser & Honneth 2003, Andersen 2014, Coulthard 2014). One of the challenges in enabling self-determination for Australia's Indigenous peoples stems from the increasing influence of neoliberalism in Indigenous policy (Altman 2007, Humpage 2008, Howard-Wagner 2010).

The prevalence of neoliberalism in academic and policy discourse is evident from the increasing amount of scholarly writing on the topic (Peck & Tickell 2002, Humpage 2008, Boas & Gans-Morse 2009, Venugopal 2015). Boas and Gans-Morse (2009: 143–45) offer four approaches in which neoliberalism has been used in the literature, including to examine economic reform policies, as a development model, to denote an ideology and to characterise an academic paradigm. Notwithstanding how neoliberalism has been operationalised within the different approaches, the case in point is the permeation of key values, ideals and norms associated with neoliberalism into the social, economic and political sphere. In this section, fellow contributors offer examples of how legislation provisions in Australia are imbued in principles and values of neoliberalism, arguing that neoliberalism as a guiding philosophy of Indigenous policy undermines Indigenous self-determination. The spread of neoliberalism in indigenous policy is also evident in New Zealand and Canada (see Humpage, O'Sullivan and Altamirano-Jiménez, this volume).

Policies aimed at improving Indigenous wellbeing in Australia through the monitoring of Indigenous socio-economic outcomes according to specific ideals and values from the dominant society can be seen as an extension of neoliberalism. The governing, measurement and evaluation of all domains of society according to a set of principles associated with the market results in benchmarking of society against an idealised vision of a 'good market', which includes a good job, healthy lifestyles and consumer rationality (Mirowski 2009, Davies 2015: 301). Yet, these idealised visions do not reflect notions of wellbeing for Indigenous peoples.

Aspects of wellbeing for many Indigenous peoples

The literature on Indigenous wellbeing points to wellbeing as both a process and outcome, that is achieved and maintained as a collective and relationally. Furthermore, the literature reveals the importance of maintaining connection to country and culture and self-determination over matters concerning one's self, one's family, community and country (Greiner et al. 2005, Durie 2006, Grieves 2007, Panzironi 2007, Ganesharajah 2009, Yu 2012, McCubbin et al. 2013, Murphy 2014).

Indigenous worldviews and values can and should provide an alternative foundation to understanding rights and self-determination for Indigenous peoples. This alternative set of values requires the direct inclusion of Indigenous voices and requires engagement with Indigenous peoples' historical experience of colonisation (Watene 2016). This chapter offers a broader perspective of rights and self-determination through working with the Yawuru community in Broome to model co-production of knowledge from the ground up. This model has its foundation in Yawuru worldviews, privileges Yawuru voices and starts with *mabu liyan*, Yawuru's philosophy for living well. Through a participatory mixed methods approach, the findings will illustrate that self-determination for the Yawuru is both an aspect of *mabu liyan* and also a pathway towards achieving and sustaining *mabu liyan*.

Indigenous peoples and self-determination

Self-determination is a basic human right that also carries instrumental value for individual wellbeing (Sen 1999, Webb 2012). Perhaps unsurprisingly, the principles of self-determination underpin the United Nations Declaration of the Rights of Indigenous Peoples (UNDRIP), an international standard-setting mechanism to support indigenous peoples' rights to a development paradigm that reflects their collective sense of identity, built on the strength of their culture and identity and in balance with the environment.[1]

The principles of and rights to self-determination for indigenous peoples have been discussed at length within the legal and political space in Australia and internationally (Panzironi 2007). At these levels, rights and recognition for indigenous peoples may come in the form of indigenous representation or allocated seats at the table, such as the dedicated Māori seats in the New Zealand Parliament or the Sami Assembly. In Australia, representative bodies of Indigenous peoples such as the former Aboriginal and Torres Strait Islander Commission and, more recently, the National Congress of Australia's First Peoples are important vehicles for Indigenous Australians.

However, the claims and expressions to self-determination may extend beyond these domains (Panzironi 2007). Watene (2016) and Davis (2013) argue that, to fully capture self-determination, engagement with Indigenous peoples and communities about their perspectives on self-determination are necessary. This chapter echoes the sentiment of both scholars and argues that to fully understand self-determination,

---

1   For the full text of the United Nations Declaration of the Rights of Indigenous Peoples, see www.un.org/development/desa/indigenouspeoples/declaration-on-the-rights-of-indigenous-peoples. html.

an important starting point is for Indigenous communities to express what constitutes a life where Indigenous peoples are able to pursue their economic, political and cultural rights as set out in UNDRIP.

In the 1970s, self-determination for Indigenous Australians was proposed as the guiding principle for Indigenous affairs following a period of paternalistic policies of assimilation (HREOC 2002). Land rights legislation, native title and the emergence of an Indigenous sector signalled a promising shift towards self-determination for Indigenous Australians (HREOC 2002, Sanders 2002, Rowse 2012). That promise, however, was short-lived, with the introduction of policies such as the Northern Territory Emergency Response affecting any progress towards Indigenous control over matters concerning their lives (Altman & Hinkson 2010).

The ambiguities surrounding what it means to be self-determining within the legal and political context has challenged the implementation of policies that truly facilitate self-determination of indigenous communities (Sanders 2002, Anaya 2004, Webb 2012). For many indigenous peoples, self-determination is fundamentally about the right and freedom to live the life they value, and to participate in the process of decision-making concerning them (Daes 2000). As the Human Rights and Equal Opportunity Commission (HREOC) notes, 'self-determination as the centre piece of Indigenous policy has to a large extent been a statement of intention rather than of action. Real self-determination has never been tried' (HREOC 2002: 3).

Indigenous wellbeing and the politics of recognition in Australia

Despite the continuous call by Indigenous Australians to have the rights to set their own development agenda, the policies pertaining to them in the last decade have focused on achieving statistical equality with their non-Indigenous counterparts to improve their wellbeing (Taylor 2008, Jordan et al. 2010, Kukutai & Walter 2015). As a result, much of the research and data collection efforts at informing the evidence base tend to focus on government programs designed to reduce disadvantage faced by Indigenous Australians. What is 'recognised' as evidence is often considered synonymous with official data collected and analysed for the purposes of informing government reporting (Taylor 2008, Kukutai &

Walter 2015). Such research often uses a top-down approach, and may be expertly driven or derived with very little input from communities or from the peoples who are the beneficiaries of government policies and programs.

The tension that exists between the worldviews of indigenous peoples and government reporting frameworks is what Taylor has termed 'the recognition or translation space' (Taylor 2008). It is this area of intersection between the two spaces where meaningful and substantive engagement and measurement is necessary (Taylor 2008). More importantly, 'recognition' is a vital human need, and misrecognition can be seen as another form of oppression (Taylor 1992: 25).

The 'recognition space' is where two or more forms of law, knowledge, culture and worldview encounter or intersect (Pearson 1997, Mantziaris & Martin 2000, Ermine 2007, Taylor 2008). In essence, most authors describe 'the space' as a means through which Indigenous worldviews and aspirations can become 'recognised' within the broader political, legal and statistical reporting frameworks. Kukutai and Walter (2015) further offer five recognition principles to increase information functionality for Indigenous peoples: recognising cultural diversity, recognising geographical diversity, recognising different ways of knowing indigenous peoples, mutual capacity-building and indigenous decision-making. These five principles are important in the process of operationalising the 'recognition space' to elicit indigenous articulations of self-determination and to challenge the normative definitions of self-determination.

Self-determination on the ground

What self-determination might mean within the lived experiences, strengths and challenges faced by Australian Indigenous communities on the ground has remain largely unexplored amid the large body of literature on self-determination (Behrendt 2002, Davis 2013, Watene 2016). Indigenous and non-Indigenous scholars have argued that the concept of self-determination needs to be understood and expressed within an alternative framework that recognises relational aspects of self-determination, in particular relating to the natural world, to the collective and to sustainability (Behrendt 2002, Anaya 2004, Corntassel 2008, Coulthard 2014, Murphy 2014).

The former Chair of the United Nations Working Group on Indigenous Populations, Professor Erica-Irene Daes, offered the following definition of self-determination:

> Self-determination means the freedom for indigenous peoples to live well, to live according to their own values and beliefs, and to be respected by their non-indigenous neighbours …

> the true test of self-determination is not whether indigenous peoples have their own institutions, legislative authorities, laws, police and judges. The true test of self-determination is whether indigenous peoples themselves actually feel that they have choices about their way of life. (Daes 2000: x)

This suggests that the starting point surely is to first understand what it means to live well for indigenous peoples according to their own values and beliefs. For the Yawuru that is *mabu liyan*.

Mabu liyan (good *liyan*) reflects Yawuru's sense of belonging and being, emotional strength, dignity and pride. Expressions of *liyan* are articulated based on collective structures: it is a model of living well in connection with country, culture, others and with oneself (McKenna & Anderson 2011, Yap & Yu 2016a). Starting with *mabu liyan* as the central focus of Yawuru wellbeing is recognising that there is a different way of understanding what wellbeing is, and how rights and self-determination might operate within the philosophy of *mabu liyan*.

Yawuru rights and responsibilities—standing in two worlds

The Yawuru people are the traditional owners of the lands and waters in and around Rubibi (the town of Broome) from Bangarangara to the *yalimban* (south) to Wirrjinmirr (Willie Creek) to the *guniyan* (north), and *banu* (east) covering Roebuck Plains and Thangoo pastoral leases, in the Kimberley region of northern Western Australia (Yawuru RNTBC 2011).

In 2010, after 20 long years, the Yawuru secured native title, recognising Yawuru's enduring relationship with their land. The Native Title Determination has provided Yawuru with the opportunity to have a say over the land and its usages and to have an input into issues affecting Yawuru in local and regional settings (Yawuru RNTBC 2011). Within the Western and political legal frameworks, the Yawuru have to consider how their rights and entitlements can be exercised and negotiated. However, for the Yawuru, there is a set of cultural rights and responsibilities that arise from the *bugarrigarra*,[2] the core of Yawuru cosmology. Self-determination, for Yawuru, cannot be disconnected from the broader rights and responsibilities of looking after country and fulfilling one's cultural obligations as Yawuru.

The Yawuru Wellbeing Project—exercising self-determination in the 'recognition space'

The importance of self-determination and autonomy is critical within a research paradigm to ensure that power relations are transformed, whereby Indigenous peoples as holders of knowledge, expert on their own lives, meaningfully participate in the process to co-produce knowledge as collaborators and partners, not as research subjects or participants (Yap & Yu 2016a). In operationalising the 'recognition space' to understand what constitutes wellbeing for the Yawuru, rights and self-determination are exercised in two stages. First, in the process aspect, whereby Yawuru are co-producers of knowledge to conceptualise what rights, recognition and wellbeing means for Yawuru. Second, through the grounding of rights, recognition and self-determination measures informed through narratives by Yawuru women and men. Together, they seek to reveal understandings of living well through Yawuru's worldviews into the recognition space.

Yawuru's participation—a necessary and critical element

Working with the Yawuru as a distinct language group is recognising that there is geographical and cultural diversity within Indigenous Australians as a collective. Yawuru's participation in the Yawuru Wellbeing Project research[3] was critical, and thus interwoven throughout the process,

---

2   *Bugarrigarra* is the time before time, when the creative forces shaped and gave meaning and form to the landscape, putting the languages to the people within those landscapes and creating the protocol and laws for living within this environment (Yawuru RNTBC 2011: 13).

3   The Yawuru Wellbeing Project combined stories of Yawuru women and men with findings from the Yawuru Wellbeing Survey to paint a localised and multi-dimensional picture of wellbeing. The project aimed to provide a baseline for Yawuru people as a collective to plan and design programs around what might bring about improvements in wellbeing. Please see www.healthinfonet.ecu.edu. au/key-resources/programs-projects?pid=3245.

from research content to survey design and collection, to ensure that understandings about self-determination from the ground up are privileged (Behrendt 2002, Watene 2016, Yap & Yu 2016b).

The various ways in which Yawuru's worldviews, aspirations and participation has been prioritised in this research has been outlined elsewhere (Yap & Yu 2016a). As a first step, Yawuru's own agenda to measure wellbeing according to their worldviews, together with a PhD research proposal by a non-Indigenous student, which aimed to develop culturally relevant measures of wellbeing, provided a common group for forming a collaborative partnership between this chapter's two authors (Yap & Yu 2016a). The setting up of the Yawuru Guidance and Reference Committee ensured that the information generated through the research reflected local aspirations and values and, most importantly, was functional for Yawuru needs. Yawuru's participation in the research was critically interwoven throughout the process, from research content to survey collection, to ensure Indigenous decision-making as a principle was operationalised in the recognition space.

Mutual capacity building is a necessary element in enabling self-determinations. The employment of 10 local research assistants and purchase of iPads facilitated through Bankwest Curtin Economics Centre enabled this. The mutual capacity building built into the research with Yawuru women and men further ensured that knowledge is co-produced from the ground up, bringing together different ways of knowing, both traditional and Western, in a manner that is consistent with the recognition space.

Conceptions of rights, recognition and self-determination by Yawuru

From stories to indicators to measures

Underpinning Yawuru's wellbeing is the notion of *liyan*. There was general consensus from Yawuru women and men that *liyan* is a *feeling*, not just in one sense but all senses. Yawuru derive *mabu liyan* from touching, eating, feeling, being and doing. *Liyan* is also about how one relates to others, to the surroundings, and to the environment. As a result, values that bring about the maintenance of good relations with others and one's surroundings were important as a Yawuru philosophy of being. There were several key themes arising from what brings about *mabu liyan* for Yawuru. They include family, connection to country and culture, standard of living, health, safety and respect, community, and rights and recognition. This chapter will not reproduce all the themes outlined in previous publications (see Yap & Yu 2016a, 2016b). Instead, it will focus on expressions and conceptions of rights, recognition and self-determination for Yawuru.

These concepts of rights and recognition critically laid the foundation for the grounding of indicators and survey questions according to Yawuru's worldviews. The grounding of the indicators from the stories by Yawuru women and men further created a sense of 'ownership' in the operation of the 'recognition space' and allow for further expressions of self-determination by Yawuru (see Table 5.1).

Table 5.1: The development of indicators of rights of recognition for Yawuru

Themes	Examples of interview	Indicators	Selected/not selected by focus groups	Translated to survey question
Rights and recognition	'Being respected by other people, both Aboriginal and non-Aboriginal is a part of self-determination'	Feel respected by Indigenous and non-Indigenous people in my community	Picked by Yawuru women Picked by Yawuru men	I felt respected and my opinions valued most or all of the time
	'We need to keep the seasons going by looking after the country as best we can by communicating it and sharing it with others so that they can understand as well why it is important, why we need access to those parts of country'	Sharing Yawuru culture with Indigenous and non-Indigenous peoples	Picked by Yawuru women Picked by Yawuru men	In the last 12 months, did you share Yawuru culture with Indigenous and non-Indigenous peoples ? (E.g. have a yarn, cultural tour, welcome to country)

Source: Adapted from Yap (2017) and Yap & Yu (2016b).

Rights and respect

Having human rights is fundamental to Yawuru's sense of wellbeing. These include having basic human rights, feeling respected, having autonomy and control and being free from discrimination.

> Having human rights is fundamental for wellbeing. Rights that were denied to our grandparents. We have some so far since then and there is still room for improvement (Yawuru female, 34 years old).[4]

For many Indigenous peoples, the right to maintain one's distinct cultural identity is a fundamental human right. For the Yawuru, an aspect of this is speaking the Yawuru language.

> Language is the basis of identity, the basis of confidence and culture … We need to keep our language strong and reinvigorate it for us who were not able to learn it properly as kids for whatever reason. We shouldn't feel ashamed of that. We need to say to our people that—It is okay that we didn't learn to speak our language properly. It was a time when we were not allowed to speak our language, where it was great pressure on us to not speak our language. That shouldn't stop us from learning our language or teaching our children language (Yawuru male, 58 years old).

The narrative above suggests that Yawuru people, like many other Indigenous language groups, did not have the opportunity to learn or were not permitted to speak their Indigenous language growing up. As a result, the number of Yawuru speakers declined to a critical level. The language efforts driven by Yawuru through the establishment of the Yawuru Language Centre alongside the concerted effort towards building a cohort of Yawuru speakers and teachers has led to a revitalisation of the Yawuru language.

Respect is an important element of Yawuru conceptions of self-determination and wellbeing. This includes showing respect towards others and also being respected by others. Feeling free from discrimination is also critically important for self-determination. As one woman describes:

> Being respected by other people, both Aboriginal and non-Aboriginal is a part of self-determination. Getting rid of racism is part of self-determination (Yawuru female, 34 years old).

---

4   All quotes taken from participants in the Yawuru Wellbeing Project except where otherwise specified.

For Yawuru, the importance of being traditional owners and the responsibility over traditional country is another dimension of respect for territory, respect for country and respect for other Aboriginal groups' connections to their land, and the need for others to respect Yawuru's responsibility for their traditional country.

> Respect should be handed down and respect is involved with culture, family and kinship. The land provides for you, so you respect the land because it looks after you. Country will look after you if you look after country. I am not just talking about Yawuru country, I am talking about every part of Australia. Where ever I go to someone else's country, I will respect the land because one, it is not mine and two because its's the black fella way (Yawuru male, 30 years old).

Connectedness to country and culture

Not dissimilar to other indigenous groups around the world, the Yawuru people describe a deep physical, cultural and spiritual connection to their country in which they live but also identify with. Knowing about land and sea, hunting and fishing, eating bush tucker and seasonal catch, spending time with elders, sharing and receiving of catch and kill are all dimensions of connection to culture and country for Yawuru women and men.

As a result, management of country and culture is a responsibility and right which arises through Yawuru's intrinsic connection to the land, both physically, emotionally and spiritually:

> not only the trees provide us with the tools, medicine, food, but the connection to that biodiversity, the birds everything that utilise the area … lizards … when you start to draw the picture. People start to see it's not just a piece of rubbish, desolate savannah … these are the animals, reptiles and things that reside here … and when you give it cultural significance, you give it a living landscape … Yawuru people and the land are intrinsically connected … and wellbeing are intrinsically connected. Anything done to the land, it's like hurting them because of the connection to land (Yawuru male, 41 years old).

The ability to exercise rights and self-determination to maintain a healthy country and fulfil one's cultural obligation is dependent on a range of factors, one of which is access to country:

> Once upon a time we used to have access to go down to the beach to our favourite fishing grounds or camping grounds. But you can't do it anymore. It is blocked off. They put fences up to block you off … We are

> Yawuru people, saltwater people. We have fished in this area for hundreds of years. They come along and tell you that you are not allowed to throw your net there ... (Yawuru female, 70 years old)

However, many individuals further noted that if they had some say or control over what is happening, that may go some way to negating the impacts on their wellbeing.

> How do we develop or negotiate or implement programs to make us feel like we can feed that *liyan* feeling. If we are worried about it ... Implement the program—water monitoring or strategy where ranger group helps inform the mining company. How do we develop a spin off to try and have control over the process (Yawuru male, 41 years old).

While there are the more formal ways of contributing to the management of country and culture through attendance at meetings and representations in programs, an important way in which Yawuru exercise control over and maintains their connection to country and culture is through the sharing of Yawuru culture with other Indigenous and non-Indigenous groups.

> We need to keep the seasons going by looking after the country as best we can by communicating it and sharing it with others so that they can understand as well why it is important, why we need access to those parts of country (Yawuru male, 52 years old).

Table 5.2: Expressions of self-determination by Yawuru women and men

Indicators of self-determination for the Yawuru	Females (%)	Males (%)
Felt respected and opinions valued most or all of the time	51.0	63.6
Felt vulnerable to being discriminated against none or little of the time	74.4	76.4
Having total/quite a lot of control over what happens on my country	18.4	19.3
Having total/quite or a lot of control over what happens to my family	50.0	42.9
Having total/quite or a lot of control over what happens to me	90.8	82.8
Attended community meetings	39.8	46.6
Attended community rally/call for action	33.7	31.0
Voted at Yawuru meetings	31.6	36.2
Voted at state/national elections	48.0	46.6
Shared Yawuru culture with Indigenous and non-Indigenous people	48.0	56.9
Feel able to access country to hunt and fish	80.6	79.3
Feel able to access country to practice traditional culture	62.2	69.0

Source: Yawuru Wellbeing Survey 2015. See Yap (2017) and Yap & Yu (2016a, 2016b).

Table 5.2 provides some indicators of self-determination as expressed by Yawuru. It is evident that the majority of Yawuru women and men felt they were vulnerable to being discriminated against none or a little of the time. However, a lower share of the population felt respected by others and felt their opinions were valued most or all of the time.

Around a third of Yawuru women and men reported having voted at Yawuru meetings on matters concerning Yawuru, but as high as 57 per cent of Yawuru men reported having shared Yawuru culture with Indigenous and non-Indigenous peoples in the last 12 months. This suggests there is a need to facilitate a broader understanding of expressions of self-determination.

Conclusion

Self-determination has both intrinsic and instrumental value for Indigenous Australian peoples, including Yawuru. To understand and enable self-determination, there is a need to first understand what it means to live well, to make decisions, to have autonomy over the lives that Indigenous men and women value at the grassroots level. While there are important efforts needed at the national and international level, this chapter echoes the argument that it is self-determination facilitated at the local level with Indigenous communities that will ensure that the effectiveness of UNDRIP flows across multiple sectors and levels, rather than being confined to being an instrument of rights within the political and legal sphere with minimal impact on the lives of Indigenous communities on the ground.

Acknowledgements

The authors would like to acknowledge that this work was undertaken on Yawuru country and extend their gratitude to all the Yawuru women and men who have generously given their time to share their ideas, views and thoughts for advancing the research, in particular the Yawuru Reference and Guidance Committee who have been a guiding compass to ensure the research is fit for purpose for community needs and aspirations. We would also like to acknowledge the Yawuru Wellbeing Survey 2015 team of research assistants without whom the findings in Table 5.2 would not be possible. The research received both financial and in-kind support from the following organisations to which the authors are very grateful: Centre for Aboriginal Economic Policy Research (The Australian National University), Kimberley Institute Limited, Bankwest Curtin Economics Centre, Nulungu Institute (University of Notre Dame), Nyamba Buru Yawuru, Nagula Jarndu, Bottles of Australia and Yawuru Prescribed Body Corporate.

References

Altman JC (2007). *The Howard Government's Northern Territory Intervention: Are neo-paternalism and Indigenous development compatible?* Topical Issue 16/2007, Centre for Aboriginal Economic Policy Research, The Australian National University, Canberra.

Altman J & Hinkson M (2010). *Culture crisis: Anthropology and politics in Aboriginal Australia*, UNSW Press, Sydney.

Anaya J (2004). *Indigenous peoples in international law*, Oxford University Press, Oxford.

Andersen C (2014). *Metis: Race, recognition and the struggle for indigenous peoplehood*, University of British Columbia Press, Vancouver.

Behrendt L (2002). Unfinished business: Indigenous self-determination. *Arena Magazine* 58(April–May):24–7.

Boas T & Gans-Morse J (2009). Neoliberalism: From new liberal philosophy to anti-liberal slogan. *Studies in Comparative International Development* 44(2):137–61, doi.org/10.1007/s12116-009-9040-5.

Corntassel J (2008). Toward sustainable self-determination: Rethinking the contemporary indigenous-rights discourse. *Alternatives* 33:105–32, doi.org/10.1177/030437540803300106.

Coulthard G (2014). *Red skin, white masks: Rejecting the colonial politics of recognition*, University of Minnesota Press, Minneapolis, doi.org/10.5749/minnesota/9780816679645.001.0001.

Daes E (2000). Striving for self-determination for indigenous peoples. In Kly Y & Kly D (eds), *In pursuit of the right to self-determination*, Clarity Press, Geneva.

Davies W (2015). Spirits of neoliberalism: 'Competitiveness' and 'wellbeing' indicators as rival orders of worth. In Rottenburg R, Merry S, Park S & Mugler J (eds), *The world of indicators: The making of governmental knowledge through quantification*, Cambridge Studies in Law and Society, Cambridge, doi.org/10.1017/CBO9781316091265.011.

Davis M (2013). Community control and the work of national Aboriginal community controlled health organisation: Putting meat on the bones of the UNDRIP. *Indigenous Law Bulletin* 8(7):11–14.

Durie M (2006). *Measuring Māori wellbeing*, New Zealand Treasury Guest Lecture Series, New Zealand Treasury, Wellington.

Ermine W (2007). The ethical space of engagement. *Indigenous Law Journal* 6(1):193–203.

Fraser N & Honneth A (2003). *Redistribution or recognition? A political–philosophical exchange*, Verso, London.

Ganesharajah C (2009). *Indigenous health and wellbeing: The importance of country*. Native Title Research Report, Report No. 1/2009, Australian Institute of Aboriginal and Torres Strait Islander Studies, Canberra.

Greiner R, Larson S, Herr A, & Bligh V (2005). *Wellbeing of Nywaigi traditional owners: The contribution of country to wellbeing and the role of natural resource management*. CSIRO Sustainable Ecosystems, Townsville.

Grieves V (2007). *Indigenous wellbeing: A framework for governments' Aboriginal cultural heritage activities*. Report prepared for the NSW Department of Environment and Conservation, Sydney.

Howard-Wagner D (2010). From state of denial to state of emergency: Governing Australian indigenous communities through the exception. In Fassin D & Pandolfi M (eds), *Contemporary states of emergency: The politics of military and humanitarian interventions*, Zone Publishing, New York.

HREOC (Human Rights and Equal Opportunity Commission) (2002). Chapter 2: Self-determination—the freedom to 'live well'. *HREOC Social Justice Report 2002*, Australian Human Rights Commission.

Humpage L (2008). Relegitimating neoliberalism? Performance management and Indigenous affairs policy. *Policy and Politics* 36(3):413–29, doi.org/10.1332/030557308X313688.

Jordan K, Bullock H & Buchanan G (2010). Exploring the tensions between statistical equality and cultural difference in Indigenous wellbeing frameworks: A new expression of an enduring debate. *Australian Journal of Social Issues* 45(3):333–62, doi.org/10.1002/j.1839-4655.2010.tb00183.x.

Kukutai T & Walter M (2015). Recognition and indigenising official statistics: Reflections from Aotearoa New Zealand and Australia. *Statistical Journal of the IAOS* 31:317–26, doi.org/10.3233/sji-150896.

Mantziaris C & Martin D (2000). *Native title corporations: A legal and anthropological analysis*, Federation Press, Sydney.

McCubbin L, McCubbin H, Zhang W, Kehl L & Strom I (2013). Relational wellbeing: An Indigenous perspective and measure. *Family Relations* 62:354–65, doi.org/10.1111/fare.12007.

McKenna V & Anderson K (2011). Kimberley dreaming: Old Law, new ways—finding new meaning, Presentation to World Congress for Psychotherapy, Sydney, 24–28 August.

Mirowski P (2009). Postface: Defining neoliberalism. In Mirowski P & Plehwe D (eds), *The road from Mont Pelerin: The making of the neoliberal thought collective,* Harvard University Press, Cambridge, Massachusetts, doi.org/10.4159/9780674054264.

Murphy M (2014). Self-determination as a collective capability: The case of Indigenous peoples. *Journal of Human Development and Capabilities: A Multidisciplinary Journal for People Centred Development* 15:320–34, doi.org/10.1080/19452829.2013.878320.

Panzironi F (2007). Indigenous peoples' right to self-determination and development policy. PhD thesis, University of Sydney, NSW.

Pearson N (1997). The concept of Native Title at Common Law. *Australian Humanities Review* 5.

Peck J & Tickell A (2002). Neoliberalizing space. *Antipode* 35(3):380–404, doi.org/10.1111/1467-8330.00247.

Rowse T (2012). *Rethinking social justice: From 'peoples' to 'populations',* Aboriginal Studies Press, Canberra.

Sanders W (2002). *Towards an Indigenous order of Australian government: Rethinking self-determination as Indigenous affairs policy,* Discussion Paper 230, Centre for Aboriginal Economic Policy Research, The Australian National University, Canberra.

Sen A (1999). *Development as freedom*, Knopf Press, New York.

Taylor C (1992). The politics of recognition. In Guttmann A & Taylor C (eds), *Multiculturalism and the 'politics of recognition'*, Princeton University Press, Princeton.

Taylor J (2008). Indigenous peoples and indicators of well-being: Australian perspectives on United Nations global frameworks. *Social Indicators Research* 87(1):111–26, doi.org/10.1007/s11205-007-9161-z.

Venugopal R (2015). Neoliberalism as concept. *Economy and Society* 44(2):165–87, doi.org/10.1080/03085147.2015.1013356.

Watene K (2016). Indigenous peoples and justice. In Watene K & Drydyk J (eds), *Theorising justice: Novel insights and future directions*, Rowman and Littlefield International, London.

Webb J (2012). Indigenous peoples and the right to self-determination. *Journal of Indigenous Policy*, 13:75–102.

Yap M (2017). In pursuit of culturally relevant indicators of Indigenous wellbeing: Operationalising the Recognition space. PhD thesis, The Australian National University, Canberra.

Yap M & Yu E (2016a). Operationalising the capability approach: Developing culturally relevant indicators of indigenous wellbeing—An Australian example. *Oxford Development Studies* 44(3):315–331, doi.org/10.1080/136 00818.2016.1178223.

Yap M & Yu E (2016b). *Community wellbeing from the ground up: A Yawuru example*, Bankwest Curtin Economics Centre Research Report 3/16.

Yawuru RNTBC (2011). *Walyjala-jala buru jayida jarringgun Nyamba Yawuru ngan-ga mirlimirli [Planning for the future: Yawuru cultural management plan]*, Pindan Printing Pty Ltd, Broome.

Yu P (2012). *The power of data in Aboriginal hands*, Topical Issue 4/2012, Centre for Aboriginal Economic Policy Research, The Australian National University, Canberra.

PART 2

Pendulums and contradictions in neoliberalism governing everything from Indigenous disadvantage to Indigenous economic development in Australia

6

Missing ATSIC: Australia's need for a strong Indigenous representative body

Will Sanders

Introduction

The idea of market liberalism within government has been influential since the 1980s, but its interaction with other more established ideas in Australian Indigenous affairs is a matter for debate. I tend to the view that Australian Indigenous policy was for a decade or more protected from neoliberalism by the idea of self-determination, which had become influential in the 1970s. This other policy idea led the Australian Commonwealth Parliament in 1989 to create a statutory authority, the Aboriginal and Torres Strait Islander Commission (ATSIC). As well as a permanent staff of public servants, ATSIC had an extensive structure of elected Indigenous regional councillors, who in turn elected zone and national commissioners. This made ATSIC a significant Indigenous representative body within Australian political institutions. Through its programs and spending, ATSIC also encouraged community-based Indigenous organisations to take on service delivery, asset holding and representative roles. Rowse referred to these organisations as the 'Indigenous sector', which he argued was 'one of the defining material products of the Australian public policy change from "assimilation" to "self-determination"' in Indigenous affairs (Rowse 2004: 39, see also

Rowse 2002). Going further, I suggested that ATSIC and the supported Indigenous organisations could together be thought of as moving 'towards an Indigenous order of Australian government' (Sanders 2002). This terminology had been used in Canada in the 1996 Royal Commission on Aboriginal Peoples and also seemed appropriate to Australia. Particularly since the High Court recognition of common law native title in the Mabo case in 1992, it seemed possible to think of law and governmental authority in Australia as flowing from Indigenous sources as well as from Commonwealth and state legislatures and their constitutions. These ideas and language potentially gave ATSIC and Indigenous organisations strong long-term foundations within Australian political institutions. This, however, was not to be. Through a convergence of circumstances detailed below, ATSIC was abolished in 2004–05. In the decade since, ideas of market liberalism have overrun those of self-determination in Australian Indigenous affairs, leading to continuing challenges to the roles of Indigenous community organisations (Sullivan 2011: 48–66).

This chapter revisits some of these ideas over a decade after ATSIC. It argues that some law and governmental authority in Australia *must* flow from Indigenous peoples and their precolonial history. As a consequence, Australia needs a strong Indigenous representative body within its political institutions. The ATSIC experiment was an attempt to develop such a body, which we are now missing. The chapter begins with some history of the abolition of ATSIC and developments since in public policy towards Indigenous Australians. The emergence of the National Congress of Australia's First Peoples as a new Indigenous representative body is recounted and analysed, and so too is the push towards recognition of Aboriginal and Torres Strait Islander peoples in the Australian Constitution. Both are argued, as of 2016, to have achieved weaker recognition of Indigenous peoplehood and rights than ATSIC. Australian public policy is thus still trying to recover from the abolition of ATSIC over a decade on.

The administrative location of Indigenous-specific programs within government in recent years is also discussed and compared with the ATSIC era. Looking forward, the question for Australian Indigenous policy becomes: how can a strong Aboriginal and Torres Strait Islander representative body be redeveloped as an appropriate recognition of Indigenous peoplehood rights within Australian political institutions? While answering that question proves beyond the scope of this chapter, hopefully I will at least establish that this is a good question to be asking. For during the decade since ATSIC, there has not even been acknowledgement of the appropriateness of this question.

Rather than neoliberalism, the broad sociological term I find most helpful in Indigenous affairs is decolonisation. I resist the term neoliberalism as it seems to foreclose, rather than open, possibilities. While there is no denying the rise of market liberalism in ideas about government since the 1980s, other ideas have also still had a presence, such as decolonisation and a 'peoples' approach. Framing and labelling are important, and it may be that insisting that this is still the age of decolonisation, as well as neoliberalism, is a way to keep alive ideas about the recognition of Indigenous rights.

Losing ATSIC and self-determination in Australian Indigenous policy

For almost three decades from the early 1970s to the late 1900s, the central terms of Indigenous policy in Australia were self-determination and the slightly less assertive self-management. This use of a foundational right of peoples drawn from international law as an element of Australian Indigenous policy was widely accepted, if at times a little cautiously. The second 'object' of the ATSIC Act passed in 1989 was 'to promote the development of self-management and self-sufficiency among Aboriginal persons and Torres Strait Islanders'. If this was less than a whole-hearted embracing of the right to self-determination of Indigenous peoples, this was less evident in 1992 when the Australian Government and ATSIC made contributions to the 10th session of the United Nations Working Group on Indigenous Populations, which was developing a draft Declaration of the Rights of Indigenous Peoples. As the CEO of ATSIC put it, the 'Australian delegation' argued for retaining the right to self-determination of Indigenous peoples within the draft so long as this took place 'within the framework of existing nation States'. This 'recognition of the right of self-determination' within the proposed Declaration would help Indigenous peoples 'to overcome the barriers to full democratic participation in the political process' (ATSIC 1992: vii). This position was maintained until the late 1990s, when the Howard Coalition Government began to retreat from supporting self-determination in the draft Declaration and in Indigenous policy more generally (Dodson & Pritchard 1998, ATSIC 1999).

Even with this retreat, ATSIC seemed to be growing stronger as an Indigenous representative body. From 1995, it was accredited with non-government organisation (NGO) status in the United Nations, giving access to international forums independent of the Australian Government. In 2000, ATSIC gained its first elected chairperson, Victorian Indigenous leader Geoff Clark. With Clark re-elected as chair for a second term in early 2003, ATSIC seemed secure. But controversy surrounding a pub brawl and a publicly funded trip to Ireland during 2002 soon caught up with Clark, as too did legal proceedings relating to allegations of rape back in the 1970s. Allegations of nepotism and funding impropriety among the elected representatives more generally saw ATSIC stripped of its financial decision-making powers in April 2003 and a broader review undertaken. Clark was suspended as chair by Minister Ruddock in August 2003, leaving ATSIC in the vulnerable position of having an acting chair.

The 2003 review of ATSIC was conducted by two white male ex-politicians and an Indigenous woman academic. The reviewers proposed with some 'urgency' a 'reform package' that would provide ATSIC with 'a new leadership structure and a boost to its morale' (Hannaford et al. 2003: 7). This would do away with zone commissioners and instead make the 35 Regional Council chairs ATSIC's national 'governing body'. The national chair and deputy chair would be elected from this body and, like Regional Council chairs, would be able to 'be removed by a no-confidence vote in them, carried by a statutory majority of their respective electing bodies' (Hannaford et al. 2003: 13).[1] While these were significant changes, the reviewers began with two 'over-arching' recommendations that indicated foundational support for ATSIC: that the 'existing objects of the ATSIC Act should be retained' and that 'ATSIC should be the primary vehicle to represent Aboriginal and Torres Strait Islander peoples' views to all levels of government' (Hannaford et al. 2003: 8). The Review was in fact calling for the strengthening of ATSIC as a national Indigenous representative body, rather than in any way diminishing it. It talked of ATSIC representing the 'voice and interests of Aboriginal and Torres Strait Islander peoples within government' and of this 'advocacy role' extending 'internationally' through ATSIC's NGO status at the

---

1   This suggestion probably grew out of uncertainty around the position of Geoff Clark as ATSIC chair during late 2003. When Clark was suspended by Minister Ruddock in August 2003, the ATSIC Board was left with an acting chair, Lionel Quartermaine, for many months. Clearly, this put the board in a rather weak position, unable to move decisively to a new chair by its own vote.

UN (Hannaford et al. 2003: 18). This supportiveness was not, however, how the Review report was interpreted and used by either the Howard Coalition Government or the Latham Labor opposition.

In late March 2004, with a federal election looming later that year, Opposition Leader Mark Latham announced that, if elected, a Labor Government would abolish ATSIC, its own creation of 15 years earlier, and 'establish a new framework for Indigenous self-governance and program delivery' (Latham & O'Brien 2004). A couple of weeks later, the Howard Coalition Government seized the opportunity to do likewise. The ATSIC 'experiment in separate representation' had, it argued, been a 'failure' (Howard & Vanstone 2004). It was to be 'abolished' and would not be replaced by 'another elected structure' (Vanstone 2004a). 'Specialist Indigenous programmes' would be 'retained' but 'devolved to mainstream Departments', while 'existing mainstream programmes' would also be pushed to 'perform better'. To this end a Ministerial Taskforce would be 'established immediately' and a 'new Office of Indigenous Policy Coordination' would 'provide policy advice and monitor the performance of mainstream agencies' (Vanstone 2004a).

Five days after these ministerial announcements, the Secretary of the Australian Government Department of the Prime Minister and Cabinet (PMC), Peter Shergold, made the new arrangements in Indigenous affairs the central example of a speech on 'Connecting Government'—a report on how Australia would adopt 'whole-of-government responses' to its 'priority challenges'. Shergold identified five 'characteristics' of the 'new whole-of-government mainstreaming' in Indigenous affairs: collaboration, a focus on regional need, flexibility, accountability and leadership. Under the first of these he referred not only to the Ministerial Taskforce, but also to a 'Secretaries' Group in Canberra' and a 'network of regional offices around the nation' in which 'all the services delivered by key departments—employment, education, community services, legal aid and health—will be represented'. These 'Australian government indigenous coordination centres' would be 'tasked to work with indigenous communities to deliver services in a coordinated way' using 'Framework Agreements' in which 'government and community work as partners to establish goals and agree their shared responsibilities' (Shergold 2004).

Establishing these new arrangements in Indigenous affairs proved both complex and simple. Faced with a Bill to abolish ATSIC in June 2004, the Labor opposition pulled back from immediate support and moved instead for a Senate Committee inquiry. This extended the legislative process for abolition past the election held in November and into 2005 (SCAIA 2005). The administrative process, however, was effected far more simply by machinery of government changes from 1 July 2004. From that day, ATSIC's programs and legislated responsibilities were assigned to 13 different Commonwealth agencies (Vanstone 2004b). This left ATSIC a mere shell during the last year of its legislative existence.

Mainstreaming and whole-of-government logics in the new arrangements

During the Senate Committee inquiry, and more generally in 2004, it was often noted that the involvement of mainstream Commonwealth agencies and programs in servicing Indigenous people was not new. It had been common ever since the Commonwealth became involved in Indigenous affairs on a national scale after the 1967 constitutional alteration referendum. Indigenous-specific programs in Indigenous-specific agencies, like the Department of Aboriginal Affairs and ATSIC, had existed alongside the service delivery efforts of line agencies through both general programs and some Indigenous-specific ones. The question was thus posed of how the 'new mainstreaming' would differ from the 'old' (Altman 2004). Shergold was optimistic that, through the whole-of-government idea, this new approach could in fact be quite different from the old pattern of 'each department' making 'its own decisions in a non-coordinated way' (SCAIA 2005: 82). Others, however, were more sceptical. Bill Jonas, the Aboriginal and Torres Strait Islander Social Justice Commissioner whose five-year term was just ending, argued that while 'accountability for service delivery by mainstream government departments and agencies' was to be 'commended' and was progressing 'in fledgling stages', there were 'issues that remain to be addressed before success is assured' (Jonas & Dick 2004: 13). He saw the bigger challenge as 'ensuring meaningful participation of Indigenous peoples in government processes' in the absence of a national Indigenous representative body. The successor Aboriginal and Torres Strait Islander Social Justice Commissioner, Tom Calma, took a similar line when he identified 'the fundamental flaw of the new arrangements' as 'the absence of principled engagement with Indigenous peoples' (Calma 2007: 107).

A 2009 study of the whole-of-government push in Australian Indigenous affairs by public administration scholars judged it to have 'under-performed due to entrenched barriers', including a lack of 'supportive architecture', a 'programmatic focus' and 'the maintenance of centralized decision-making'. This was so despite there being strong crafted 'leadership' for the approach and the 'cultivation of rich networked relationships'. These scholars argued that within the 'broad trend' of under-performance there were some 'resounding stories of success' (O'Flynn et al. 2011: 247–51). But their ultimate conclusion was that 'with all the best of intentions, deeply embedded bureaucratic characteristics impede attempts at working across boundaries and of connecting outside of silos' (O'Flynn et al. 2011: 253).

Sullivan's more anthropological study around the same time noted that 'mainstreaming' actually leads to the 'fragmentation of Indigenous affairs' and is, therefore, in 'tension' with the whole-of-government idea. He judged that while mainstreaming was 'delivered', a whole-of-government approach was not. He argued that devising 'hierarchical structures' for a whole-of-government approach was 'relatively easy', but that 'few conceptual and organisational tools were available to the subordinate reaches of the bureaucracy charged with putting policy into effect' (Sullivan 2011: 46–7).

My approach to the whole-of-government idea in Indigenous affairs was more sceptical from the outset. I thought it overlooked why government is divided into departments in the first place: so that its parts can focus on doing one thing and not another. It is one thing to observe, as Shergold often did, that education is related to health and community order in Indigenous affairs, but it is quite another to argue that all these things should be attended to together. Running a health clinic is not like running a school or a community policing patrol, and there is only a limited sense in which these services can be coordinated, let alone combined. Holism, I argue, is unhelpful counsel of perfection and impossibility within government that, when resorted to, distracts from the lack of other more important guiding principles—like engaging with Indigenous people (Gray & Sanders 2006).

By contrast, my approach to mainstreaming has long been more sympathetic and strategic. Back in 1993, in response to the Royal Commission into Aboriginal Deaths in Custody complaining about the 'multiplicity of agencies' within government involved in Indigenous affairs, I warned against the alluring idea of returning to a single dominant source of Indigenous funding. There was much to be gained, I argued, from the involvement of many government agencies in Indigenous servicing, either through general programs or through Indigenous-specific ones. This multiplicity potentially increased the 'manoeuvrability' of Indigenous interests in relation to government and also the 'amount' of accessible resources. It could also help cater for the 'diversity of Aboriginal circumstances' and, in the case of general programs, reduce the 'visibility' of spending through Indigenous-specific services that could be labelled as 'special' (Sanders 1993, see also Anderson & Sanders 1996 on health spending and services). This was not an argument against Indigenous-specific programs and organisations, but rather an argument for using Indigenous-specific resources sparingly and strategically in conjunction with mainstream or general resources that could also be accessed by Indigenous interests.

Twenty years on, my thoughts on mainstreaming have shifted a little. I have watched disappointedly as line departments in housing and employment have turned the very different Indigenous-specific programs they inherited from ATSIC into much more standardised versions of their own general programs (Sanders 2014). It was still, however, with a sense of foreboding that I watched the Abbott Coalition Government elected in 2013 bring the vast majority of Indigenous-specific programs into the PMC. This centralisation was, I thought, a bad idea that would probably lead to a reduction in the resources available to Indigenous people, both through the central department and through line departments. To the extent that this centralisation was promoted and seen as another version of the whole-of-government approach, this simply confirmed my scepticism about the naivety of this idea. Corralling most Indigenous-specific funding within the PMC has, in my judgement, proved to be very adverse to Indigenous interests, and the sooner we return to a more dispersed administrative model of funding Indigenous services, the better. The whole-of-government idea in Indigenous affairs has long been oversold, while the very different strategic potential of the involvement of mainstream or line departments of government in Indigenous servicing has, conversely, long been under-appreciated.

Rediscovering decolonisation and a 'peoples' approach to Indigenous affairs

Beyond debates about the administrative organisation of Indigenous affairs, when attempting to take a broader sociological view I often turn to ideas about decolonisation. In 2006, when assessing the Howard Government's first decade in office, the phrase that seemed appropriate was 'defying decolonisation' (Sanders 2006). With ATSIC gone and the administrative revolution of the new arrangements proceeding apace, what the Howard Government seemed to lack was any sense of the larger colonial context of Indigenous affairs and the way in which modern Indigenous policy is, in many ways, an allegorical attempt at decolonisation. This entails recognising that contemporary Indigenous Australians are 'peoples' descended from precolonial political communities, rather than just a 'population' segment within Australian society. Rowse (2012) has charted the changing relative strengths of these two 'idioms' in Indigenous affairs in a collection of recent essays, arguing that the peoples approach was on the rise during the late 20th century but that the populations approach has risen to prominence again in the early years of the 21st century. What is needed in contemporary Australian Indigenous policy is some re-recognition of the attempt at decolonisation and the contribution that a peoples approach can make.

ATSIC, it should be noted, always sat rather awkwardly between the populations and peoples idioms. Created by the Commonwealth with a franchise for Indigenous people based on regions of residence, ATSIC for some could only ever be another imposition of the colonial 'status quo' (Bradfield 2006). But, as noted above, ATSIC did, over time, assert autonomy from its Commonwealth creator and start to use the language of First Nations and peoples. While the Howard Coalition Government resisted this move, and drove the relative rise of the populations idiom during most of its 11-and-a-half-year reign, ironically at the end it also set some ground for the reinvigoration of a peoples approach. In the lead-up to the 2007 election, Howard slightly shifted his ground on Indigenous policy and reconciliation. While repeating his support for the 'Indigenous responsibility agenda' and 'unified Australian citizenship', Howard now committed to a referendum 'within 18 months' to 'formally recognise Indigenous Australians in our Constitution—their history as the first inhabitants of our country, their unique heritage of culture and languages, and their special (though not separate) place within a reconciled, indivisible nation' (Howard 2007: 4). This ever so slight move back towards a peoples approach gave the Rudd and Gillard Labor governments and the Abbott and Turnbull Coalition governments new room for manoeuvre.

The National Congress of Australia's First Peoples: Not yet strong

During its turbulent two-and-a-half years, the first Rudd Government did two things that moved Australian Indigenous policy back towards a peoples approach. It changed Australia's 'position' on the United Nations Declaration on the Rights of Indigenous Peoples (UNDRIP), voted on in the General Assembly in September 2007, from opposition to 'support' (Macklin 2009a: 2). And it supported Indigenous people, through the Aboriginal and Torres Strait Islander Social Justice Commissioner, in the development of a new national Indigenous representative body. Rather than a statutory creation of the Commonwealth Parliament, the new National Congress of Australia's First Peoples became an incorporated company. The Rudd Government supported its establishment with AU$6 million initially and another AU$23.2 million for operations to the end of 2013 (Macklin 2009b). In the May 2013 Budget, the Gillard Government committed to another AU$15 million over three years, but the Abbott Coalition Government elected in September indicated in December that it was withdrawing that commitment (Harrison 2013). This left the National Congress struggling to survive financially from the beginning of 2014.

In June 2016, during the next federal election campaign, the National Congress joined with 17 other Indigenous organisations to issue 'The Redfern Statement', a 'call for urgent Government action'. This called for the 'restoration of funding to the National Congress of Australia's First Peoples', as well as the establishment of national Indigenous peak bodies in the areas of education, employment and housing. It also called for specific policy actions in the areas of health, justice, preventing violence, early childhood and disability.[2] While the National Congress has clearly survived and is establishing some presence in Australian politics, it is not yet a strong national Indigenous representative body. Perhaps strength can only develop slowly, through persistence when the political climate

---

2   See nationalcongress.com.au/redfern-statement/, viewed 28 October 2016.

is unfavourable and through cautious opportunism in more favourable times. After six years, the National Congress of Australia's First Peoples is still a young Indigenous representative body fighting to institutionalise itself within Australian politics. It will be many years before this institutionalisation can be assessed, but, unlike ATSIC, Congress will not be able to be abolished by the Commonwealth Parliament. While the National Congress of Australia's First People is not yet strong, it is also not vulnerable to complete destruction by adverse government action. Indeed, it has already survived some adverse times and demonstrated a growing strength.

With individual and corporate members and two chambers of elected representatives, Congress, like ATSIC before it, sits ambiguously between the populations and peoples idioms. Proposals have been floated for an Assembly of First Nations that would supplement and extend Congress into a fuller peoples structure, but as yet these have come to little (McAvoy 2014). Decolonisation in settler majority societies is clearly never simple, and Indigenous activists can legitimately work in both the populations and peoples idioms.

Constitutional recognition: Not yet done

The Gillard Government's major contribution to Indigenous affairs was to advance the idea of constitutional recognition. In December 2010, it established an Expert Panel on Recognising Aboriginal and Torres Strait Islander Peoples in the Constitution, which reported in January 2012. This suggested that the existing Commonwealth 'race' power should be repealed along with one other reference to race in the Constitution. It recommended a new power for the Commonwealth to make laws 'with respect to Aboriginal peoples and Torres Strait Islander peoples' with several statements of recognition in its preamble (Dodson & Leibler 2012: 133, 153). The Expert Panel also recommended that a prohibition of racial discrimination be added to the Constitution, plus a recognition of Aboriginal and Torres Strait Islander languages alongside English as the national language (Dodson & Leibler 2012: 133, 173). While these were modest, well-argued ideas for constitutional change, this was not how they were portrayed in the ensuing public debate.

Aboriginal lawyer and member of the Expert Panel Noel Pearson has commented that he was 'surprised at the negative reaction' to these recommendations for constitutional change of which he was a 'strong proponent'. The proposed 'racial non-discrimination clause' came in for particular criticism from 'the right side of politics' as a 'one clause bill of rights' that would 'improperly empower the judiciary to strike down parliament's laws' (Pearson 2016: 173). The cause of constitutional recognition never recovered from these adverse reactions despite almost two years further work by a parliamentary committee (Joint Select Committee on Constitutional Recognition of Aboriginal and Torres Strait Islander Peoples 2015). Indeed, it now seems certain that the 50th anniversary of the previous constitutional alteration referendum concerning 'aboriginal natives' will pass in May 2017 without further change. From seeming possible in the early Gillard years, constitutional recognition has now lost impetus.

In trying to reposition the debate on constitutional recognition, Pearson has turned away from rights that could be tested in courts to the idea of a 'guarantee of Indigenous participation and consultation in the political processes with respect to Indigenous affairs, creating an ongoing dialogue between Indigenous peoples and the parliament' (Pearson 2016: 174). This 'Indigenous representative mechanism' would be 'constitutionally modest' but 'could provide the impetus for a profound paradigmatic shift between Indigenous peoples and the state', with 'statements of recognition' then being made 'outside the Constitution', possibly in a 'statute of reconciliation' that 'could perhaps be enacted with the concurrence of all the parliaments, and with the active agreement of Indigenous peoples' (Pearson 2016: 174). These ideas and phrases are somewhat vague and speculative, but that is arguably their strength as Australians struggle to find some common ground around constitutional recognition for Aboriginal and Torres Strait Islander peoples. They are also strangely reminiscent of what ATSIC did and was during its 15-year life; Indigenous people talking back to the settler state and, through some settler recognition, also at times being heard.

Conclusion: The importance of language and Indigenous representation

I began by saying that I would revisit the idea of an Indigenous order of Australian Government, as well as the need for a strong Indigenous representative body. This was language used in the 1996 Canadian Royal Commission on Aboriginal Peoples that attracted my attention around the turn of the millennium as also appropriate to Australia. It is language that still attracts me to this day, although I gather it has not greatly caught on even in Canada.[3] What has flourished in Canada, as I understand it, is the language of nation-to-nation relationships in Indigenous affairs. A peoples or peoplehood approach is another element of this idiom. Perhaps what is most important is recognising how this political communities approach in Indigenous affairs is so vastly different from the disadvantaged populations idiom. The language of political communities, peoples and First Nations opens a whole other terrain in Indigenous affairs, as too does the language of colonisation and decolonisation. Without these languages, Indigenous affairs conducted solely in the populations idiom is severely lacking.

Finally, I note that in the decade since ATSIC's abolition, the numbers of Indigenous representatives in Australia's federal, state and territory parliaments have increased significantly. One ATSIC Commissioner, Alison Anderson, was a Northern Territory parliamentarian for the next 11 years, becoming a minister in governments of each major party persuasion before retreating to the cross bench as a disappointed independent. In the Australian Parliament, there are now Indigenous members of the House of Representatives in both major parties and two Indigenous Labor Senators.[4] While this increased Indigenous parliamentary representation is to be applauded, as Maddison argued

---

3   I have partly wanted to revisit this language to correct a mistake of numbering made by the Canadians, which I extended. The Canadian Royal Commission referred to indigenous nations as a third order of government, but I argue that this is conceptually incorrect. There are logically just two orders of government in countries like Canada and Australia, an indigenous order of precolonial origins and a colonial order brought by the settlers of the 18th and 19th centuries. Through federalism within the colonial order, there are two *levels* of government within both Canada and Australia that claim some independence from each other, but these are not two orders of government. Rather, they are simply two levels within the colonial order. This helps us see that there can be different levels within the indigenous order of government as well, ranging from very localised individual First Nations to groupings of First Nations at larger geographic scales.

4   This leaves aside Senator Jacquie Lambie's claim to Indigenous heritage, which has been controversial among the Tasmanian Aboriginal community.

in a review of Indigenous parliamentarians, this form of representation places major constraints on Indigenous people. Indigenous parliamentary representation will never, 'without structural transformation', she argues, 'be an adequate vehicle for representing Indigenous needs and concerns in the postcolonial state' (Maddison 2010: 663). For that, a strong, separate Indigenous representative body will be needed, something like ATSIC was becoming before it was so ill advisedly abolished.

Postscript 2017: The Abbott and Turnbull governments on constitutional recognition

While a self-proclaimed prime minister for Indigenous Affairs, Tony Abbott did little during his two years at the top that advanced the cause of constitutional recognition. As replacement Coalition Prime Minister, Malcom Turnbull attempted a bipartisan reopening of Indigenous constitutional recognition. In December 2015, together with Labor Opposition Leader Bill Shorten, Turnbull established a Referendum Council to 'advise on the next steps towards a successful referendum' on constitutional recognition (Referendum Council 2017: 46).

In early 2017, the Referendum Council held 12 First Nations Regional Dialogues around Australia and a culminating National Constitutional Convention at Uluru in central Australia. This resulted in the 'Uluru Statement from the Heart', which spoke in a collective Indigenous voice. After preliminary statements about the continuing sovereignty of 'our Aboriginal and Torres Strait Islander tribes', the major claim for recognition was a 'call for the establishment of a First Nations Voice enshrined in the Constitution' (Referendum Council 2017: i). This reflected the development of Noel Pearson's thinking; he was a member of the 2016–17 Referendum Council as well as of the 2010–12 Expert Panel. Cobble Cobble woman and Professor of Law at the University of NSW Megan Davis was another key supporter and promoter, being also a member of both the Referendum Council and the previous Expert Panel (see Davis 2016, Pearson 2017).

The Referendum Council's final report in June 2017 made two recommendations. The first was that a referendum be held to alter the Australian Constitution to provide for:

a representative body that gives Aboriginal and Torres Strait Islander First Nations a Voice to the Commonwealth Parliament (Referendum Council 2017: 2).

The second was for an 'extra-constitutional Declaration of Recognition' to be passed by all Australian parliaments as a 'symbolic statement of recognition to unify Australians' (Referendum Council 2017: 2). Reactions to these recommendations were cautious at the time, but three-and-a-half months later hopes were dashed. The Turnbull Coalition Government's official response in October was that such an 'addition to our national representative institutions' was neither 'desirable or capable of winning acceptance in a referendum' (Prime Minister, Attorney General, Minister for Indigenous Affairs 2017). After a brief moment of openness, if not optimism, constitutional recognition for Aboriginal and Torres Strait Islander peoples in Australia was, again, going nowhere.

Constitutional recognition is about decolonisation, self-determination and a peoples approach in Australian Indigenous affairs. These ideas have been in retreat in Australia over the last two decades, particularly since the abolition of ATSIC. The ascendant ideas are a mix of neoliberalism, neopaternalism, formal legal equality and overcoming socio-economic disadvantage among the Indigenous population. ATSIC, if it still existed, would be rightly pushing back.

References

Altman J (2004). Practical reconciliation and the new mainstreaming: Will it make a difference to Indigenous Australians? *Dialogue* 23(2):35–46.

Anderson I & Sanders W (1996). *Aboriginal health and institutional reform within Australian federalism*. Discussion Paper 117, Centre for Aboriginal Economic Policy Research, The Australian National University, Canberra.

ATSIC (1992). *The Australian contribution: UN working group on indigenous populations, tenth session, 20–31 July 1992 Geneva, Switzerland*, Office of Public Affairs, ATSIC, Canberra.

ATSIC (1999). *The Australian contribution 1999: The UN working group on indigenous populations, seventeenth session, 26–30 July Geneva, Switzerland*, ATSIC, Canberra.

Bradfield (2006). Separatism of status quo? Indigenous affairs from the birth of land rights to the death of ATSIC. *Australian Journal of Politics and History* 52(1):80–97.

Calma T (2007). *Social justice report 2006*, Aboriginal & Torres Strait Islander Social Justice Commissioner, Human Rights and Equal Opportunity Commission, Sydney.

Davis M (2016). Ships that pass in the night. In Davis M & Langton M (eds), *It's our country: Indigenous arguments for meaningful constitutional recognition and reform*, Melbourne University Press, Carlton Victoria.

Dodson M & Pritchard S (1998). Recent developments in Indigenous policy: The abandonment of self-determination? *Indigenous Law Bulletin*, 4(15):4–6.

Dodson P & Leibler M (2012). *Recognising Aboriginal and Torres Strait Islander peoples in the constitution: Report of the expert panel*, Department of Families, Housing, Community Services and Indigenous Affairs, Canberra.

Gray W & Sanders W (2006). *Views from the top of the 'quiet revolution': Secretarial perspectives on the new arrangements in Indigenous affairs*. Discussion Paper 282, Centre for Aboriginal Economic Policy Research, The Australian National University, Canberra.

Hannaford J, Huggins J & Collins B (2003). *In the hands of the regions: A new ATSIC*, Report of the Review of the Aboriginal and Torres Strait Islander Commission, Canberra.

Harrison D (2013). Indigenous organisation to defy Tony Abbott funding cut, *Sydney Morning Herald*, 19 December.

Howard J (2007). Address to the Sydney Institute, Sydney, 11 October.

Howard J & Vanstone A (2004). Joint press conference, Parliament House, Canberra, parlinfo.aph.gov.au/parlInfo/search/display/display.w3p;query=Source%3A%22PRIME%20MINISTER%22%20Author_Phrase%3A%22vanstone,%20amanda%22;rec=1.

Joint Select Committee on Constitutional Recognition of Aboriginal and Torres Strait Islander Peoples (2015). *Final report*, Senate Printing Unit, Parliament House, Canberra.

Jonas W & Dick D (2004). Ensuring meaningful participation of indigenous peoples in government processes: The implications of the decline of ATSIC. *Dialogue* 23(2): 4–15.

Latham M & O'Brien K (2004). *Opportunity and responsibility for Indigenous Australians*, statement by Federal Labor Leader and Shadow Minister for Reconciliation and Indigenous Affairs, Canberra, 30 March.

Macklin J (2009a). *Statement on the United Nations Declaration on the Rights of Indigenous Peoples*, Minister for Families, Housing, Community Services and Indigenous Affairs, Parliament House, Canberra, 3 April.

Macklin J (2009b). *Australian Government response to 'Our future in our hands'*, joint media release with the Hon. Kevin Rudd MP, Prime Minister, Parliament House, Canberra, 22 November.

Maddison S (2010). White parliament, black politics: The dilemmas of Indigenous representation. *Australian Journal of Political Science* 45(4):663–80, doi.org/10.1080/10361146.2010.517180.

McAvoy T (2014). An Assembly of First Nations and a Treaty. Presentation to the National Native Title Conference, Coffs Harbour. Viewed 24 December 2016 at aiatsis.gov.au/sites/default/files/docs/presentations/tony_mcavoy_pp.pdf.

O'Flynn J, Buick F, Blackman D & Halligan J (2011). You win some, you lose some: Experiments with joined-up government. *International Journal of Public Administration* 34(4):244–54, doi.org/10.1080/01900692.2010.540 703.

Pearson N (2016). There is no such thing as minimal recognition—there is only recognition. In Davis M & Langton M (eds), *It's our country: Indigenous arguments for meaningful constitutional recognition and reform*, Melbourne University Press, Carlton Victoria.

Pearson N (2017). Indigenous voice deserves to be heard: The Uluru convention has spelled out the ideal from of recognition, *Weekend Australian*, 27–28 May.

Prime Minister, Attorney General and Minister for Indigenous Affairs (2017). *Response to Referendum Council's report on Constitutional Recognition*, media release, 26 October.

Referendum Council (2017). *Final report*, Australian Government Department of the Prime Minister and Cabinet, Canberra.

Rowse T (2002). *Indigenous futures: Choice and development for Aboriginal and Islander Australia*, University of New South Wales Press, Sydney.

Rowse T (2004) [2002]. The political dimensions of community development. In Morphy F & Sanders W (eds.), *The Indigenous welfare economy and the CDEP scheme*, CAEPR Research Monograph No. 20, ANU E Press, Canberra.

Rowse T (2012). *Rethinking social justice: From 'peoples' to 'populations'*, Aboriginal Studies Press, Canberra.

Sanders W (1993). *Rethinking the fundamentals of social policy towards Indigenous Australians: Block grants, mainstreaming and the multiplicity of agencies and programs.* Discussion Paper 46, Centre for Aboriginal Economic Policy Research, The Australian National University, Canberra.

Sanders W (2002). *Towards an Indigenous order of Australian government: Rethinking self-determination as Indigenous affairs policy.* Discussion Paper 230, Centre for Aboriginal Economic Policy Research, The Australian National University, Canberra.

Sanders W (2006). *Indigenous affairs after the Howard decade: An administrative revolution while defying decolonisation.* Topical Issue 3/2006, Centre for Aboriginal Economic Policy Research, The Australian National University, Canberra.

Sanders W (2014). *Experimental governance in Australian Indigenous affairs: From Coombs to Pearson via Rowse and the competing principles.* Discussion Paper 291, Centre for Aboriginal Economic Policy Research, The Australian National University, Canberra.

SCAIA (Select Committee on the Administration of Indigenous Affairs) (2005). *After ATSIC—Life in the mainstream?* Senate Committee Report, The Senate, Parliament House, Canberra.

Shergold P (2004). A speech to launch 'Connecting government: Whole-of-government response to Australia's priority challenges', Secretary, Australian Government Department of the Prime Minister and Cabinet, Canberra, 20 April.

Sullivan P (2011). *Belonging together: Dealing with the politics of disenchantment in Australian Indigenous policy*, Aboriginal Studies Press, Canberra.

Vanstone A (2004a). *New service delivery arrangements for Indigenous affairs*, media release, Minister for Immigration and Multicultural and Indigenous Affairs, Canberra, 15 April.

Vanstone A (2004b). *Australian government changes to Indigenous affairs services commence tomorrow*, media release, Minister for Immigration and Multicultural and Indigenous Affairs, Canberra, 30 June.

7

Neoliberalising disability income reform: What does this mean for Indigenous Australians living in regional areas?

Karen Soldatic

Introduction

It is well documented that Australia's Aboriginal and Torres Strait Islander peoples have experienced some of the harshest effects of neoliberal intensification and its continuous pursuit of state welfare retraction and stigmatisation (Bielefeld this volume, Chapter 8). Given the highly racialised nature of these measures, practitioners, activists and researchers concerned with the advancing of neoliberal principles in Australia have been mostly interested in Indigenous social policy. In the meantime, other fields of social provisioning that have become increasingly important to Aboriginal and Torres Strait Islander wellbeing have received little critical attention (Gilroy & Donnelly 2016). Disability social provisioning measures, particularly disability social security income structures, is one such area. The Howard Government, as early as 2004, began to radically transform Australia's Disability Support Pension (DSP), and there has been continued bipartisan support to significantly diminish access to this payment (Morris et al. 2015). Some community advocacy organisations have recently attested that the number of people receiving the DSP has decreased overall (Soldatic & Sykes 2017). Further restrictions are predicted, with the announcement in the 2016 Budget that up to 90,000 DSP recipients would be reassessed for an estimated budgetary saving of AU$62.1 million (Morton 2016).

The impact of such changes on Aboriginal and Torres Strait Islander peoples is not directly known or understood, with attention on disability social security systems being surpassed by other urgent concerns, such as access to the new AU$22 billion National Disability Insurance Scheme (NDIS). Nonetheless, the population size affected by the DSP is almost twice that of the targeted NDIS (over 800,000 compared to an estimated 400,000); its population base has been historically much broader. Yet, emerging narrative evidence suggests that Aboriginal and Torres Strait Islander Australians with disabilities are one of the groups most affected by the retraction of the DSP. The DSP is much more generous than general social security payments, such as Newstart Allowance, and entitles recipients to access a diverse range of subsidies and concessions that alleviate the additional costs associated with living with a disability.

The interrelationship between Indigenous political rights and Indigenous health and wellbeing and the right to appropriate and adequate social protection strategies (commonly referred to as social security benefits and payments) was first formerly identified as a critical factor for indigenous self-determination and autonomy internationally within the International Labor Organization's (ILO) *Indigenous and Tribal Peoples Convention, C169*.[1] Part 5, 'Social Security and Health', consists of two distinct yet interrelated Articles, 24 and 25, that clearly illustrate the interrelationship of long-term indigenous health and wellbeing with state social protection mechanisms. Article 24, in particular, illustrates the need for states to recognise and provide appropriate mechanisms to ensure non-discrimination and accessibility to a broader diversity of social security arrangements and that, in application to indigenous persons:

> Social security schemes shall be extended progressively to cover the peoples concerned, and applied without discrimination against them (Article 24).

---

1   For the full text of the *Indigenous and Tribal Peoples Convention*, see www.ilo.org/dyn/normlex/en/f?p=NORMLEXPUB:12100:0::NO::P12100_ILO_CODE:C169.

The long-term impacts upon indigenous bodies with European invasion and colonisation has also been recognised within the United Nations Declaration on the Rights of Indigenous Peoples (UNDRIP).[2] Articles 21 and 22 of UNDRIP proclaim that particular attention be paid to 'the rights and special needs of … persons with disabilities', as well as indigenous elders, women, youth and children. While this is an attempt to address intersectionality within international law, Australia's reluctance to enact UNDRIP or support the ILO convention demonstrates the unique discriminatory processes, impacts and outcomes of its disability and Indigenous policy at the local scale.

To identify the potential impacts of these trends in disability social security retraction, this chapter first provides an overview of the changes to the DSP and then focuses on the implications for regional Australia, particularly the historical role of the DSP in sustaining regional populations in times of economic change. This section raises significant questions about the impact of the national neoliberal retraction of social policy on regional towns. It also shows the kind of adjustments and policy responses that local government authorities harness for some of their most vulnerable populations in times of economic change. Finally, the chapter discusses the potential effects on regional Aboriginal and Torres Strait Islander people with disabilities who are seeking access to the disability income support system but are frequently denied it due to the interstice of Aboriginality, disability and regionality, drawing upon theories of economic insecurity advanced by Bruce Western and colleagues (2012).

Neoliberalising the disability income system

Recent national data in relation to disability suggests that the prevalence of disability for Aboriginal and Torres Strait Islander Australians was approximately 23.9 per cent (ABS 2015), an increase from 23.4 per cent in 2012 (ABS 2012) and 21.1 per cent in 2009 (ABS 2009). The non-Indigenous population prevalence of disability has remained fairly constant at around 17.5 per cent in 2015 and 18.5 per cent in 2012 and 2009 (ABS 2017). The labour market participation of disabled people of workforce age currently stands at only 53.4 per cent, which is 30 per cent

2   For the full text of the United Nations Declaration of the Rights of Indigenous Peoples, see www.un.org/development/desa/indigenouspeoples/declaration-on-the-rights-of-indigenous-peoples. html.

lower than for the general Australian population (ABS 2015). More than 800,000 Australians with disabilities of workforce age receive a DSP (Morris et al. 2015). This raises broader questions in relation to issues of long-term illness and disability, and how Australian disability policy responds to Aboriginal and Torres Strait Islanders living with disability.

The shift of disability from the fringes to the centre of economic policy, particularly within Organisation for Economic Co-operation and Development (OECD) countries, emerged in the mid-1990s (Soldatic & Chapman 2010). With the onset of the global financial crisis, disability policy became 'a key economic policy area in most OECD countries' (OECD 2009: 1). Nearly all Western liberal democracies have undertaken large-scale disability policy restructuring in line with neoliberal welfare policy trends (Wilton & Schuer 2006, Humpage 2007, Soldatic 2013). While there is a multiplicity of local variations and deviations, international analysis suggests that neoliberal disability policy tendencies converge around the restructuring of disability social security entitlements with the primary aim of steering disabled people off disability pensions and into the open labour market (Roulstone & Barnes 2005, Grover & Piggott 2010). Australia, the UK, Canada and the USA have seen wide-ranging implementation of numerous governance technologies to 'activate' the labour market participation of people with disabilities (OECD 2009). These technologies, such as individual compacts, participation plans, sanctioning regimes and, in Australia, mutual obligation requirements, compel disability social security recipients into a set of prescribed activity tests as a condition of maintaining access to benefits (Grover & Piggott 2010, Soldatic & Pini 2012). The central purpose of these activation technologies is to: 1) reduce the number of disabled people receiving disability social security; and 2) restrict the disability eligibility criteria to curtail the future growth of disability social security and programming (Grover & Soldatic 2013).

Australia has been both leader and follower in these global trends. Indeed, since the late 1990s a plethora of strategies has been implemented to reduce the number of people accessing the DSP (Galvin 2004, Soldatic & Pini 2009, 2012), and disability social security policy has been radically reconfigured under the broad banner of national welfare reform (Mendes 2008, Soldatic & Meekosha 2012). While the most contentious of the proposed reforms proved to be politically untenable under the Howard Government, the 2011 Labor Government budget actively implemented many of its predecessor's policies. Yet, unlike its predecessor, the Labor

Government undertook a comprehensive review of the DSP medical impairment test to ascertain disabled people's partial work capacity and implemented mutual obligation requirements and activity tests—participation plans—for those people on the DSP aged under 35 years (Macklin 2011). Within a 12-month period, the number of Australians on the DSP dropped by 0.98 per cent, from 827,460 to 814,391 (Soldatic & Sykes 2017).

This drop raises the question of what entitlements people with disabilities receive if they no longer qualify for the DSP. Morris and colleagues (2015) have demonstrated that people with disabilities now on general social security payments, such as Newstart Allowance, have significantly lower weekly payments with few benefits and concession entitlements. As the Australian Council of Social Service has identified, relying on Newstart results in extreme poverty, with 55 per cent of Newstart recipients living below the poverty line (ACOSS 2016). This is based on income only and does not take into account the full gamut of costs associated with living with a disability. As Soldatic and Sykes (2017) document, disability poverty is much more complex. Drawing on Alcock's (1993) framework, they highlight that disability poverty is interrelated across four dimensions: income deprivation, inadequacy of service systems and supports, employment exploitation and discrimination, and, finally, inaccessible environments that increase costs for people with disabilities. For example, people with physical impairments are often required to use taxi services rather than public transport. Even though they may receive some type of transport subsidy, the personal outlay of using taxi services results in higher personal expenditure that they cannot afford. Therefore, income deprivation results in a range of social and economic losses, cumulating in greater personal hardship and poverty over a longer period of time. Additionally, to qualify for such subsidies, individuals must first qualify for the DSP and be deemed eligible for mobility assistance.

The move to diminish access to the DSP has pushed more disabled people onto Newstart with dire outcomes—increased rates of real poverty—as people are unable to meet the additional costs of disability; in some circumstances, this has led to the development of secondary impairments (Morris et al. 2015). Not only is the ongoing retraction of the DSP demoralising and stigmatising, but it has real impacts on the health and wellbeing of people with disabilities, diminishing their bodily capacities and sense of self-worth while denying dignity and respect. Many people with disabilities will no longer qualify for additional disability assistance, such as mobility subsidies or increased health care costs. Table 7.1 outlines these significant changes.

Table 7.1: Welfare streams for people with disabilities according to assessed work capacity

Assessment	Less than 15 hours	15–30 hours	30+ hours
Entry program	DSP	Newstart	Newstart
Payment for singles	$797.90 per fortnight	$528.70 per fortnight	$528.70 per fortnight
Pension supplement	$35.00 per fortnight minimum		
Conditions	No activity testing required if you are over 35 years DSP reduced by 50c for each dollar earned in the labour market above $164 per fortnight	Required to undergo job search and activity testing Newstart reduced by 50c for each dollar earned in the labour market above $104 and up to $254 per fortnight, then 60c in the dollar for labour market earnings above $254 per fortnight	Required to undergo job search and activity testing Newstart reduced by 50c for each dollar earned in the labour market above $104 and up to $254 per fortnight, then 60c in the dollar for labour market earnings above $254 per fortnight
Special assistance measures	Access to a range of pension benefits such as highly subsidised pharmaceuticals, rental assistance, educational supplement and subsidised transport DSP is one of the key eligibility criteria for state/territory-funded disability support services such as in-home support, disability counselling, aids and equipment, subsidised taxi scheme, and companion card	Access to a range of pension benefits such as highly subsidised pharmaceuticals, rental assistance and educational supplement Do **not** qualify for state/territory-funded disability support schemes that require the DSP for eligibility	Access to the Health Care Card, which has lower-level subsidies than those available on the DSP No access to state/territory-funded disability support schemes

Note: All dollar figures are Australian dollars.

Source: Adapted from Morris et al. (2015) and updated from Department of Human Services (2016a–e) to reflect the rules and payment rates at the time of writing (27 December 2016).

An investigative report released by the Commonwealth Ombudsman has identified that Aboriginal and Torres Strait Islander Australians are significantly disadvantaged under these new eligibility rules and criteria (Neave 2016). Two aspects are particularly discriminatory: 1) the medical evidence required for DSP assessment; and 2) the highly restrictive eligibility criteria. Aboriginal and Torres Strait Islander people are therefore more likely to be assessed for Newstart, further entrenching their structural position of poverty.

First, the new evidence requirements for a positive DSP determination presuppose extensive engagement with the formalised Australian medical system, where an individual can draw upon historical medical records and evidence to demonstrate long-term disability. As documented throughout the report, this actively discriminates against Aboriginal and Torres Strait Islander peoples' cultural engagement with their bodies and the use of Indigenous medical knowledges of healing and wellbeing (Neave 2016). Importantly, the requirements also misrecognise the lack of medical services readily available to Aboriginal and Torres Strait Islander people residing in regional and remote areas. It is well documented that regional and remote Australia is poorly serviced; in turn, residents of such areas have poorer health outcomes as they are unable to attend to the early onset of disability-creating illnesses and diseases due to lack of readily available medical services. Second, the eligibility criteria for the DSP is imbued with a set of Western normative systems of the body and, therefore, the questions asked of the individual in relation to the impact of disability do not necessarily align with Indigenous cultural engagements with the body and mind: it is 'race blind'. As noted in the report, this also has a particular spatial-cultural dimension. Aboriginal and Torres Strait Islander people with disabilities residing in regional and remote areas, close to community and country, respond to many of the eligibility questions from an Indigenous standpoint, a form of body-and-mind engagement that is outside Western understandings of what the body and mind can and cannot do.

The spatial dimension of the experience of Aboriginal and Torres Strait Islander people with disabilities residing in regional Australia is little understood, despite the significant consequences this has on their daily lives, the levels of poverty experienced and, critically, the level of social supports and services they are entitled to, to ensure a life of decency as a person with disability. It is this aspect that this chapter will now explore in greater detail.

Spatial dimensions of the DSP: Regional Australia

Regional Australia has endured extensive economic restructuring over the last 30 years (Horsley 2013). With the onset of a changing international and national economic and social landscape, many regional centres are adopting new policies and practices to regenerate their economic activity, to meet the employment demands of their communities and to sustain their local population base (Beer & Clower 2012, Rainnie et al. 2014). Processes of regeneration are increasingly framed around developing new markets to spur on economic growth, which, in many instances, are export-focused for global trade (Beer 2012). The effects of these economic processes of regional regeneration are often uneven and differentiated (Plummer et al. 2014). They are shaped by local historical structures, industries and populations, and the fluctuating global demand for local resources, products and services (Luck et al. 2011).

As Fraser and colleagues (2005: 151) suggest, economic restructuring and social change in regional Australia has stimulated 'two sharply differentiated zones, one of growth and one of decline'. This is particularly the case for regional centres in the Top End and in the lower southeast of Australia; their economies are markedly distinct (McKenzie et al. 2014). Lower southeast Australian regional centres have experienced long-term processes of mining disinvestment and deindustrialisation (Weller & O'Neill 2014). In the northern, Top End of Australia, regional economic development has been heavily tied to the resource boom alongside cultural economies, such as cultural festivals and natural tourism, in anticipation of the resource boom demise (Gibson et al. 2009, Plummer et al. 2014, Rainnie et al. 2014).

One of the key factors mitigating the negative impacts of regional economic instability and economic restructuring has been Australia's complex income support system (Beer 2012: 274). National income support systems have offered local populations a type of 'buffer zone' to navigate shifting and/or declining local labour markets while regional areas transition to new forms of economic activity (Tonts et al. 2012). The significance of these support systems in maintaining regional centres in times of economic uncertainty has been well recognised in national income support legislation and policy (Daniels 2006), particularly for the DSP. Before 2004, national DSP legislation described disability broadly, taking into account structural disadvantages including residential location and local labour market buoyancy (Soldatic 2010)—forms of structural disablement that were locally contingent, yet nationally recognised. This historical feature within the DSP added a layer of support for regional communities to withstand processes of economic restructuring and endure the often long wait until regeneration of their communities, economies and industries. In 2004, these broader structural processes of disablement were removed from the eligibility criteria of the national DSP (Soldatic 2010), making it more difficult for regional disabled people to access disability income support and associated entitlements (Soldatic & Sykes 2017). Local regional disabled populations who no longer qualify for the DSP are facing greater levels of economic insecurity as the loss of disability status means the loss of local and state government tax breaks, subsidies and entitlements specifically designed to maintain a level of support for regional disadvantaged populations (Soldatic et al. 2014).

This economic insecurity is particularly heightened for those people with disabilities and their families who reside in regional areas that are dominated by extractive industries. Local residents of mining regions tend to access jobs in 'ancillary industries or other sections [that] often earn much more modest wages and are confronted by high house prices and inflated living costs' (Beer 2012: 273). Regional residents with disabilities are often not in a position to take up mining employment due to the limited educational opportunities available within these regions (Spurway & Soldatic 2015), evident by their consistently low employment rates (ABS 2015). Even when they do work, their earnings are not sufficient to cover the daily costs of living, which have become artificially inflated with the resource boom (Chapman et al. 2014). Simultaneously, regional areas in economic decline that have lower costs of living experience an increase in low-income households with the in-migration of income support recipients (on DSP and Newstart) (ABS 2009).

The interstice of disability and regionality creates uneven and differentiated outcomes, yet this experience remains largely unknown and is little understood. Core questions remain. How do local governments, communities and economies respond to changing national redistributive social policy measures? How do regional towns and centres adjust social programming within the local landscape to address new vulnerabilities that are created with population restratification? And how do they respond to the specific needs of Aboriginal and Torres Strait Islander peoples with disabilities within their regions who are unable to access appropriate nationally assigned disability entitlements and payments? The next section identifies some of the potential issues that require further investigation.

The impact of disability income reform on Indigenous people in regional towns

Indigenous unemployment in regional Australia has largely remained static at 17.6 per cent over the last 10 years (ABS 2011), and this rate is even higher for Aboriginal and Torres Strait Islander people with disabilities residing in these areas (AIHW 2011). Tonts and colleagues (2012: 288–301) have demonstrated that regional centres with high Aboriginal and Torres Strait Islander populations have a higher proportion of low-income households dependent on income support measures.

Bruce Western and colleagues propose examining the impact of changing social security regimes on regional communities through the prism of economic (in)security. They define economic (in)security as the level of potential loss faced by households as they encounter the unpredictable events of social life (Western et al. 2012: 341). Public policies, related to unemployment benefits and disability pensions for example, alongside social policies around public housing, health care and education, play a central role in mediating the impact of negative outcomes of a changing economic landscape on individuals, their families and communities (Western et al. 2012). Economic insecurity has been on the rise globally with the intensification of neoliberalism as policy hegemony, as it radically diminishes the social provisioning structures that have historically provided household stability and wellbeing with the onset of broader economic change (growth or decline). While, in Australia, household economic insecurity has risen overall (ILO 2004), it is rural and remote regions that have most sharply felt its presence (Tonts et al. 2007).

Having a disability substantially increases all risks associated with economic insecurity, whether the disability is acquired in adult life or is an existing condition on entering the labour market (UNDESA 2008). For people with disabilities, economic insecurity is heightened due to the enduring structural discrimination embedded within the labour market (ILO 2014). Additionally, it is well recognised that due to direct and indirect forms of racism, Aboriginal Australians face particular barriers to achieving economic security via labour market participation and associated earnings. The persistence of these extensive forms of racism has significant implications for health, illness and disability and, in turn, extensively heightens Aboriginal Australians' exposure to economic insecurity when compared to the non-Aboriginal population (Scrimgeour & Scrimgeour 2008).

Diminished access to the DSP for Aboriginal and Torres Strait Islander people with disabilities in regional areas only heightens the risks associated with economic insecurity. Disability status, recognised through DSP eligibility, provides access to a range of increased supports, such as, but not limited to, prioritisation for public housing (thereby lessening long-term dependence on the private rental market); additional local government subsidies, benefits and community programs; public transport subsidies; and a range of highly subsidised health care and disability supports. These critical social benefits are broader than disability supports and care, such as those offered under the NDIS.

As Peck (2013: 248) has argued, neoliberalising the development of rural and remote economies positions the market as 'natural' through counterposing discursive structures of 'dysfunction' that publicly undermine enduring and sustainable Indigenous customary economies and practices. Yet, as Spurway and Soldatic (2015) have documented, for many Aboriginal and Torres Strait Islander people with disabilities residing in regional towns, traditional food practices and knowledges have been central in coping with the chronic economic insecurity generated by the neoliberalisation of disability income regimes. This research stresses the importance of not romanticising Indigenous food sovereignty practices when they are enacted to address chronic food insecurity caused by a changing social security landscape.

Conclusion

The eligibility rules for the DSP are not based on an objective system of disability measurement. The DSP's operationalisation is deeply embedded in political ideological commitments to a just society (positive or negative) and constructed with a particular set of normative assumptions about the body and Western medical science. Significantly, and a key area undertheorised within the disability social policy literature, the DSP has a spatial dimension. The implications of the ongoing neoliberal retraction of disability income regimes for Aboriginal and Torres Strait Islander Australians residing in regional towns has been little considered. Aboriginal and Torres Strait Islander people with disabilities living in regional Australia face serious disadvantages that have persisted over time, with few documented improvements despite the significant investment in government policy to 'close the gap'. With further changes mooted for the DSP, it is urgent that we begin to identify, examine, analyse and document the ways in which regional Australia responds to, navigates and traverses the interstices of national policy agendas and local economic imperatives for its Aboriginal and Torres Strait Islander populations with disabilities. This knowledge is critical to enable regional Australia—which has in the past heavily relied upon national income support policies for its most marginalised populations—to design, develop and implement effective local responses to substantive economic and social change that sustain the material, social and cultural wellbeing of Aboriginal and Torres Strait Islander Australians with disabilities.

Acknowledgements

This research described in this paper has been funded by an Australian Research Council DECRA Fellowship (DE160100478).

References

ABS (Australian Bureau of Statistics) (2009). *Disability, Australia*, cat. no. 4446.0, ABS, Canberra.

ABS (2011). *Census population and the characteristics of Aboriginal and Torres Strait Islander Australia*, cat. no. 2076.0, ABS, Canberra.

ABS (2012). *Australian social trends, March quarter 2012*, cat. no. 4102.0, ABS, Canberra.

ABS (2015). *Disability, ageing and carers, Australia: Summary of findings*, cat. no. 4430.0, ABS, Canberra.

ABS (2017). *Disability, ageing and carers, Australia: Summary of findings*, cat. no. 4430.0, ABS, Canberra.

ACOSS (Australian Council of Social Service) (2016). *Poverty in Australia*, ACOSS, Sydney.

AIHW (Australian Institute of Health and Welfare) (2011). *Aboriginal and Torres Strait Islander people with disability: Wellbeing, participation and support*, AIHW, Canberra.

Alcock P (1993). *Understanding poverty*, Macmillan, London.

Beer A (2012). The economic geography of Australia and its analysis: From industrial to post-industrial regions. *Geographical Research* 50:269–81, doi.org/10.1111/j.1745-5871.2012.00771.x.

Beer A & Clower T (2012). Specialisation and growth: Evidence from Australia's regional cities. *Urban Studies* 46:369–89, doi.org/10.1177/0042098008099359.

Chapman R, Tonts M & Plummer P (2014). Resource development, local adjustment and regional policy: Resolving the problem of rapid growth in the Pilbara, WA. *Journal of Rural and Community Development* 9:72–86.

Daniels D (2006). *Social security payments for the aged, people with disabilities and carers 1909 to 2006—part 1*, Social Policy Group, Parliamentary Library of Australia, Canberra.

Department of Human Services (2016a). *Income test for Newstart Allowance, Partner Allowance, Sickness Allowance and Widow Allowance*, Australian Government, Canberra, www.humanservices.gov.au/individuals/enablers/income-test-newstart-allowance-partner-allowance-sickness-allowance-and-widow-allowance.

Department of Human Services (2016b). *Newstart Allowance*, Australian Government, Canberra.

Department of Human Services (2016c). *Disability Support Pension*, Australian Government, Canberra, www.humanservices.gov.au/customer/services/centrelink/disability-support-pension.

Department of Human Services (2016d). *Income test for pensions*, Australian Government, Canberra, www.humanservices.gov.au/customer/enablers/income-test-pensions.

Department of Human Services (2016e). *Pension Supplement*, Australian Government, Canberra, www.humanservices.gov.au/customer/services/centrelink/pension-supplement.

Fraser C, Jackson H, Judd F, Komiti A, Robins G, Murray G, Humphreys J, Pattison P & Hodgins G (2005). Changing places: The impact of rural restructuring on mental health in Australia. *Health & Place* 11:157–71, doi.org/10.1016/j.healthplace.2004.03.003.

Galvin R (2004). Can welfare reform make disability disappear? *Australian Journal of Social Issues* 39(3):343–53, doi.org/10.1002/j.1839-4655.2004. tb01181.x.

Gibson C, Waitt G, Walmsley J & Connell J (2009). Cultural festivals and economic development in nonmetropolitan Australia. *Journal of Planning Education and Research* 29:280–93, doi.org/10.1177/0739456X09354382.

Gilroy J & Donelly M (2016). Australian indigenous people with disability: Ethics and standpoint theory. In Grech S & Soldatic K (eds), *Disability in the Global South: The Critical Handbook*, Springer, New York.

Grover C & Piggott L (2010). Disgusting! Understanding financial support for disabled people in the UK. Paper presented at Disability Studies 5th biannual conference, Lancaster University, Lancaster, 7–9 September.

Grover C and Soldatic K (2013). Neoliberal restructuring, disabled people and social (in)security in Australia and Britain. *Scandinavian Journal of Disability Studies* 15(3):216–32, doi.org/10.1080/15017419.2012.724446.

Horsley J (2013). Conceptualising the state, governance and development in a semi-peripheral resource economy. *Australian Geographer* 44:283–303, doi.org/10.1080/00049182.2013.817038.

Humpage L (2007). Models of disability, work and welfare in Australia. *Social Policy & Administration* 41(3):215–31, doi.org/10.1111/j.1467-9515.2007. 00549.x.

ILO (International Labor Organization) (2004). *Economic security for a better world,* ILO, Geneva, www.ilo.org/public/english/protection/ses/download/ docs/happiness.pdf.

ILO (2014). *World social protection report 2014/15*, ILO, Geneva, ilo.org/ wcmsp5/groups/public/---dgreports/---dcomm/documents/publication/ wcms_245201.pdf.

Luck G, Race D & Black R (2011). *Demographic change in Australia's rural landscapes*, Springer and CSIRO, New York and Melbourne.

Macklin J (2011). Tackling disadvantage in the midst of the boom. Ministerial keynote speech at Economic and Social Outlook Conference, Melbourne, 30 June.

McKenzie F, Haslam McKenzie F & Hoath A (2014). Fly-in/fly-out, flexibility and the future: Does becoming a regional FIFO source community present opportunity or burden? *Geographical Research* 52:430–41, doi.org/10.1111/ 1745-5871.12080.

Mendes P (2008). *Australia's welfare wars revisited*, 2nd edn, UNSW Press, Sydney.

Morris A, Wilson S & Soldatic K (2015). Hard yakka: Disabled people's experience of living on Newstart. In Grover C & Piggott L (eds), *Work, welfare and disabled people: UK and international perspectives*, Policy Press, Bristol.

Morton R (2016). Budget 2016: Welfare cuts to boost $27bn disabilities spend. *The Australian*, 4 May.

Neave C (2016). *Department of Human Services: accessibility of Disability Support Pension for remote Indigenous Australians*, Commonwealth Ombudsman, Canberra, www.ombudsman.gov.au/__data/assets/pdf_file/0024/42558/Accessibility-of-DSP-for-remote-Indigenous-Australians_Final-report.pdf.

OECD (Organisation for Economic Co-operation and Development) (2009). *Sickness, disability and work: Keeping on track in the economic downturn*, OECD Directorate for Employment, Labour and Social Affairs, London.

Peck J (2013). Polyani in the Pilbara. *Australian Geographer* 44(3):243–64, doi.org/10.1080/00049182.2013.817037.

Plummer P, Tonts M & Martinus K (2014). Endogenous growth, local competitiveness and regional development. *Journal of Economic and Social Policy* 16:1–28.

Rainnie A, Fitzgerald S, Ellem B & Goods C (2014). FIFO and global production networks: Exploring the issues. *Australian Bulletin of Labour* 40(2):98–115.

Roulstone A & Barnes C (2005). *Working futures? Disabled people, policy and social inclusion*, Policy Press, Bristol, doi.org/10.1332/policypress/9781861346261.001.0001.

Scrimgeour M & Scrimgeour D (2008). *Health care access for Aboriginal and Torres Strait Islander people living in urban areas, and related research issues: A review of the literature*, Cooperative Research Centre for Aboriginal Health, Melbourne.

Soldatic K (2010). Disability and the Australian neoliberal workfare state. PhD thesis, University of Western Australia, Perth.

Soldatic K (2013). Appointment time: Disability and neoliberal temporal rationalities. *Critical Sociology* 39:405–19, doi.org/10.1177/0896920511430168.

Soldatic K & Chapman A (2010). Surviving the assault? The Australian disability movement and the neoliberal workfare state. *Social Movement Studies* 9(2):139–54, doi.org/10.1080/14742831003603299.

Soldatic K & Meekosha H (2012). Disability and neoliberal state formations. In Watson N, Thomas C & Roulstone A (eds), *Routledge handbook of disability studies*, Routledge, London.

Soldatic K & Pini B (2009). The three Ds of welfare reform: Disability, disgust and deservingness. *Australian Journal of Human Rights* 15(1):76–94, doi.org/10.1080/1323238X.2009.11910862.

Soldatic K & Pini B (2012). Continuity or change? Disability policy and the Rudd government. *Social Policy & Society* 11(2):183–96, doi.org/10.1017/S1474746411000510.

Soldatic, K & Sykes, D (2017). Poverty and people with a disability. In Serr K (ed.), *Thinking about poverty*, 4th edition, The Federation Press, Sydney.

Soldatic K, Spurway K & Meekosha H (2014). *Hard yakka: Living with a disability in the West Kimberley*, UNSW Australia, Sydney.

Spurway K & Soldatic K (2015). 'Life keeps throwing me lemons': Aboriginal Australians with disability and food insecurity. *Local Environment* 21:1118–31, doi.org/10.1080/13549839.2015.1073235.

Tonts M, Davies A & Haslam-McKenzie F (2007). *Regional workforce futures: An analysis of the Great Southern, South west and Wheatbelt regions*, University of Western Australia, Perth.

Tonts M, Plummer P & Lawrie M (2012). Socio-economic wellbeing in Australian mining towns: A comparative analysis. *Journal of Rural Studies* 28:288–301, doi.org/10.1016/j.jrurstud.2011.10.006.

UNDESA (United Nations Department of Economic and Social Affairs) (2008). *World economic and social survey 2008: Overcoming economic insecurity*, United Nations, New York.

Weller S & O'Neill P (2014). De-industrialisation, financialisation and Australia's macro-economic trap. *Cambridge Journal of Regions, Economy and Society* 7:509–26, doi.org/10.1093/cjres/rsu020.

Western B, Bloome D, Sosnaud B & Tach L (2012). Economic insecurity and social stratification. *Annual Review of Sociology* 38:341–59, doi.org/10.1146/annurev-soc-071811-145434.

Wilton R & Schuer S (2006). Towards socio-spatial inclusion? Disabled people, neoliberalism and the contemporary labour market. *Area* 38(2):186–95, doi.org/10.1111/j.1475-4762.2006.00668.x.

8

Indigenous peoples, neoliberalism and the state: A retreat from rights to 'responsibilisation' via the cashless welfare card

Shelley Bielefeld

Introduction

Reflecting on the focus of this edited collection—indigenous rights, recognition, neoliberalism and the state—this chapter will address the reduction of Indigenous peoples' rights in the context of cashless welfare transfers. It contributes to the arguments made in this collection by exploring how neoliberal interventions can adversely affect Indigenous peoples, diminishing their consumer choices and other rights, whilst simultaneously creating benefits for entrepreneurial interests via privatisation of social security payments. It questions the purpose of the government's recognition of the lower socio-economic status of Indigenous peoples and explores who benefits from such recognition. The chapter analyses how cashless welfare transfers operate along racialised contours and implement a neoliberal approach to governance of Indigenous peoples, fostering regulation by market principles that reward entrepreneurialism and self-reliance. Like the work of Deirdre Howard-Wagner, Patrick Sullivan, Cathy Eatock and Alexander Page in this collection, this chapter highlights the increasingly precarious experience of Indigenous communities caused by insecure marketised funding arrangements with competitive processes. It progresses these themes by recommending the development of an alternative form of resource redistribution through an integrity tax based on reparation for colonial atrocities. The chapter contends that this approach is preferable to that of intensifying welfare conditionality via cashless welfare transfers.

In 2014, Andrew Forrest recommended that the federal government trial a 'Healthy Welfare Card' with 100 per cent cashless welfare for recipients of government income support except for 'age and veterans' pensions (Forrest 2014: 100–8). Forrest (2014: 102–3) claimed that Australia had 'increased the risk to its most vulnerable by paying all welfare benefits in cash', which enabled an 'incoming tide of drugs and alcohol', particularly in remote Indigenous communities, and that there was a need to 'find a technologically possible, sensible mass solution to end this unnecessary suffering'. Forrest (2014: 105) maintained that the Welfare Card would swiftly move individuals into employment and reduce 'emergency relief payments and crisis services ... through a longer-term reduction in welfare reliance'. Neoliberal notions of increased efficiency and reduced government expenditure on income support were therefore an important aspect of his advocacy for overhauling the Australian welfare system. Forrest (2014: 107) also envisioned that 'existing data mining technology' be used 'to monitor use of the card to detect any unusual sales or purchases, with ... on-the-spot penalties on retailers and individuals for fraudulent use of the card'.

The federal government decided to implement aspects of the Healthy Welfare Card via the *Social Security Legislation Amendment (Debit Card Trial) Act 2015* (Cwth) (the DCT Act), with some variations to Forrest's formulation. Initially described by government as the 'Healthy Welfare Card', the epithet they now favour is the 'cashless debit card' (CDC) (Commonwealth of Australia 2015: 2). This corresponds with the government's representation of this card as 'an everyday mainstream debit card' (Commonwealth of Australia 2015: 3). However, critics of the scheme have come up with alternative nomenclature: the 'cashless welfare card' (ACOSS 2014a), 'Welfare Debit Trial Card', the 'Unhealthy Welfare Card', the 'Economic Apartheid Card' (Say NO to the Welfare Debit Card Ceduna[1]) and the 'White Card' (Klein & Razi 2017: 13).

---

1   For more information about the Say NO to the Welfare Debit Card Ceduna resistance group, see their Facebook page: www.facebook.com/groups/1486363324991953/?notif_t=group_r2j_approved &notif_id=1469193406809130.

Rather than being applied to all welfare recipients, the scheme is being trialled in communities with large numbers of Indigenous welfare recipients: Ceduna, Kununurra and Wyndham (DSS 2016). Indigenous people comprise 565 of the 752 people subject to the Welfare Card in Ceduna and 984 of the 1,199 people on the card in Kununurra and Wyndham (Aboriginal and Torres Strait Islander Social Justice Commissioner 2016: 91–2). Indigenous social security recipients are consequently disproportionately impacted by the Welfare Card, which raises the issue of violation of the right to be free from racial discrimination and other significant rights, including rights to privacy, equality and social security (Gooda 2015, Parliamentary Joint Committee on Human Rights 2015: 24, 27–8).

The DCT Act Explanatory Memorandum (2015) states the trial aims to restrict access to cash to 'reduce the habitual abuse and associated harm resulting from alcohol, gambling and illegal drugs'. Substance abuse has featured heavily in the government's rationalisation for the trial, which unjustly stigmatises trial participants. Yet the Welfare Card does not simply target people with addiction issues. Instead, the card has wide application to welfare recipients residing in geographical locations selected for the trial. There is grassroots resistance in Ceduna to the blanket imposition of the card (Ceduna Anti Card Group 2016, Say NO to the Welfare Debit Card Ceduna), which makes no distinction between the financial capacities or behaviours of affected welfare recipients. The government states that the Welfare Card is being implemented at the behest of Indigenous leaders (Commonwealth of Australia 2015: 2), yet if there was community consent to the scheme there would be no need for broad compulsory application of the card. Indeed, some Indigenous leaders of Ceduna have stressed that there was no support in their communities for the card to be universally applied to all welfare recipients in the region (Smart and Peters in Davey 2017). Rather, they emphasise that any community support was qualified and conditional; however, this ultimately was not reflected in government policy. Similar feedback has been forthcoming from Kununurra (MG Corporation 2017: 1–4).

Although the new legislation allows welfare recipients to voluntarily choose the Welfare Card (DCT Act s. 124PH), there is broad compulsory subjection to the scheme through ministerially determined 'trigger' payments for people of 'a particular class' who reside in 'a particular trial area' (DCT Act s. 124PG). A 'trigger payment' is broadly defined and covers most payment types except for the 'mature age allowance'

(DCT Act s. 124PD). The amount of restricted income under this new system is 80 per cent of a welfare recipient's payment (DCT Act s. 124PJ). Those subject to the Welfare Card can appeal to a community panel to have the restricted amount reduced to 'a percentage in the range of 50% to 80%' (s. 124PK), at the panel's discretion. Feedback from Ceduna indicates that this is a protracted and often unsatisfactory process. Some of those affected have expressed concern that this outsourcing process involves members of the community panel being given substantial power over peoples' lives without providing a rationale for decisions made, intensifying the arbitrary exercise of power (Kakoschke-Moore in Community Affairs Legislation Committee 2016: 98) and surveillance over welfare recipients.

Practical problems and consumer issues

In the second reading speech introducing the DCT Act, the government claimed that:

> the cashless debit card will work as similarly as possible to any other bank card. The trial will seek to ensure the card can work at all existing terminals and shops, except those selling the restricted products of alcohol and gambling, as well as online where possible. The only difference will be that it will not allow the purchase of alcohol and gambling products or allow cash withdrawals (Commonwealth of Australia 2015: 3).

However, feedback from those affected in the trial site of Ceduna indicates that people subject to the card have had trouble paying for items that were meant to be permitted expenditure via the card (Pav in Fedorowytsch & Iggulden 2016). For example, in May 2016, the Ceduna Anti Card Group met and relayed that there had been problems with people being unable to pay their bills at their local post office with their Welfare Card (Ceduna Anti Card Group 2016). This meant that people were presented with the impossible challenge of trying to pay their bills with their 20 per cent cash allowance. The group reported that many people were experiencing delayed payments of eight to 12 hours by financial services provider Indue Ltd. One person was said to have experienced 'having funds disappear from her card account without her knowledge and permission at the rate of 100 dollars at a time' (Ceduna Anti Card Group 2016). Problems paying off credit cards were also a cause of distress, as this leads to more debt with penalties for overdue payments and additional interest.

Inability to pay bills normally was reported to create feelings of shame and humiliation (Ceduna Anti Card Group 2016). This led the group to ask 'how are people to pay their bills normally? … Will we have to go and beg every time we need to pay a bill?' (Ceduna Anti Card Group 2016). Further reported problems include people being unable to purchase food during blackouts (ABC Editorial 2016) and people with previously sound rental payment records falling behind in rent due to the card (Haseldine in Gage 2016).

Other concerns include consumer issues. These are twofold. First, those who had previously preferred to pay for items in cash in order to avoid transaction fees are now forced into a situation where they have to pay additional merchant surcharge fees for goods and services because they are paying by card. This is difficult for people already experiencing challenges associated with a low income. The government has not offered to pay these additional sums nor have they prohibited merchants from charging such fees in the trial sites or in Australia more broadly. This means that *the cashless welfare card makes social security income more expensive for welfare recipients to use.* This is a crucial point that has not been addressed satisfactorily by the government. When the issue of diminished consumer rights under the Welfare Card was drawn to the attention of Alan Tudge, the Minister for Human Services, he denied that this was the case, pointing out that 'of the 16 merchants in Ceduna with surcharges or minimum spends, only eight will continue to implement these fees' (Tudge 2016: 3). Yet those additional merchant charges from even eight outlets are enough to break a budget for welfare recipients living on below 'poverty line' payments (ACOSS 2014b: 8). Moreover, like other members of Australian society, welfare recipients travel when seeking employment and maintaining relationships necessary for social inclusion. Extra costs due to card surcharges associated with such travel could well increase difficulties for those on low incomes, as occurs with compulsory income management in the Northern Territory (Bray et al. 2014: 136–7).

The second consumer issue is that people who had previously been free to choose the banking service into which their social security payments were made are now coerced to have a contractual relationship with Indue Ltd, a financial services provider that is not a bank. Indue does not offer the range of accounts to suit low-income earners that banks have developed. When contacted about these issues by the CEO of the Consumer Action Law Centre, Gerard Brody, the CEO of the Australian Bankers Association (2016) Steven Münchenburg responded that:

consumer choice is a valuable right which should be protected and choosing the right banking product or service that is suitable to individual needs should continue to be a pivotal consideration. Currently, some Australian banks offer 'basic bank accounts' that are suitable for disadvantaged and low-income customers and the banking industry strongly supports the promotion of these accounts. The ABA [Australian Bankers Association] also supports ensuring competition in the market which is most likely to lead to innovations that maximise consumer choices. (Australian Bankers Association 2016)

Instead of fostering consumer choice, the government has created a captured market for Indue Ltd as the entity charged with orchestrating this new technological 'panopticon', where those subject to the Welfare Card are under omnipresent inspection (Bentham 1995: 31, 43–5). This has led to strongly worded concerns. For instance, David Tennant (2015) has suggested that this move may lead to 'a new banking underclass' in Australia.

Who benefits?

The launch of the cashless welfare card raises significant questions. Given that the concept was derived from Forrest's Indigenous jobs and training review, it must be asked for what purpose is the lower socio-economic status of Indigenous people recognised and who benefits from such recognition? Indue Ltd's early stage contract figures were AU$2,870,675.50 for the CDC IT build and a further contract of AU$7,939,809 for implementation of the CDC trial.[2] These sums were part of a reported AU$18.9 million (excluding GST) allocated to the CDC, costing approximately AU$10,000 per participant (Conifer 2017). Considering that this was for a trial of the cashless welfare card for no more than 10,000 welfare recipients (Explanatory Memorandum 2015: 4) from '1 February 2016' to '30 June 2018' (DCT Act s. 124 PF), this sum is hefty indeed. Indue Ltd's implementation contract has since risen to AU$13,035,581.16.[3] If this trial is expanded then Indue Ltd and possibly other like institutions will stand to benefit considerably as Australia's social security payments are privatised. This fits with 'the

---

2   The reference numbers for these contracts between the Department of Social Services and Indue Ltd are CN3323493-A1 and CN3290604 respectively, published on AusTender, www.tenders.gov.au.

3   Reference number CN3323493-A2, published on AusTender, www.tenders.gov.au.

normative neoliberal vision of market provision' of services traditionally provided by governments (Cahill 2014: 27, 54). That the government has an eye towards this possibility is signalled by the second reading speech, which states that 'The trial … will make a vital contribution towards informing … future arrangements for income management' (Commonwealth of Australia 2015: 3).

While the benefits of the CDC for Indue Ltd are clear, the same cannot be said for government income support recipients subject to the card. The Final Evaluation report on the CDC by Orima consultants (DSS 2017a) reveals some troubling consequences for numerous cardholders who participated in the surveys. These include increased difficulties paying bills, running 'out of money to buy food', problems paying for housing needs, having insufficient funds to pay for educational items for children, and running out of money to pay for essentials for children (e.g. 'nappies, clothes and medicine') (DSS 2017a: 72). Other problems included card malfunction, inability to participate as desired in the cash-based economy, trouble checking card account balances, some merchants refusing to accept the card for purchase of everyday items, and embarrassment when the card does not work (DSS 2017a: 89). Unsurprisingly, 32 per cent of card users said the CDC 'had made their lives worse' (DSS 2017a: 6). None of these problems have been emphasised by government in their media releases on the card. Also, significant given the government rationale for the card, the majority of CDC participants reported either no change in alcohol consumption, gambling or illegal drug use since using the CDC or an increase in these behaviours (DSS 2017a: 43).

For numerous welfare recipients subject to it, the coercive nature of the CDC may impair any possible benefits envisioned by government because health research indicates that autonomy is a core human need directly linked with favourable health outcomes. Marmot (2015: 249) indicates that 'control over one's life and opportunities for meaningful social engagement are necessary for health'. He contends (2015: 248) that '[a]utonomy and social participation are so important for health that their lack leads to deterioration in health'. Autonomy is clearly undermined by the cashless welfare card, which denies users freedom of choice and, as previously mentioned, the additional cost of living incurred by those who use the card may also detrimentally affect their capacity for social inclusion. Mick Gooda (2015) also contends that '[a]ny possible benefits must be weighed against the sense of disempowerment people report, the stigma they feel and punitive perceptions'.

It has been noted by the Parliamentary Joint Committee on Human Rights (2015: 23) that the cashless welfare card 'is very similar to the existing program of income management' currently operating in the Northern Territory and other select trial areas in Australia. Empirical research reveals that income management is ineffective in 'changing people's behaviours' or 'spending patterns, including food and alcohol sales' (Bray et al. 2014: xxi). Nor does income management facilitate 'improvement in financial wellbeing … reductions in financial harassment or improved financial management skills' (Bray et al. 2014: xxi). There is also no robust evidence to suggest that community wellbeing has been enhanced by compulsory forms of income management (Bray et al. 2014: xxi, Hunt 2017: 2–3).

The cashless welfare card has the same deficiency-based philosophical foundation as the income management system that has now had an extremely protracted trial for thousands of (mostly) Indigenous welfare recipients in various trial sites. As of 25 August 2017, 79 per cent of the 25,009 welfare recipients nationwide subject to income management identified as Indigenous (DSS 2017b). According to this 'deficit' model, any socio-economic vulnerability experienced by welfare recipients is due to their irresponsible spending patterns. This is a misrepresentation of the budgetary capacity of many welfare recipients and constitutes simplistic and destructive negative stereotyping. Nevertheless, this 'deficit'-based dynamic is consistent with broader neoliberal Indigenous policy trends in Australia, elaborated upon by numerous scholars, who highlight how this model assumes that coercive disciplinarian interventions are warranted to reshape behaviours of Indigenous peoples (Walter 2009: 7, 11–12, Watson 2009: 89, Howard-Wagner & Kelly 2011: 115, 120, Altman 2013: 88–9, 116, 139, Lovell 2014: 234, Strakosch 2015: 88–90, 105, 134). This approach has clear benefits for government in terms of reinforcement of state power over Indigenous peoples. The language of Indigenous deficiency allows the state to obscure the complexities 'of Aboriginal disadvantage and its own complicity in the maintenance of such poverty and disadvantage' (Walter 2009: 12, also see Watson 2009: 90–1).

Neoliberalism and responsibilisation: The antithesis of necessary reparations for First Peoples

As previously mentioned, the government's rationale for implementing the Welfare Card is that it is to reduce 'the social harm caused by welfare-fuelled alcohol, gambling and drug abuse' (Commonwealth of Australia 2015: 2). This portrayal of welfare income and welfare recipients as problems requiring intensive regulation is a long familiar theme of neoliberal governance, whereby the poor are portrayed as the sole authors of their impoverished circumstances. Within this framework, they are tasked with 'responsibilisation', urged to take responsibility for their failure to flourish in 'the neoliberal race to riches', and charged with the task of 'undertaking the correct strategies of self-investment and entrepreneurship for thriving and surviving' (Brown 2015: 24, 133). Wendy Brown (2015: 133) explains that responsibilisation 'discursively denigrates dependency and practically negates collective provisioning for existence' whilst situating 'the individual as the only relevant and wholly accountable actor'.

The Welfare Card reflects neoliberal governmentality in that the aim of 'responsibilisation' is to reconstitute and reorient individuals 'for a neoliberal order' (Brown 2015: 133). Foucault (2008: 145) points out that neoliberal governance aims not to 'correct the destructive effects of the market on society' but instead to facilitate 'regulation of society by the market'. He highlights that for neoliberals, '[t]he *homo oeconomicus* sought after is not the man of exchange or man the consumer; he is the man of enterprise and production' (Foucault 2008: 147). This perhaps explains why Australia's cashless welfare card architects tend to trivialise or ignore the reduction of consumer rights for income-managed welfare recipients. If entrepreneurial interests require that consumer rights are diminished in their pursuit of profit then neoliberal governments are accommodating.

The objective of neoliberal governmentality is to construct *homo oeconomicus* as 'someone who is eminently governable' (Foucault 2008: 270); and, as Edward Said (1994: 327) notes, '[t]o be governed people must be … ruled in regulated places'. Whilst Australia's consumer landscape has long been regulated, cashless welfare card transfers add rocky new terrain where welfare recipients are differentiated in public places and exposed to greater stigma and surveillance.[4] This is aligned with neoliberalism's continuous 'institutional transformation, involving … destruction and reconstruction of regulatory architectures, and the overlaying of these upon existing institutions' (Cahill 2014: 28). This ushers in what Peck describes as 'neoliberal*isation*' with 'an open-ended and contradictory process of politically assisted market rule' (Peck 2012: xii). Thus, in the name of creating more autonomous subjects, the autonomy of welfare recipients is undermined.

Indigenous welfare recipients who do not conform to the neoliberal ideal of *homo oeconomicus* have been portrayed as deficient, irresponsible and antisocial (Moreton-Robinson 2009: 70). They have been represented as particularly in need of the intensive regulation offered by the Welfare Card (Commonwealth of Australia 2015: 2) and of income management via the BasicsCard (Bielefeld 2014: 287–289). This is part of a broader welfare reform agenda to decrease the number of people in receipt of government income support by ensuring that 'income from work' is 'more favourably treated than income from other sources' (DSS 2014: 9).

Welfare conditionality programs like income management via the BasicsCard and the cashless welfare card also expose a neoliberal fixation on return for investment. Foucault (2008: 256) explains that 'according to the neoliberal theory of consumption', society is portrayed as 'the producer of conforming behaviour with which it is satisfied in return for a certain investment'. Thus, there has been an intensification of welfare conditionality in order to create a political impression that it facilitates the production of conforming behaviour. In a colonial context, this amounts to a quest to complete the government's long cherished ideal of assimilation of Indigenous peoples. In terms of neoliberal governance, where disadvantage remains, this is seen as an outcome for which Indigenous peoples are to take 'responsibility' (Watson 2009: 90).

While 'disciplining Indigenous life to the cold rationality of market principles' (Coulthard 2014: 13) has long featured in colonial projects, neoliberal governance proffers new challenges for Indigenous peoples as they are confronted with a host of proposals that are '[p]unitive … and

---

4   The effortless public identification of Indue card holders engaging in purchases has been confirmed by fieldwork conducted in the East Kimberley. Klein and Razi (2017: 12) note the presence of separate cash registers in some venues that must be used by CDC users.

obsessed with employment despite the absence of good jobs' (Fraser 2013: 113). Such policies foster insecurity for the most marginalised while cementing elite privilege.

Colonial governments are well served by neoliberal governmentality because its ahistoricism allows accumulated layers of privilege and disadvantage to be left undisturbed. However, there is a need to critique the filters through which we attempt to comprehend causes of poverty and possibilities for its redress. To position the socio-economic challenges Indigenous communities experience as the consequence of pathological individual or community behaviour can detract focus from significant structural factors contributing to poverty. Structural contributors include the paucity of adequately paid employment in remote communities and lingering legacies of colonialism that have resulted in underfunded essential services for Indigenous communities (Altman 2013: 40, Watson 2009: 90–1). Interventions such as the Welfare Card also arguably distract attention away from alternative redistributive possibilities, such as a reparations fund for Australia's First Peoples based on their experience of colonial atrocities. This is characteristic of Australia, where there has been a 'long tradition of framing domestic welfare policy as the "solution" to settler colonial conflicts' (Strakosch 2015: 3).

Yet, such framing need not be treated as inevitable. An alternative type of policy framing is possible. For instance, James Ferguson (2015: 10, 165) proposes that a new 'politics of distribution' be developed where resource redistribution is based on the concept of the 'rightful share'. This is important in colonial contexts worldwide where government and corporate interests continue to profit vastly from mineral extraction and other exploitative enterprises while millions of people who have undergone the nightmare of colonisation remain greatly impoverished. Ferguson (2015: 26) explains that according to the rightful share approach:

> Distributive claims … are rooted in a conviction that citizens (and particularly poor and black citizens) are the *rightful owners* of a vast national wealth (including mineral wealth) of which they have been unjustly deprived through a historic process of racialized dispossession—a conception that provides a very different, and much more politicized, justification for cash payments than is available in the usual framework of 'social assistance' as generous help for the needy.

If adopted in Australia, this framework would likely improve the socio-economic circumstances of remote living Indigenous peoples, including those currently subject to a range of punitive welfare conditionality programs in addition to income management, such as penalty-heavy workfare imposed as part of the Community Development Program (Fowkes & Sanders 2016: 10). Welfare conditionality programs individualise responsibility for 'structural violence' (Bielefeld 2014/2015: 99–118). They are therefore incapable of addressing the root causes of socio-economic disadvantage. Something else is necessary.

Drawing inspiration from an international context, a possible reparation funding model can be seen in the Dene/Métis proposal put to the Canadian government, that 'to ensure economic self-sufficiency … 10 per cent of all resource revenues derived in the territory be collected and paid into a "Dene Heritage Fund" managed by the Dene' (Coulthard 2014: 74). The Dene/Métis stipulated that national resource use should encompass 'a "firm commitment to renewables"' and that use of non-renewables only be permitted if the '"well-being of the people and resources of Denendeh"' were ensured (Coulthard 2014: 74). The Dene argued for this economic reparation model in relation to their traditional lands. This could be considered as a type of 'integrity tax' owed by colonial governments to First Peoples as part of a process of decolonisation. It is a concept that may well resonate across multiple jurisdictions where indigenous peoples continue to experience ongoing socio-economic deprivation.

In the Australian Indigenous policy context, Virginia Marshall has suggested a somewhat similar idea with respect to water resources. She contends that 'the concept of water royalties' should 'be included in the policy framework on Aboriginal water rights' (Marshall 2017: 163). Marshall (2017: 163) explains that '[a] water royalty would ensure certainty in economic planning in Aboriginal communities where third parties seek to access and use water on Aboriginal owned lands'. This is one way to ensure Indigenous peoples' access to ongoing economic resources—without the multitude of hoops imposed by oppressive and stigmatising welfare conditionality policy frameworks. This is important because the combination of welfare conditionality programs presently affecting Indigenous peoples 'replicates past discriminatory treatment they experienced as non-citizen wards of the state: ineligible for award wages and paid in kind with rations rather than cash' (Altman 2017).

If Australia is to attain a genuinely postcolonial status, then redressing the power imbalance over Indigenous peoples' access to economic resources is essential. Application of this integrity tax principle in Australia has the potential to address Indigenous socio-economic disadvantage in a way that bolsters Indigenous self-determination. Nationwide application is crucial in order to account for the effects of colonial dispossession, with many Indigenous peoples being forced off their lands, and practices of coerced child removal resulting in the Stolen Generations. When political elites bemoan that Indigenous peoples do not contribute enough economically, they exclude a highly significant contribution that Indigenous peoples have made to Australia's economy—their land and their forced labour (Bielefeld 2014/2015: 100–3).

In Australia, this integrity tax could be derived from a percentage of resource revenues obtained within the nation, including renewable energy and water resources, subject to the caveats Australia's First Peoples thought appropriate. Repressive regulation in the form of welfare conditionality embodies coloniality and neoliberal governmentality. This integrity tax could potentially provide a pathway out of current approaches designed to colonise, regulate and subjugate Indigenous peoples. It may provide a way to sustain long-term funding for Indigenous communities and end the destructive cycle of endless grant applications for short-term funding under competitive schemes like the Indigenous Advancement Strategy (IAS). The IAS funding fiasco that resulted in major fiscal shortfalls for Indigenous run organisations is aptly critiqued by Alexander Page in this edited collection (see Chapter 10).

While space does not permit full elaboration of how these integrity tax ideas might be implemented, further work on alternative frameworks to poverty surveillance and welfare conditionality will be facilitated by the author's Australian Research Council–funded project in coming years.[5] Preliminary analysis suggests that any Australian reparations fund would need to be controlled by Indigenous communities, not by the state. The Aboriginals Benefit Account (ABA) stands as a cautionary tale of what can occur when government has control over such finances. The ABA is a scheme by which a percentage of mining royalties from Aboriginal lands in the Northern Territory are placed in an account for the benefit of Indigenous communities. The use of the ABA to facilitate 99-year

---

5   ARC DECRA, 'Regulation and Governance for Indigenous Welfare: Poverty Surveillance and its Alternatives' (DE180100599).

leases of Aboriginal lands back to the federal government in exchange for essential services has met with merited criticism (Altman 2013: 98, Altman 2014: 135–6). Indeed, it could be seen as the federal government unconscionably requiring Indigenous landholders to ransom their land in exchange for essential services available to other citizens without like conditions.

Conclusion

Arguably the cashless welfare card is a new technology of power reinscribing a long-established socio-economic hierarchy with racialised consequences. Yet, Australia needs '[a]n ambitious plan to redress injustice' rather than 'simply managing inequality with the latest tools from economists and technocrats' (Farmer 2005: 244–5). Alternative forms of resource redistribution ought to be explored rather than engaging in expensive intensive surveillance that is central to welfare conditionality. The cashless welfare card consumes scarce resources based upon an unproven assumption that welfare recipients are untrustworthy/deviant subjects who require constant paternalistic oversight. Resource-intensive income management reforms are unlikely to cut long-term costs if that is the government's aim.

There are many questions that remain as to what the cashless welfare card will achieve. Is this Welfare Card yet another example of colonial powers 'co-opting Indigenous Peoples' (Watson 2015: 3) into their regulatory regimes? And, if so, at what price? What other possibilities are not explored if the Welfare Card is presented as the poverty solution? Although the federal government and Forrest assert that the Welfare Card is a modern mechanism to address socio-economic disadvantage, and a Senate Inquiry has recently recommended its expansion (Senate Community Affairs Legislation Committee 2017: 29),[6] the CDC can more credibly be understood as yet another regulatory intervention designed to impose a Eurocentric and neoliberal script. In the East Kimberley, this is reflected in the reframing of the CDC by those forced to use it—they describe it as the 'White Card' due to it being 'imposed by white people' (Klein & Razi 2017: 13).

---

6   With dissenting reports by the Labor Committee members (Senators Lisa Singh and Murray Watt) and the Greens Committee member (Senator Rachel Siewert).

The preliminary work undertaken by the cashless welfare card is considerable. First, by pathologising poverty it rationalises existing economic injustices, what Bourdieu (1998: 98, 62) refers to as 'the *structural violence* of unemployment' and 'the uncontrolled violence of … markets'. Second, it creates a new industry for 'poverty profiteers' (Bielefeld 2017: 31) to mine as other geographically land-based mines face a future of inevitable exhaustion. This is one way of understanding why a mining magnate such as Forrest was chosen by the federal government for the Indigenous jobs and training review and why government has been willing to adopt his recommendation for a welfare system overhaul, despite this recommendation clearly being outside the terms of reference of that review. Third, it forecloses discussion about alternative redistributive possibilities, such as a reparations fund for Australia's First Peoples. However, a reparations framework for Australia's First Peoples funded by the kind of integrity tax outlined in this chapter is preferable to shoring up existing inequality via technological panopticonism, and a new 'politics of distribution' (Ferguson 2015: 10) is arguably long overdue.

Acknowledgements

The author thanks the 'Indigenous Rights, Recognition and the State in the Neoliberal Age' symposium participants for their stimulating and helpful feedback on an earlier draft.

References

ABC Editorial (2016). Blackout causes 'mayhem' in Ceduna as phones, internet and eftpos cut. *ABC News*, 10 September, www.abc.net.au/news/2016-09-10/families-leave-food-in-supermarket-after-eftpos-blackout/7833338.

Aboriginal and Torres Strait Islander Social Justice Commissioner (2016). *Social justice and native title report 2016*, Australian Human Rights Commission, Sydney.

ACOSS (Australian Council of Social Service) (2014a). *Groups call for rejection of Healthy Welfare Card: Joint statement.* 13 December, www.acoss.org.au/media_release/groups_call_for_rejection_of_forrest_review_healthy_welfare_card.

ACOSS (2014b). *Poverty in Australia 2014*, ACOSS, Redfern.

Altman JC (2013). Arguing the Intervention. *Journal of Indigenous Policy* 14:1–151.

Altman JC (2014). Tracking Indigenous policy, 2011–2014. *Journal of Indigenous Policy* 15:1–155.

Altman JC (2017). Modern slavery in remote Australia? *Arena Magazine*, arena.org.au/modern-slavery-in-remote-australia-by-jon-altman/.

Australian Bankers Association (2016). Correspondence by letter from Steven Münchenburg CEO of the Australian Bankers Association to Gerard Brody CEO of the Consumer Action Law Centre, 7 July.

Bentham J (1995). *The Panopticon writings*, Verso, London & New York.

Bielefeld S (2014). Income management and indigenous peoples—nudged into a stronger future? *Griffith Law Review* 23(2):285–317, doi.org/10.1080/103 83441.2014.979421.

Bielefeld S (2014/2015). Compulsory income management, Indigenous peoples and structural violence—implications for citizenship and autonomy. *Australian Indigenous Law Review* 18(1):99–118.

Bielefeld S (2017). Cashless welfare cards: Controlling spending patterns to what end? *Indigenous Law Bulletin* 8(29):28–32.

Bourdieu P (1998). *Acts of resistance—against the tyranny of the market*, The New Press, New York.

Bray J, Gray M, Hand K & Katz I (2014). *Evaluating new income management in the Northern Territory: The final report*, Social Policy Research Centre UNSW, Sydney.

Brown W (2015). *Undoing the demos: Neoliberalism's stealth revolution*, Zone Books, New York.

Cahill D (2014). *The end of laissez-faire? On the durability of embedded neoliberalism*, Edward Elgar Publishing, Gloucestershire & Massachusetts.

Ceduna Anti Card Group (2016), email correspondence from group member to the Keep Income Management Accountable Network, 7 May.

Commonwealth of Australia (2015). Parliamentary Debates, House of Representatives, 19 August (Alan Tudge, Parliamentary Secretary to the Prime Minister).

Community Affairs Legislation Committee (2016). Senate Estimates, 20 October (Skye Kakoschke-Moore, Senator for South Australia).

Conifer D (2017). Centrelink cashless welfare card trial costing taxpayers $10,000 per participant, *ABC Radio*, 2 May, www.abc.net.au/news/2017-05-02/cashless-welfare-trial-costing-taxpayers-$10k-per-participant/8488268.

Coulthard GS (2014). *Red skins, white masks: Rejecting the colonial politics of recognition*, University of Minnesota Press, Minnesota & London, doi.org/10.5749/minnesota/9780816679645.001.0001.

Davey M (2017). 'Ration days again': Cashless welfare card ignites shame, *Guardian*, 9 January, www.theguardian.com/australia-news/2017/jan/09/ration-days-again-cashless-welfare-card-ignites-shame.

DSS (Department of Social Services) (2014). *A new system for better employment and social outcomes—Interim report of the reference group on welfare reform to the minister for social services*, Commonwealth of Australia, Canberra.

DSS (2016). *Cashless debit card trial—Overview*, DSS, Canberra, www.dss.gov.au/families-and-children/programmes-services/welfare-conditionality/cashless-debit-card-trial-overview.

DSS (2017a). *Cashless debit card trial evaluation: Final evaluation report*, Orima Research, Canberra.

DSS (2017b). *Income management and cashless debit card summary (25 August 2017)*, DSS, Canberra, www.data.gov.au/dataset/income-management-summary-data/resource/b898777c-8a2b-4094-b378-cdb48346a110.

Explanatory Memorandum (2015). *Social Security Legislation Amendment (Debit Card Trial) Bill 2015 (Cth)*, parlinfo.aph.gov.au/parlInfo/download/legislation/ems/r5520_ems_91404ffb-3b40-4be1-a67e-2c5f2e6a1eeb/upload_pdf/503546.pdf.

Farmer P (2005). *Pathologies of power: Health, human rights and the new war on the poor*, University of California Press, Berkeley, Los Angeles & London.

Fedorowytsch T & Iggulden T (2016). Malcolm Turnbull praises cashless welfare card trial on Ceduna visit. *ABC News,* 31 October, www.abc.net.au/news/2016-10-30/malcolm-turnbull-praises-cashless-welfare-card-trial-in-ceduna/7978758.

Ferguson J (2015). *Give a man a fish: Reflections on the new politics of distribution*, Duke University Press, Durham & London, doi.org/10.1215/9780822375524.

Forrest A (2014). *Forrest review: Creating parity*. Report to the Commonwealth of Australia, Canberra.

Foucault M (2008). *The birth of biopolitics: Lectures at the College De France 1978–1979*, Palgrave Macmillan, New York.

Fowkes L & Sanders W (2016). *Financial penalties under the Remote Jobs and Communities Program*. Working Paper No. 108, Centre for Aboriginal Economic Policy Research, The Australian National University, Canberra.

Fraser N (2013). *Fortunes of feminism: From state-managed capitalism to neoliberal crisis*, Verso, London.

Gage N (2016). Ceduna's cashless welfare card a 'massive inconvenience', but council sees improvements. *ABC News*, 12 September, www.abc.net.au/news/2016-09-12/ceduna-cashless-welfare-card-'massive-inconvenience'/7836942.

Gooda M (2015). Cashless welfare card opens old wounds for Indigenous Australians. *The Drum, ABC News*, 16 October, www.abc.net.au/news/2015-10-16/gooda-healthy-welfare-card-opens-old-wounds-for-indigenous/6859588.

Howard-Wagner D & Kelly B (2011). Containing Aboriginal mobility in the Northern Territory: From 'protectionism' to 'interventionism'. *Law Text Culture* 15:102–34.

Hunt J (2017). *The cashless debit card evaluation: Does it really prove success?* Topical Issue 2/2017, Centre for Aboriginal Economic Policy Research, The Australian National University, Canberra.

Klein E & Razi S (2017). *The cashless debit card trial in the East Kimberley.* Working Paper No. 121, Centre for Aboriginal Economic Policy Research, The Australian National University, Canberra.

Lovell M (2014). Languages of neoliberal critique: The production of coercive government in the Northern Territory intervention. In Uhr J and Walter R (eds), *Studies in Australian political rhetoric*, ANU Press, Canberra, doi.org/10.22459/SAPR.09.2014.11.

Marmot M (2015). *Status syndrome: How your place on the social gradient directly affects your health*, Bloomsbury, London, Oxford, New York, New Delhi & Sydney.

Marshall V (2017). *Overturning aqua nullius: Securing Aboriginal water rights*, Aboriginal Studies Press, Canberra.

MG Corporation (2017). *Submission No 6 to the Senate Standing Committee on Community Affairs, Social Services Legislation Amendment (Cashless Debit Card) Bill 2017*, October.

Moreton-Robinson A (2009). Imagining the good Indigenous citizen: Race war and the pathology of patriarchal White sovereignty. *Cultural Studies Review* 15(2):61–79, doi.org/10.5130/csr.v15i2.2038.

Parliamentary Joint Committee on Human Rights (2015). *Human rights scrutiny report: Twenty-seventh report of the 44th parliament*, 8 September, Canberra.

Peck J (2012). *Constructions of neoliberal reason*, Oxford University Press, Oxford.

Said E (1994). *Culture and imperialism*, Vintage Books, New York.

Senate Community Affairs Legislation Committee (2017). *Social Services Legislation Amendment (Cashless Debit Card) Bill 2017*. Commonwealth of Australia, Canberra.

Strakosch E (2015). *Neoliberal Indigenous policy: Settler colonialism and the 'post-welfare' state*, Palgrave Macmillan, Hampshire, doi.org/10.1057/9781137405418.

Tennant D (2015). Is the cashless welfare card the forerunner to a banking underclass? *Pro Bono Australia*, 29 October, www.probonoaustralia.com.au/news/2015/10/cashless-welfare-card-forerunner-banking-underclass.

Tudge A (2016). Correspondence by letter to Simon Schrapel, 6 May.

Walter, M (2009). An economy of poverty? Power and the domain of Aboriginality. *International Journal of Critical Indigenous Studies* 2.

Watson I (2015). *Aboriginal peoples, colonialism and international law: Raw law*, Routledge, Abingdon & New York.

Watson V (2009). From the 'quiet revolution' to 'crisis' in Australian Indigenous affairs. *Cultural Studies Review*, 15(1):88–109, doi.org/10.5130/csr.v15i1.2055.

9

Ideology vs context in the neoliberal state's management of remote Indigenous housing reform

Daphne Habibis

Introduction

Reforms to the delivery of housing services to remote Aboriginal communities in Australia have resulted in radical changes to housing management. Commencing in 2008, the National Partnership Agreement on Remote Aboriginal Housing (NPARIH) was a 10-year, AU$5.5-billion housing management and capital works program of new housing, and refurbishment of existing housing, in remote Indigenous communities. As well as increasing the quality and quantity of housing stock, the reforms included the transfer of housing from Indigenous Community Housing Organisations (ICHOs) to state and territory governments, with the goal of improving the standard of housing and housing maintenance by bringing tenancy management up to public housing standards (COAG 2008).

Drawing on Sanders' (2009) framework for analysing policy principles in Australian Indigenous affairs, this chapter argues that as the process of implementing NPARIH rolled out, remote housing delivery became a site in which competing policy principles of guardianship, equality and choice were played out. Equality was evident in NPARIH's goal of normalising remote Aboriginal communities so that housing standards are comparable to those that apply in other regions of Australia. There were also elements of adaptation that resulted in some principles of choice and recognition. But these tendencies were accompanied by coercive measures that reflect policy principles of guardianship: first, in their requirement for Aboriginal people to give up some of their land rights by agreeing to government leases over their land; and second, in the emphasis on individual behavioural change and self-responsibility in meeting the same tenancy obligations as apply in mainstream public housing.

The analysis concludes that, despite evidence that an adaptive approach that recognises Aboriginal lifeworlds works best in Aboriginal service delivery, the normalising imperatives of the neoliberal state overwhelmingly support the continuation of the colonising project and the transformation of remote Aboriginal Australia along white 'settler' lines. As argued by others in this volume (Eatock, Chapter 3, Sanders, Chapter 6, Howard-Wagner, Chapter 12), this shows that although neoliberal governance may allow some lacunas of difference, it is fundamentally aligned with the overarching, enduring and continuing project of colonisation.

Policy tensions within Aboriginal affairs

Sanders' account of the history of Australian Indigenous affairs argues it involves a triangular relationship between three policy principles of equality, guardianship and self-determination. These compete for dominance, and although one principle may be dominant for decades, it always exists in tension with the other two (Sanders 2009). Equality forms the top apex of the schema, with equality of opportunity the most dominant form, although both socio-economic and legal equality are significant. Sitting on the bottom right corner of the triangle is the principle of guardianship. This operates when 'governments believe that particular people within their jurisdictions are not competent judges of their own best interests' (2009: 8). This involves top-down, paternalistic policies that may include elements of coercion. At the bottom left corner is the principle of choice, in which there is an emphasis on difference and diversity, individual and collective agency and forms of self-determination. Each of these principles contains problematic elements. Equality tends to deny the significance of difference and diversity, guardianship operates with a negative understanding of difference and ignores the significance of freedom and choice, while choice may lead to white exploitation of Aboriginal people or negative constructions of Aboriginal agency (ibid.).

Looked at through the lens of neoliberalism, these three principles can be understood in terms of neoliberal goals to eradicate difference through the assimilation and normalisation of communities (equality), to reduce dependence on the state through the regulation of the poor via paternalistic and disciplinary measures (guardianship), and to encourage the creation of self-determining citizens who are empowered to operate as free agents within the market (choice).

Sanders shows that although these principles are partly aligned to the political positions of left and right, they cannot be reduced to these, with both political perspectives embracing elements of these principles, depending on whether industrial society is viewed with enthusiasm or scepticism. Further, although the dominance of particular policy principles map broadly onto the major Indigenous public policy eras of protection, assimilation and self-determination, at any one time, all three principles are in play.

This framework provides a helpful schema for understanding the trajectory of remote Indigenous housing policy, and is used in this chapter to argue that, since 2007, equality and guardianship have been the prevailing policy principles operating in remote Indigenous housing, with equality understood in individualistic terms as equality of opportunity. However, their dominance has not entirely silenced the principle of choice, with jurisdictions applying some adaptive measures that recognise the collective principles that underpin Aboriginal lifeworlds and their embedded and enduring nature.

Methods

The data for this analysis comes from two Australian Housing and Urban Research Institute–funded investigations into NPARIH undertaken between 2013 and 2015. The first investigated how these reforms were progressing, what forms the new arrangements were taking and what factors influenced these decisions (Habibis et al. 2014); the second examined how well the new arrangements were working (Habibis et al. 2016).

The study used a mixed-methods approach, involving five case studies undertaken at Ngukkur in the Northern Territory; Mimili, Amata and Pipalyatjara, in the Anangu Pitjantjatjara Yankunytjatjara (APY) Lands of South Australia; Bayulu and Yakanarra in the Fitzroy Valley in Western Australia and at communities in and around Kununurra in Western Australia; and at Wujal Wujal and Hope Vale in the Cooktown region of Queensland (see Figure 9.1).

Across the case studies, a total of 144 tenant surveys, 138 tenant interviews, 37 housing provider interviews and 34 stakeholder interviews were undertaken (see Table 9.1).

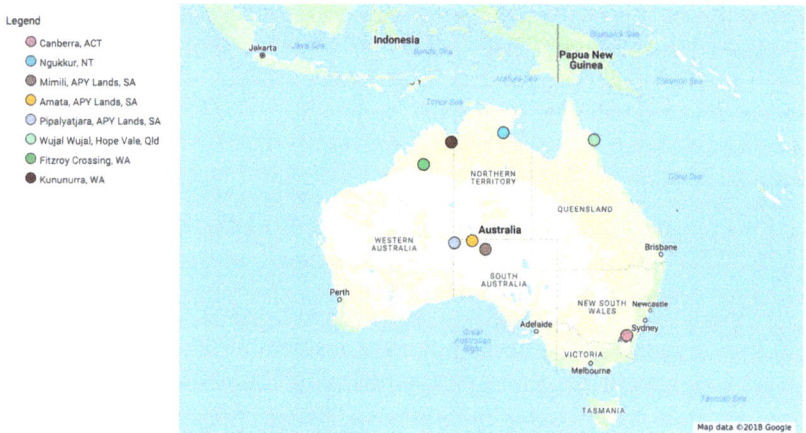

Figure 9.1: Remote tenancies case study communities
Source: Author's extrapolation of data from Google Maps.

The data collection period for each case study site was three weeks, undertaken in blocks of one to two weeks in 2014.

Policy principles in the evolution of Australia's remote Indigenous housing programs

NPARIH can be understood as the culmination of a shift in Aboriginal housing policy that commenced in the 1990s in which principles of choice and self-determination were replaced by those of equality and guardianship. From this time, in urban settings, state-owned and managed Indigenous housing was increasingly integrated into mainstream public housing programs (see Milligan et al. 2016: 76–8). But, in remote communities,

Indigenous housing remained under the control of ICHOs, which had first emerged in the late 1960s under policies of self-determination. These Aboriginal-controlled organisations were funded by the Community Housing Infrastructure Program (CHIP), which was managed by the Aboriginal and Torres Strait Islander Commission (ATSIC). Following the dismantling of ATSIC in 2004, responsibility for CHIP was transferred to the Australian Government Department of Families, Housing, Community Services and Indigenous Affairs (FaHCSIA). In 2007, an Australian Government–initiated review of CHIP found that the program was failing to provide adequate housing for remote-living Indigenous people and recommended its abolition and replacement with a program managed by state housing authorities (FaHCSIA 2007). This coincided with the Northern Territory Emergency Response (NTER), in which media and public policy constructed remote Aboriginal communities as universally chaotic and dysfunctional, and in need of government regulation and control (Proudfoot & Habibis 2015). This justified the introduction of a guardianship approach to housing management on remote Aboriginal communities in the Northern Territory, including the transfer of remote Aboriginal housing management from the ICHO sector to Territory Housing and the imposition of compulsory 99-year leases over prescribed Northern Territory communities.

Table 9.1: Case study field visits: Respondent numbers

Respondents		N
All		
Tenants	Survey	144
	Interview	138
Housing provider	Interview	37
Stakeholders	Interview	34
Ngukkur, Northern Territory		
Tenants	Survey	30
	Interview	29
Housing provider	Interview	6
Stakeholders	Interview	8
Cooktown region, Queensland		
Tenants	Survey	30
	Interview	23
Housing provider	Interview	5
Stakeholders	Interview	7

Respondents		N
APY Lands, South Australia		
Tenants	Survey	29
	Interview	28
Housing provider	Interview	9
Stakeholders	Interview	4
Fitzroy Valley, Western Australia		
Tenants	Survey	29
	Interview	33
Housing provider	Interview	11
Stakeholders	Interview	12
Kununurra and surrounds, Western Australia		
Tenants	Survey	26
	Interview	25
Housing provider	Interview	6
Stakeholders	Interview	3

Source: Habibis et al. (2014, 2016).

Some of the authoritarian elements of the NTER were included in NPARIH when it was introduced to all states and the Northern Territory the following year. Government investment in housing infrastructure was only available if the owners of Aboriginal land agreed to lease their land to the states and the Northern Territory, while tenants were required to meet behavioural requirements through regularised tenancy agreements that included paying rent at public housing settings, maintaining their homes to public housing standards and meeting obligations for good behaviour.

There were also elements of equality within NPARIH because of its concern to improve living standards for remote-living Aboriginal people by bringing a systemic approach to remote tenancy and property management and to establish a uniformity of housing standards across remote communities that were the same as those that applied in other parts of Australia (COAG 2008). Under ICHO management, few tenants were protected by *Residential Tenancies Act* (RTA) legislation. Inadequate resources and structural problems relating to the small size of most ICHOs, as well as a lack of housing management skills within the sector, had meant many tenants had paid little or no rent, reducing already inadequate funding for housing maintenance. Consequently, this was often minimal (Eringa et al. 2009). NPARIH addressed this by requiring state housing agencies to ensure compliance with RTA legislation, to introduce effective repairs and maintenance regimes and to apply rent payment regimes in line with those in public housing.

This imposition of a public housing model on remote Aboriginal communities reflects the neoliberal state's modernising imperative and its emphasis on the normalisation of cultural and geographic difference. With important exceptions, there was little attempt to adapt this model to the kin-based nature of remote Aboriginal communities, and the collective norms that underpin daily life. Despite its being developed in vastly different urban contexts, most state and territory housing managers assumed that NPARIH should be implemented as a centralised, one-size-fits-all program, little different from mainstream public housing program and policy settings. This was in tension with elements of the National Partnership Agreements that supported a degree of choice and self-determination, and was also impractical and inefficient when it came to implementation.

Ideology vs context in the implementation of NPARIH

NPARIH was a top-down policy intervention, developed in Canberra with minimal consultation with Aboriginal people, including those it directly affected. It contributed substantially to the decline of the ICHO sector, with the number of organisations falling nationally from 496 in 2006 to 330 in 2012 (Habibis et al. 2016: 20), weakening one of the main avenues for Aboriginal choice and self-determination. From the perspective of governance theory, this willingness to deny Aboriginal agency can be understood as deriving from the view that Aboriginal people, being outside the market economy, are therefore in need of pedagogical discipline (see also Altman & Hinkson 2007, Ford & Rowse 2012, Howard-Wagner 2012, Strakosch 2015). While authoritarian and coercive measures are not necessary for those subject to the normalising impact of the labour market, this is not the case for those who stand outside it. Instead, such citizens may be subject to special measures to encourage greater autonomy and self-regulation, and a reduction in dependence on the state (Helliwell & Hindess 2002).

The changes expected of tenants under the regulatory regimes of government housing agencies were considerable. Under ICHO management, most tenants had paid little or no rent, maintenance regimes were minimal or non-existent, property damage was not penalised, and because housing was usually on Aboriginal land, the distinction between ownership and renting was blurred. Housing decisions, such as allocations and transfers, were mostly undertaken locally, through informal consultation with family and community. This was vastly different from the formal, centralised policy practices of government housing agencies.

But if NPARIH represented a radical change for Aboriginal people, it was also challenging for the states and the Northern Territory, where it was imposed by the Australian Government in a rapid policy shift. In the Northern Territory, the government housing agency's housing portfolio doubled, virtually overnight, from 5,000 to 10,000, with many remote community properties in a deteriorated condition (Habibis et al. 2016). Within state and territory housing agencies, the skills and capacity to manage Aboriginal housing was limited, as these had been largely lost following the mainstreaming of Aboriginal housing that had occurred in the urban sector over the previous two decades.

These difficulties were compounded by the conditions of housing delivery in remote communities (Memmott et al. 2003, Milligan et al. 2011, Habibis 2013, Habibis et al. 2014). In most remote Aboriginal communities, there is no housing market, so constructs such as 'market rent' and 'housing market' do not apply. The collective nature of Indigenous land tenure meant that, in most locations, residential tenancy legislation had to be altered before it could apply, and native title considerations and limited or non-existent service infrastructure restricted where buildings could be located.

The delivery of housing services is also impacted by distance, the absence of a skilled workforce, poor transport structure and the often harsh terrain and weather conditions, making everything more costly. Communities are often located many kilometres from service centres, with unsealed roads that are dangerous and difficult to travel. This creates occupational health and safety and practical challenges, impacts on staff time and makes it difficult to establish local offices and to recruit, oversee and support community-based staff. Limited mobile and internet coverage make establishing effective communication systems difficult. Repairs and maintenance are constrained by a low rent base, extreme weather events and expensive contractor services. Travel times can rapidly blow-out a community's repairs and maintenance budget and distances make accurate scoping of jobs and monitoring and regulation of suppliers challenging.

Remote Indigenous populations are also very different from urban populations. Communities are mostly comprised of extended families and other kin, households are large and comprised of multi-family households. This, together with a shortage of housing, creates high levels of crowding, which generates costly repairs and maintenance needs. Frequent population movement between houses and communities makes identifying occupants and collecting rent difficult. Residents of communities often have low skills and educational achievement, high levels of disability, and language and cultural differences.

Given these differences, it is hard to understand why most states and the Northern Territory provided their services through a model designed for white, urban populations that was poorly aligned with the population needs and the conditions that operated in remote communities. Explanations include a politicised context following the controversy that surrounded the NTER and the failures of the capital works program that followed it (the Strategic Indigenous Housing Infrastructure Program). This generated federal government pressure on the states to rush policy implementation, so there was little time to develop innovative policies that were appropriately calibrated to the conditions. In some states, there was a strong ideological commitment to mainstreamed service delivery as more cost-effective and efficient, as well as an assumption within many of the states and the Northern Territory that, following the experience with CHIP, services should be provided directly (Habibis et al. 2014). It was also the case that, in some locations, there was no alternative organisation with the skills and capacity to provide housing services.

In South Australia, the Northern Territory and Queensland, service delivery was largely centralised with little adjustment to local conditions. For example, in Queensland, despite language differences, and most houses not having a street address, tenants notified repairs and maintenance requirements via a blue phone connected to the public housing state-wide call centre. In all locations, despite the high cost of living in remote communities, and the high level of poverty, rent settings were designed to gradually increase until they were the same as applied in urban settings.

But within these predominantly mainstreamed models of housing service delivery, there were some elements of choice and recognition. NPARIH policy required leases to be voluntary and for community consultation to occur. South Australia's rent model was initially in line with the 'chuck-in' system that had prevailed under ICHO management (Eringa et al. 2009), with per capita rents applied to all adult tenants. Eligibility for housing was also treated as a largely community matter, with criteria related to kin and language. For this reason, there were no caps on income eligibility (Habibis et al. 2014: 40–1). In the Northern Territory, some Indigenous organisations, as well as shire councils, were used for some aspects of tenancy management in some regional centres and town camps. Similarly, in Queensland, the Department of Housing contracted some Indigenous shire councils to deliver some housing services. The jurisdiction where choice and recognition were most evident was Western Australia, where there were six regions in which the housing department established a hybrid service delivery arrangement, in which five ICHOs and a community housing provider were contracted to manage housing. It also developed a consultation strategy involving clear protocols that ensured investment and engagement by both parties and inclusion of community priorities.

How well did NPARIH work?

What do the findings suggest about how well these arrangements worked? Overall, they show that NPARIH went a considerable way in establishing public housing–like standards in some remote Indigenous communities, and there were improvements in the lives of tenants where NPARIH investments took place (see Habibis et al. 2016: 44–98 for a detailed presentation of the findings). Most tenants who participated in our study agreed that housing and living conditions had improved and that overall things in the community were better. Respondents understood key aspects of their tenancy agreement and were keen to maintain their new and refurbished homes in good condition. But there were many areas that required improvement, including allocations, tenant support programs, tenants' understanding of their rights and timely information about rent arrears. Crowding remained high in many locations, especially the Northern Territory and South Australia. There were problems of fairness and efficiency in the application of mainstream rent settings, and centralised repairs and maintenance systems were slow and inefficient. Many small communities outside of NPARIH arrangements faced an uncertain future, with no commitment from the states or the Commonwealth to the provision of housing and essential services.

When it came to the question of satisfaction with housing management, overall the response was positive. Figure 9.2 presents survey rating averages for some of these items and shows that among those surveyed, levels of satisfaction were generally quite high (5 equals very satisfied; 3 equals neither satisfied nor unsatisfied; 1 equals very unsatisfied), especially in relation to how rent was collected, the quickness of repairs and treatment by housing officers. Satisfaction was lowest in relation to wait times for repairs and maintenance, provision of information about rent payments and the way housing officers responded to complaints.

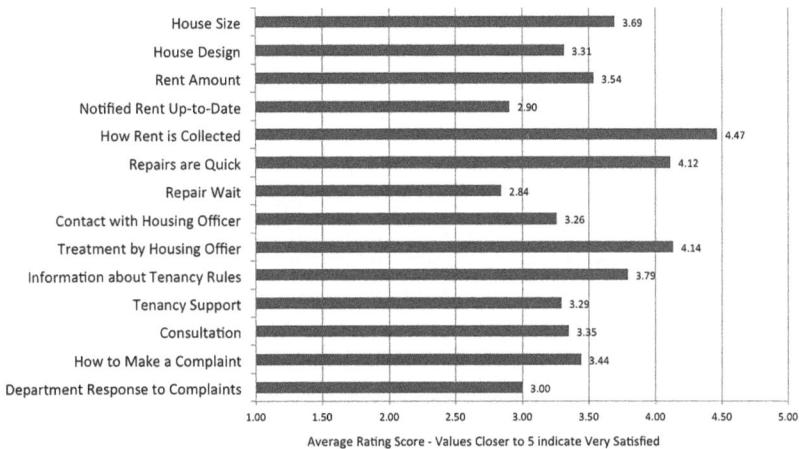

Figure 9.2: Satisfaction with housing and housing management – All jurisdictions
Source: Habibis et al. (2014, 2016).

However, analysis by case study location shows substantial differences between jurisdictions in areas including house size and house design, ease of arranging repairs, repair wait times, frequency of contact with housing officers and levels of consultation (see Table 9.2). Satisfaction levels are highest for the Western Australia sites of Fitzroy Crossing and Kununurra and surrounds. This is also the case for views on whether the condition of houses in the community had improved where these two case study sites showed the strongest positive response (Figure 9.3). Across all the data sources, there is a consistent pattern that these locations are operating with the greatest levels of community acceptance and perceptions of service quality. While there is insufficient space to provide the detail here, our cost analysis also shows there are significant savings to be made if services can be locally provided (Habibis et al. 2016: 94–7). These findings support other Aboriginal housing research (Milligan et al. 2011, Moran et al. 2016) that housing services to Aboriginal people work best when they are adapted to local contexts, delivered by Aboriginal people and provide strong mechanisms for communication and consultation with tenants and communities.

These findings are based on single case studies, and are influenced by many contextual factors, including the quality and quantity of existing housing, the community's prior experiences of housing management and its distance from service centres. The findings from Ngukkur were affected by high levels of tenant occupancy, with logistic regression of the survey findings showing household density influenced levels of satisfaction (Habibis et al. 2016: 87–90). The Western Australian Government also contributed additional funding to NPARIH, allowing a degree of discretionary investment. But the strength and consistency of the findings suggest the local model of service delivery, with high levels of Aboriginal employment, played an important part in explaining differences in case study results. In both Western Australian case study sites, housing services, including repairs and maintenance were delivered through local partners with high numbers of Indigenous employees. At Fitzroy Crossing, the partner was a large, relatively well-resourced ICHO that had been delivering housing services in the pre-NPARIH era whose staff was almost entirely Indigenous. In Kununurra, the partner was Community Housing Limited, which employed local Aboriginal staff who were well regarded and trusted in the communities. The Western Australia Department of Housing took a capacity-building approach to working with its partners, supporting them to develop their IT systems, seconding staff experienced in working with Aboriginal tenants and establishing specialist positions to support compliance.

This approach contrasted with the other case study communities where services were delivered in a largely centralised, non-adaptive way. In Queensland's Cooktown communities, there was no local office; instead, services were provided on a drive-in, drive-out basis, repairs and maintenance were centralised and there was a siloed approach to tenancy, maintenance, procurement and asset management. Little attention was paid to tenant support, education or community engagement. In Ngukkur, levels of local control and employment were low and there was little provision of tenant education and support.

Table 9.2: Comparison of rating averages of satisfaction levels with housing and housing management

Item	NT	Qld	SA	WA-FC	WA-K
House size	3.89	3.32	2.73	4.43	4.15
House design	2.63	3.21	2.82	4.07	4.07
Rent amount	3.35	3.75	3.14	3.80	3.58
How easy arrange repairs	3.63	3.88	3.55	4.54	4.80
Repair wait time	2.07	2.92	2.28	3.26	3.80
How often see housing officer	3.60	3.04	2.55	2.93	3.96
How treated by housing officer	4.03	4.00	3.93	4.22	4.35
Information about tenancy rules	3.42	3.36	3.67	4.31	4.16
Tenancy support	2.96	3.33	3.14	3.73	3.24
How well consulted	2.82	2.53	3.92	3.74	3.63

Source: Habibis et al. (2014, 2016).

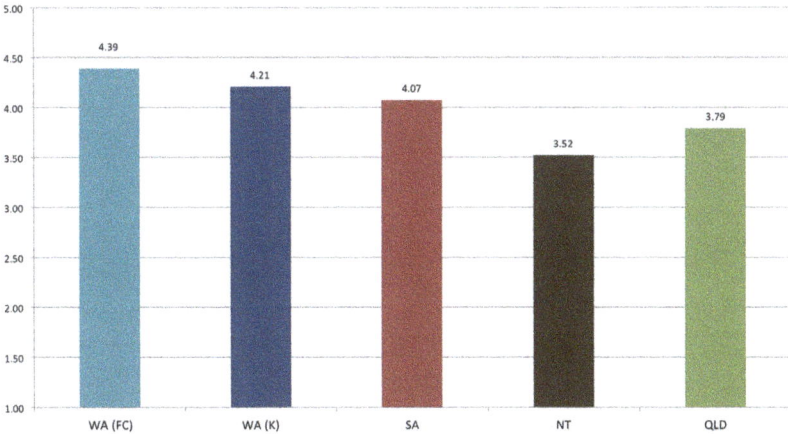

Figure 9.3: Rating averages of improvements in housing conditions
Source: Habibis et al. (2014, 2016).

Beyond NPARIH: Another policy punctuation or the continuation of mainstreaming?

NPARIH amounted to a radical experiment in managing housing on remote Indigenous communities. It was the first time that the states and the Northern Territory had taken on these responsibilities and it took time for services to be established. The early years of the program focused on capital works, and it was only once these were underway that attention shifted to tenancy management (Habibis et al. 2014). As the new systems became established there were changes to some arrangements (see Habibis et al. 2016). The Northern Territory developed a local approach to repairs and maintenance; in Queensland, a new regional housing office was established in the Cooktown region to enable local delivery of services. In Western Australia, the housing agency extended its contract to a mainstream community housing provider to provide housing management services in Kalgoorlie, Halls Creek, Exmouth and the Goldfields. In the Ngaanyatjarra Lands, in response to pressure from the local Aboriginal community, it agreed to a rent model closer to arrangements that had applied under ICHO management.

A return to recognition or continuing colonisation?

This account presents a picture in which the state's goals to normalise remote Aboriginal Australia through policies of guardianship and equality have achieved partial success. In accepting leases over their land—justified in terms of the need to protect the Commonwealth's investment and to ensure the longevity of housing infrastructure (COAG 2008: 5)— Aboriginal people have been required to trade hard-won land rights for improvements in services and living conditions that are routinely provided elsewhere. Tenants have similarly accepted the trade-off of new or refurbished homes in return for acceptance of mainstream tenancy obligations. At the same time, the regularisation of housing on remote Aboriginal communities retains elements of choice and recognition through a degree of consultation, some adaptation to local conditions and some limited Aboriginal control over housing management.

To the extent that policy principles of choice in the sense of Aboriginal self-determination have been present, they are arguably due, not so much to any policy commitment to this goal, but to a pragmatic response to the realities of housing service provision in remote communities, where partnering with knowledgeable third-party providers makes sound economic and strategic sense, especially when it includes employment of local Aboriginal people. It is also important to acknowledge Aboriginal resistance to the efforts of the state to normalise remote communities along white settler lines. This can be seen in the survey findings that show lower levels of satisfaction with mainstreamed service delivery and an overwhelming preference for housing services to be delivered by community organisations, especially those operated by Aboriginal people (see Habibis et al. 2016: 90–4). Resistance is apparent in the protests to the closure of smaller communities (Howitt & McLean 2015) and in continuing efforts by Aboriginal organisations to control their own housing services (APONT 2015). In the Northern Territory, Aboriginal pressure has resulted in some commitment to maintain smaller communities, albeit with strict guidelines and funding limits (NT Government 2017), and there are some moves to explore innovative models of housing delivery. It is too early to say what this will deliver, but the history of Aboriginal–state relations in the Northern Territory suggest Aboriginal people's distrust of government bureaucracy, their preference for services to be delivered by Aboriginal people and Aboriginal organisations, and their determination to remain on country, will remain a potent force.

This analysis reveals the capacity of neoliberalism to tolerate small spaces of contestation within a larger trajectory towards the denial of difference and diversity. The overwhelming policy push is for the normalisation of Aboriginal communities as part of the incorporation of Aboriginal people into market society (Howard-Wagner 2012: 5). This is evident in continuing pressure on smaller communities and the concentration of funding in regional communities. The National Partnership on Remote Housing that replaced NPARIH encourages greater mobility of remote residents to better labour markets, increases requirements to enforce mainstream tenancy obligations and recommends the reform of land tenure to allow commercial investment and home ownership (COAG 2016). There is also little to suggest any broad change to the application of mainstream rent settings or substantial moves towards local management and delivery of repairs and maintenance.

Sanders' chapter in this volume points to the importance of retaining the concept of colonisation because of its significance for Indigenous recognition (Sanders this volume, Chapter 6) and elsewhere, Spiers Williams writes of the way neoliberalism complements the objectives of colonialism, boosting its continued trajectory of colonisation (2016: 14). This analysis of reforms to housing in remote Aboriginal Australia supports these arguments, demonstrating that, despite some limited contrary trends towards recognition and self-determination, the overarching trajectory is towards the assimilation of the Indigene whose identity is incompatible with the demands and expectations of the Australian neoliberal state.

The findings from our study point to the perversities inherent within this agenda. These suggest the most effective and financially efficient arrangement for the delivery of remote Indigenous housing is not one that is standardised and centrally driven, but rather one that supports local economies and communities and that acknowledges rather than eradicates difference. Effective housing in remote Indigenous communities requires adaptive policies that recognise and respect Aboriginal culture and that manage housing through partnerships between governments and local providers. Unfortunately, there is little to suggest the Australian state is listening to the evidence base. The future direction of housing policy to remote Indigenous communities is likely to follow the national direction, in which the influence of new public management is resulting in governments divesting their role in social housing supply and management by increasing the role of the community sector (Pawson et al. 2015). In remote Indigenous housing policy there is no indication that increasing the role of the community sector will include any emphasis on building the ICHO sector, despite the considerable efforts of Aboriginal people to push for more consultation and control. This does not bode well for the future of housing on remote Aboriginal communities, and increases the likelihood that within a decade or so, with the divestment of the state, we will once again witness a housing crisis in remote Aboriginal Australia, at considerable cost to the people who live there.

References

Altman J & Hinkson M (eds) (2007). *Coercive reconciliation: Stabilise, normalise, exit Aboriginal Australia*, Arena Publications, Melbourne.

APONT (Aboriginal Peak Organisations of the Northern Territory) (2015). Aboriginal Remote Housing Forum, 12–13 March, Darwin, www.amsant. org.au/apont/wp-content/uploads/2015/02/APONT-Housing-Forum-12-13-March-2015-Report_LOW_RES.pdf.

COAG (Council of Australian Governments) (2008). *National Indigenous Reform Agreement (Closing the Gap)*, www.federalfinancialrelations.gov.au/content/npa/health/_archive/indigenous-reform/national-agreement_sept_12.pdf.

COAG (2016). *National partnership on remote housing*, Council on Federal Financial Relations, www.federalfinancialrelations.gov.au/content/npa/housing.aspx.

Eringa K, Spring F, Anda M, Memmott P, Long S & West M (2009). *Scoping the capacity of Indigenous community organisations*. AHURI Final Report No. 125, Australian Housing and Urban Research Institute, www.ahuri.edu. au/research/final-reports/125.

FaHCSIA (Families, Housing, Community Services and Indigenous Affairs) (2007). *Living in the sunburnt country—Indigenous housing: Findings of the review of the Community Housing and Infrastructure Programme*, report prepared by PricewaterhouseCoopers, Department of Families, Community Services and Indigenous Affairs, www.dss.gov.au/sites/default/files/ documents/05_2012/livingsunburntcountry.pdf.

Ford L & Rowse T (2012). *Between settler and Indigenous governance*, Routledge, London.

Habibis D (2013). Australian housing policy, misrecognition and Indigenous population mobility. *Housing Studies* 28(5):764–81, doi.org/10.1080/0267 3037.2013.759545.

Habibis D, Phillips R, Phibbs P & Verdouw J (2014). *Progressing tenancy management reform on remote Indigenous communities*, AHURI Final Report No. 223, Australian Housing and Urban Research Institute, Melbourne, www.ahuri.edu.au/research/final-reports/223.

Habibis D, Phillips R, Spinney A, Phibbs P & Churchill B (2016). *Identifying effective arrangements for tenancy management service delivery on remote Indigenous communities*, AHURI Final Report No. 271, Australian Housing and Urban Research Institute, Melbourne, www.ahuri.edu.au/research/final- reports/271.

Helliwell C & Hindess B (2002). The empire of uniformity and the government of subject peoples. *Cultural Values* 6(1–2):139–42, doi.org/10.1080/ 1362517022019784.

Howard-Wagner D (2012). Using theory to 'speak back' to neoliberal performativity: The Northern Territory Intervention and the inventing of a neoliberal subject as a case in point. *Theorising Indigenous Sociology: Australian Perspectives* series, University of Sydney, Sydney.

Howitt R & McLean J (2015). Towards closure? Coexistence, remoteness and righteousness in Indigenous policy in Australia. *Australian Geographer* 46(2):137–45, doi.org/10.1080/00049182.2015.1020992.

Memmott P, Long S, Chambers C & Spring F (2003). *Categories of Indigenous 'homeless' people and good practice responses to their needs*, AHURI Final Report No. 49, Australian Housing and Urban Research Institute Limited, Melbourne, www.ahuri.edu.au/research/final-reports/49.

Milligan V, Martin C, Phillips R, Liu E, Pawson H & Spinney A (2016). *Profiling Australia's affordable housing industry*, AHURI Final Report No. 268, Australian Housing and Urban Research Institute, Melbourne, doi.org/ 10.18408/ahuri-7108401.

Milligan V, Phillips R, Easthope H, Lui E & Memmott P (2011). *Urban social housing for Aboriginal people and Torres Strait Islanders: Respecting culture and adapting services*, AHURI Final Report No. 172, Australian Housing and Urban Research Institute Limited, Melbourne, www.ahuri.edu.au/research/ final-reports/172.

Moran M, Memmott P, Nash D, Birdsall-Jones C, Fantin S, Phillips R & Habibis D (2016). *Indigenous lifeworlds, conditionality and housing outcomes*, AHURI Final Report No. 260, Australian Housing and Urban Research Institute, Melbourne, www.ahuri.edu.au/research/final-reports/260.

NT (Northern Territory) Government (2017). *Services to remote communities and homelands,* Department of Housing and Community Development.

Pawson H, Milligan V, Wiesel I & Hulse K (2015). *Public stock transfers to community housing the best option for a sustainable and financially supportable housing system*, AHURI Research and Policy Bulletin No. 184, Australian Housing and Urban Research Institute, Melbourne, www.ahuri.edu.au/ research/research-and-policy-bulletins/184.

Proudfoot F & Habibis D (2015). Separate worlds: A discourse analysis of mainstream and Indigenous populist print media accounts of the Northern Territory emergency response in 2007. *Journal of Sociology* 51(2):170–88, doi.org/10.1177/1440783313482368.

Sanders W (2009). *Ideology, evidence and competing principles in Australian Indigenous affairs: From Brough to Rudd via Pearson and the NTER*, Discussion Paper 289, Centre for Aboriginal Economic and Political Research, The Australian National University, Canberra.

Spiers Williams M (2016). Neoliberalism as 'system upgrade' in Australian colonialism: A story told of two legislative provisions. Paper presented at the Indigenous Rights, Recognition and the State in the Neoliberal Age Conference, The Australian National University, 21–22 November.

Strakosch E (2015). *Neoliberal Indigenous policy: Settler colonialism and the 'post-welfare' state*, Palgrave Macmillan, New York, doi.org/10.1057/ 9781137405418.

10

Fragile positions in the new paternalism: Indigenous community organisations during the 'Advancement' era in Australia

Alexander Page

> We are now witnessing one of the largest scale 'upheavals' of Aboriginal and Torres Strait Islander affairs
>
> —Mick Gooda (2014: 16)

The introduction and continuation of the Indigenous Advancement Strategy (IAS) by the Abbott and Turnbull Coalition governments has reconstructed the Commonwealth's relationship with the Indigenous sector.[1] The IAS brought a dramatic upheaval for Aboriginal and Torres

---

1   The Indigenous sector is the estimated 8–9,000 community-run or community-based organisations (Bauman et al. 2015) that deliver localised, culturally appropriate services and perform advocacy roles with and for many Aboriginal and Torres Strait Islander peoples across the country (Rowse 2012). They form a unique political entity in the Australian polity, following their dramatic growth in the 1970s as a response to a lack of Indigenous-specific service provision by state and federal governments (Rowse 2012: 104–5; Holcombe & Sullivan 2013). Aboriginal community organisations are specific projects made by and for Indigenous peoples that speak back to top-down government policymaking through their democratic voluntary association models that practice various forms of grassroots decision-making. Importantly though, the conceptualisation of an Indigenous sector is at best an 'ideal type' (Weber 1949: 90–1). It cannot possibly capture the myriad variety in geographical, socio-historical, economic, political and cultural differences in each organisation, let alone in their relations with the various levels of Australian government and the peoples or populations they serve (Walter & Andersen 2013: 19). Instead, it is used here to discuss the racialised construction of these organisations by the Australian Government for which policy is then administered.

Strait Islander community organisations, with many facing potential closure at the introduction of a new competitive funding application with no consultation prior to implementation. Following recent debate regarding Indigenous constitutional recognition, a change in prime minister and the most recent federal election, there seems to be little discussion of the IAS in the broader Australian polity. However, the continuing need to critique the IAS as currently enacted policy is vital (Altman 2014, Cox 2014, Bond 2015, Dodson 2015, Hudson 2016). This analysis seeks to explain the current set of practices used by the Australian Government in its IAS, and the damaging effects of this policy relative to the right of Indigenous peoples' self-governance in early 21st-century Australia.

This chapter first critically assesses the introduction and rollout of the IAS (2014 to present). Next, by identifying several glaring issues in contemporary Indigenous affairs policymaking through the process, reactions and results of its introduction, a narrative of top-down, undemocratic, racist and unaccountable programming by the Commonwealth is illustrated. Finally, such an approach to Indigenous affairs is recognised as continuing the neoliberal governance mechanisms and audit technologies used by the Commonwealth in Indigenous affairs policy practice from the mid-2000s, following the dissolution of the Aboriginal and Torres Strait Islander Commission (ATSIC) as a pillar in an 'Indigenous order of Australian government' (Sanders 2002: 8, this volume Chapter 6) and a 'shield' from many major changes in Australian public administration (Sullivan 2011: 70, Strakosch 2015: 33). This chapter argues that during the present 'Advancement' era, the Commonwealth has continued its neo-paternalistic (Altman 2007: 13) practice onto Aboriginal community organisations through neoliberal forms of settler colonial micromanagement and domination (Howard-Wagner 2015: 88). This attempted control of Indigenous political capacity through the Commonwealth's allegory of deficiency—including an implicit and mandatory requirement for Indigenous 'Advancement'— prescribes an 'apolitical' logic of economic rationalism as its 'legitimate' and 'natural' remedy (Pusey 1991: 68). The 'Advancement' sought by the Commonwealth is a reproduction of racialised policymaking with strong parallels to the Protectionism era (Howard-Wagner & Kelly 2011: 107–10), which then explicitly reproduces the legitimising racial narratives of the Australian state (Goldberg 2002: 10). This chapter records and explains how this neopaternalistic framework has developed since 2013.

Through an evaluation of the intention of this 'Advancement', the ISA is revealed as a clear example of ongoing domination through 'race in action' (Wolfe 2016: 18) in current Indigenous affairs policy.

The Indigenous Advancement Strategy (2014 to present)

> We will eliminate red tape and streamline programmes to move away from the complex web of overlapping initiatives that have failed to end disadvantage [and legislate] … real action so that indigenous Australians get the services they need.
>
> —Liberal Party of Australia (2013: 43)

The fragile position of the Indigenous sector under the current Australian Government's IAS originated prior to its introduction in 2014. The new Abbott Liberal–National Coalition Government, elected on 18 September 2013, committed to audit and significantly cut federal spending in their first budget (Liberal Party of Australia 2013: 4). The National Commission of Audit (NCA)[2] was engaged to investigate potential government savings that could be accommodated. In their report, *Towards responsible government*, the NCA (2014: 174) reviewed Indigenous-specific programs, services and spending, concluding there were 'too many disparate and fragmented Commonwealth Indigenous programmes [and a] creeping overlap of responsibilities between the Commonwealth and State [governments]'. The NCA (2014: 177) recommended 'consolidation' and 'rationalisation' of Indigenous services from 150 to 'no more than six or seven programs'. In aiming to improve the oversight and strategic coordination of Indigenous Affairs, the NCA pushed for the establishment of a new agency that would report directly to the Australian Department of the Prime Minister and Cabinet (PMC). While mirroring the calls of many recent government reports,[3] the NCA provided no analysis or supporting evidence of its own in its calculations. Furthermore, the repeated use of the word 'likely' in the report regarding savings and service improvement for Indigenous populations that would potentially result from these changes revealed a lack of confidence in

---

2   The NCA was headed by then chairman of the Business Council of Australia, Tony Shepard.

3   See Australian National Audit Office (2012: 19–24), Department of Finance (2011: 12), Productivity Commission (2010: xxvi, 116).

their success (NCA 2014: 172–7). Regardless, the Abbott Government enthusiastically took up the recommendations of the NCA in its first budget wholesale.

Budget 2014–15 (May 2014) introduced a restructuring of the relationship between the Indigenous sector and the Australian Government under the newly announced IAS. Major changes included a AU$534.4 million cut in service delivery funding 'through efficiencies resulting from the rationalisation of Indigenous programmes'. The 150 programs and services previously run by a range of departments were centralised into PMC and the Department of Health. These programs and their new funding applications would now fall into five overarching categories: 'Jobs, Land and the Economy; Children and Schooling; Safety and Wellbeing; Culture and Capability; and Remote Australia Strategies' to 'eliminate waste and duplication' (Australian Government 2014: 185, PMC 2014a: 11–17, 2015: 6–8). In just six months, the Abbott Government had centralised the state–sector funding relationship in a near-complete reversal of the 'whole-of-government' and mainstreaming approach to Indigenous-specific funding and programs introduced by the Howard Coalition Government in 2004–05 (Sullivan 2011: 49). Following the dismantling of ATSIC as a 'central Indigenous affairs agency' since its establishment in 1990, Indigenous-specific programs had been placed into multiple federal government departments in an effort to 'mainstream' services (Sullivan 2011: 50). However, this new centralisation (Janet Hunt, pers. comm, November 2016) under the IAS put Indigenous affairs policy directly at the apex of the Australian Public Service: from eight departments, directly into PMC (Hudson 2016: 8).

With no prior consultation, Aboriginal community organisations across the country had only six weeks to reapply for their funding through a brand-new application system, with little instruction, or face potential closure (Gooda 2014: 28, Oscar 2014, FPARC 2016: 40). This 'new flexible programme structure' (PMC 2014b: 9) aimed to construct a single funding agreement for organisations with the department to reduce extensive bureaucratic overlap and auditing requirements that have burdened the sector for decades (Hudson 2016: 9). The most significant change was the PMC's adoption of 'open competitive grants rounds' (FPARC 2016: 6) for existing service providers. Over the next several months though, many Indigenous communities would actively campaign to maintain their services under this new bureaucratic regime, due to its tumultuous rollout and the Commonwealth's lack of engagement with the pre-existing Indigenous sector.

The fragile position of community organisations: Process, reactions, results

> You can't just say 'oh well, scrap that'. What do we do, take the money back? The IAS is a great step forward … we have picked the best providers
>
> —Nigel Scullion MP, Minister for Indigenous Affairs
> (cited in Morgan 2015)

The ad hoc implementation of the IAS was significantly destabilising for many Indigenous community organisations. The Commonwealth's attempt to 'rationalise' and 'reduce red tape' (Scullion 2014, PMC 2015: 8) faced protest and public disapproval from communities, organisations, and peak bodies during its rollout. The IAS created much confusion and funding chaos in this process by adding new layers of bureaucratic oversight, and centralised control in the Minister for Indigenous Affairs, Nigel Scullion (FPARC 2016: 14). Over time, this control directly increased the possibility of closures for many Indigenous organisations, prompting negative evaluations from organisations who lacked instructions on how to comply with the application to continue funding services deemed vital by communities (Gooda 2014: 20–8, Anderson 2015). One day prior to submitting the application, June Oscar (2014) detailed the process as having 'a distinct absence of Aboriginal inclusion, participation, and local self-determination in devising these outcomes', the IAS being a 'classic case of government policy incoherence that Indigenous people have been dealing with for decades'.

By early 2015, the first IAS funding allocation announcement saw many within the Indigenous sector express disappointment, with government departments, 'universities, churches, and … sporting organisations' receiving the majority of funding (Henderson 2015) rather than local Indigenous organisations who had been delivering their own successful culturally specific programs for many years (Davis 2015, *The Redfern Statement* 2016: 5).[4] Multiple protests outside the minister's office (Everingham 2015) eventually pushed the Commonwealth into reversing

---

4   A total of AU$860 million of funding was allocated to '964 organisations delivering 1,297 projects in 2015' (Scullion 2015). A list of the organisations who received funding approval in 2014 under the IAS, including the program component and value of that agreement is available (see PMC 2014c). A list of individual grants approved in financial years 2014–15 and 2015–16 is also available (see PMC 2016a).

some of the proposed cuts to funding, such as to Aboriginal legal services (Murphy-Oates 2016). At present though, the majority of funding is yet to be restored (Russell 2016: 4).

Public anger regarding funding cuts and application process confusion resulted in an inquiry by the Senate Finance and Public Administration References Committee (FPARC 2016). The inquiry highlighted substantial problems and consequences of the IAS, finding that no consultation was undertaken with organisations regarding the changes, resulting in the many 'non-compliant' IAS applications. All contracts were extended for six months as a result (FPARC 2016: 9, 14–15, 36–40, Scullion 2014). The 'quick transition' also created significant 'uncertainty in the sector', with many smaller organisations closing due to staffing difficulty and lacking the considerable resources required to fill in the extensive application form (FPARC 2016: 45). Even as applications were filled, the five aforementioned funding streams were unable to account for complex social issues and programs for some organisations (FPARC 2016: 18–19). If organisations received over AU$500,000 in funding, they were also now required to incorporate under the *Corporations (Aboriginal and Torres Strait Islander) Act 2006* (Cwth), thus increasing their reporting requirements unless demonstrating they were 'well-governed' and 'high-performing' (Bond 2015, PMC 2015: 19). Finally, the competitive tender model also disadvantaged already administratively overburdened local organisations, now competing with each other for contractual funding from a reduced funding pool (FPARC 2016: 21–3).

In creating this new 'rationalised' process the now central PMC improvised to ensure the delivery of vital services of many organisations. Personal phone calls to and from the minister and organisations were required in some cases to make sure service gaps were filled in this process (PMC 2014a: 9, FPARC 2016: 5–11). Even within PMC, the framework created issues for Indigenous public servants, with Biddle and Lahn (2016: 8) noting that many fell into the 'deeply uncomfortable position as the "messenger of bad news" to Indigenous organisations and communities' on behalf of the Australian Government's IAS.

During the federal election campaign of July 2016, Indigenous Affairs Minister Scullion said nothing about the IAS, maintaining what Langton (2016) called a 'very loud silence' about their 'disastrous new model of funding for the Indigenous Sector'. While the department held public consultation forums in October 2015 (Scullion 2015), resulting in the competitive nature of grants being downplayed, there has been little else done to ameliorate this situation. This is despite dozens of national Indigenous peak bodies calling on the government to reform the IAS through a restoration of funding and a 'greater emphasis on … local Aboriginal and Torres Strait Islander organisations as preferred providers' (Davidson 2016, *The Redfern Statement* 2016: 5). As government ignores voices of the Indigenous sector resisting, negotiating and rejecting this policy, an examination of the underpinning values of the IAS and its restructuring of the state–sector relationship is vital to highlight the ongoing racialised framework of this 'Advancement' era.

The neopaternalism of the 'Advancement' era

> While we are expected to meet every compliance requirement, how do we ensure equal accountability on the part of this government?
>
> —June Oscar (cited in Davis 2015)

After the abolition of ATSIC in 2004–05, the Commonwealth continues to 'Advance' a particular style of governance and policy regime *onto* Aboriginal and Torres Strait Islander populations, whereby neoliberalism and settler colonial paternalism are combined (Howard-Wagner & Kelly 2011, Strakosch 2015: 33–50). The practice of neoliberal settler colonial policymaking, as evidenced by the introduction of the IAS, has two major components I wish to highlight here. First is the vigorous integration of new public management mechanisms into government interaction with Indigenous organisations (Sullivan 2011: 70). This includes a highly strict auditing culture, specific governance rules monitored by overseer and legislation, and control of the direction of programs and services that can be offered through centralised decision-making (Rowse 2012: 121, Holcombe & Sullivan 2013: 499, Adams 2014: 274). Second, ongoing settler colonial policy formation, and the framing of those mechanisms through this lens, means policy is racialised in particular ways for Aboriginal and Torres Strait Islander peoples and Indigenous community organisations (Howard-Wagner & Kelly 2011: 119–20). They are tailored specifically for the Indigenous sector through a deficit narrative, whereby Indigenous peoples are supposedly lacking agency and political capacity (despite the very nature and continued existence of the Indigenous sector), thus requiring significant governmental intervention (Bielefeld 2016: 158, Wolfe 2016). As the existence of the Indigenous sector undermines Commonwealth legitimacy by challenging its attempt to control all policymaking and delivery from the ground up (Page 2015), the IAS continues to erode the political capacity of grassroots community organisations who seek to improve Indigenous wellbeing through democratic, self-determining means.

Such a policy framework manifests itself as neopaternalism, which here denotes policy regimes that are 'imposed without consultation, [as] top-down, racist, non-discretionary, [and] disempowering' (Altman 2007: 13) for Indigenous peoples who are deemed in need of 'intense supervision because they are less inclined to adhere to mainstream behavioural norms' (Bielefeld 2016: 156). The language of paternalism then is a link to previous caustic policy regimes of control, domination and oppression by Australian governments over the last two centuries (Altman 2007, Howard-Wagner & Kelly 2011, Bond 2015). Aboriginal and Torres Strait Islander peoples were excluded, dispersed and then 'protected' by state governments, being forced into missions where they had little control over their own lives and no civil rights, and were denied cultural and social maintenance (Broome 2010: 149–226, Howard-Wagner & Kelly 2011: 107–9). An 'authoritarian paternalism' has been gaining precedence since the abolishment of ATSIC, manifesting explicitly following the Northern Territory Emergency Response of 2007, whereby Indigenous 'dissent [is] repositioned as dysfunction' and an incapacity to comply with a non-negotiable rationalised contract results in further legitimised 'paternalistic intervention' (Strakosch 2015: 162–3). The legislative arithmetic of the largely bipartisan nature of Australian politics, where both major parties largely agree on Indigenous affairs policy, also means there is little accountability for policymakers when implementing these new policy regimes *onto* Indigenous lives (Davis 2015, 2016). Neopaternalism then is able to use and reproduce these racist frameworks in early 21st-century policy, as 'regimes of race' are constructed as ongoing and 'ever-incomplete projects' (Wolfe 2016: 18).

Racialised new public management mechanisms that flow from this neopaternalism take specific shape for the Indigenous sector (Adams 2014: 272–89, Howard-Wagner 2015: 93, Sullivan this volume, Chapter 11). Even as the Indigenous sector fills the gaps of state services and provides alternatives in culturally relevant ways, the Commonwealth's neoliberal settler colonialism disregards this contribution of Indigenous peoples and is unable to understand grassroots, place-specific, 'culturally informed local third-sector organisations' (Sullivan this volume, Chapter 11).

The IAS amplified total financial control, an extensive auditing culture, rigorous bureaucratic oversight and a newly required incorporation into Indigenous-specific legislation, moving back towards economic and political 'guardianship' as seen under the assimilationist and protectionist eras (Sanders 2014: 168). Antithetically, the Commonwealth's IAS makes decisions *for* Indigenous peoples on the 'logic' of a seemingly invisible racialised and 'neutralised' economic rationalism (Pusey 1991: 68), with the minister ultimately facing no accountability to the communities it affects. The Commonwealth has 'picked the best providers' (Scullion, quoted in Morgan 2015) in a way that is anarchic, chaotic and at the minister's personal discretion, while expecting a total assimilation of organisations into strict, non-negotiable regulatory frameworks, all on the government's terms (Anderson 2015: 58, Lea 2008, 2012: 116, Sullivan 2011). When combined with the non-consultative, total 'upheaval' (Gooda 2014: 14) of implementation, this severely damages the ability of Indigenous peoples to govern their own lives via culturally specific organisations (Davis 2015), under the guise of 'benevolent intentions' towards economic development (Bielefeld 2016: 157).

The Australian racial state continues this approach through dual narratives of racial hierarchy, both of which frame indigeneity as deficiency: naturalism, or 'the claim of inherent racial inferiority' of Indigenous peoples, and historicism, whereby Indigenous peoples are in need of 'progression' for their wellbeing (Goldberg 2002: 74). Policy is then made via this framing to maintain the state's own distinct nationalism, which legitimised the paternalistic 'Advancement' of Indigenous people. Through this allegory of deficiency, Indigenous peoples are assumed to have no political capacity, or civil society, in order to maintain the narrative of Australian nationalism and white hegemony and control over policy settings and service delivery mechanisms (McCallum 2011: 609, Strakosch 2015: 67–9). This allows the Commonwealth to continue practising racist strict regulation, governance and economic management of Indigenous peoples' lives under the IAS as 'Advancement' through a veil of economically rational legitimacy (Goldberg 2009: 355–56), while simultaneously facing very little accountability for the damage of this relationship (Sullivan 2009: 62, Howard-Wagner 2015) and in the denial of public servants' own agency in the process (Lea 2008: 18–19). The 'Advancement' era then 'rationalises' this ongoing racialisation process of the Australian state as normal.

The IAS reveals how these actively racialised mechanisms are utilised by 21st-century Australian governments as neoliberal practice positioned as natural, logical and rationalised. Indigenous populations of Australia face the dual impact of this process: the settler state's continuing reproduction of, and exclusion by, white hegemony (Goldberg 2002: 104), and in utilising neoliberal policymaking, becoming 'more robust in its controlling than enabling or caretaking conditions, more intrusive, more repressive [in an] intensification of [the capitalist state's] core features' (Goldberg 2009: 333). Such programs then reproduce a 'long-established socio-economic hierarchy with racialised consequences' (Bielefeld this volume, Chapter 8). For example, funding reliance means it is difficult for Indigenous sector organisations to survive while providing culturally specific services (Adams 2014: 271). The Indigenous sector then continues to negotiate, resist and comply within a policy framework, which demands organisations never-endingly seek an impossible 'earned autonomy' (PMC 2016b: 22) as evidence of their own 'Advancement' in whatever means a largely unaccountable, racist and dominating Australian Government decides.

'Advancement' for whom, to where?

> Make no mistake, Indigenous Affairs is in deep crisis
>
> —Noel Pearson (2016)

With little change to the IAS at the time of writing, and the recent announcement of AU$52.9 million in IAS funding in Budget 2017–18 to create an 'Enhanced Research and Evaluation in Indigenous Affairs' program to evaluate its processes (Haughton 2017), the 'Advancement' era's mechanisms of neoliberal settler colonialism and the dismantling of the rights of Indigenous peoples to self-govern continues. The IAS does little to foster the unique facets of Indigenous civil society, instead damaging Indigenous capacity via new bureaucratic demands that an already overburdened sector must now negotiate. It reproduces a continuing power inequity between government and the Indigenous sector, pushing away opportunities for a trusting and productive relationship of government and the Australian Public Service *with* Aboriginal and Torres Strait Islander peoples and organisations. Instead, the Commonwealth practices neopaternalism for populations it views as incapable of making their own decisions about what governance and service delivery arrangements work best for them (Sullivan 2011).

This paternalism undertaken in the name of 'Advancement' then is purely 'race in action' (Wolfe 2016: 10), reproducing a continuing narrative in Indigenous affairs policy of 'the "good" white [knowing] what is best for the deficient, "dysfunctional" Indigenous "other"' (Howard-Wagner & Kelly 2011: 120) behind a thin veil of 'neutralised' economic rationalism (Pusey 1991: 68). The IAS reveals the Australian Government's power to act unilaterally in attempting to constrain Indigenous political capacity, while Aboriginal and Torres Strait Islander peoples must continue to negotiate this attempted control through community organisations in the pursuit of social justice, in an increasingly precarious position. The allegory of deficiency gives government a 'legitimated' impetus to continue this neopaternalism, resting upon the de-legitimation and continued attempts to exclude and remove Indigenous sovereignty, authority and legitimacy over the past 200 years. The persistence of the Indigenous sector's survival and negotiation contradicts this framing. Despite the sector's success in providing relevant services to Indigenous peoples for over four decades, the Australian Government seems only to be 'listening, but they are not hearing' (Davis 2016: 82). While organisations across the country will continue to actively negotiate with the Commonwealth as a funding provider, the Indigenous sector will become more precarious if there is no change to the responsibilities that govern this relationship. Australian Government mechanisms such as the IAS entrench racial power disparity and do nothing to 'Advance' Aboriginal and Torres Strait Islander peoples' right to self-governance.

References

Adams E (2014). Losing ground? Issues of autonomy in an urban Indigenous organisation. PhD thesis, The Australian National University, Canberra.

Altman JC (2007). *The Howard government's Northern Territory Intervention: Are neo-paternalism and Indigenous development compatible?* Topical Issue Paper 16/2007, Centre for Aboriginal Economic Policy Research, The Australian National University, Canberra.

Altman JC (2014). Abbott's back to the future policy for Aboriginal advancement. *New Matilda*, 17 June, newmatilda.com/2014/06/17/abbotts-back-future-policy-aboriginal-advancement/.

Anderson I (2015). The crisis of Australia's Indigenous policy. *Meanjin* 74(3):54–9.

Australian Government (2014). *Budget 2014–15: Budget measures budget paper no. 2 2014–15*, Commonwealth of Australia, Canberra.

Australian National Audit Office (2012). *Australian government coordination arrangements for Indigenous programs*, Commonwealth of Australia, Canberra.

Bauman T, Smith D, Quiggin R, Keller C & Drieburg L (2015). *Building Aboriginal and Torres Strait Islander governance: Report of a survey and forum to map current and future research and resource needs*, Australian Institute of Aboriginal and Torres Strait Islander Studies, Canberra.

Biddle N & Lahn J (2016). *Understanding Aboriginal and Torres Strait Islander employee decisions to exit the Australian public service*, Working Paper 110, Centre for Aboriginal Economic Policy Research, The Australian National University, Canberra.

Bielefeld S (2016). Neoliberalism and the return of the guardian state: Micromanaging Indigenous peoples in a new chapter of colonial governance. In Sanders W (ed.), *Engaging Indigenous economy: Debating diverse approaches*, ANU Press, Canberra, doi.org/10.22459/CAEPR35.04.2016.12.

Bond C (2015). Nothing new in Indigenous reform agenda. *Croakey Blog*, 16 March, blogs.crikey.com.au/croakey/2015/03/16/unfair-and-arbitrary-is-the-only-thing-new-in-the-indigenous-advancement-strategy-a-new-round-of-a-massive-funding-cuts/.

Broome R (2010). *Aboriginal Australians: A history since 1788,* 4th edn, Allen & Unwin, Sydney.

Cox E (2014). What works—and why the budget measures don't. *Journal of Indigenous Policy*, 16:1–112.

Davidson H (2016). 'We vote too': Indigenous groups warn both parties they want action. *Guardian*, 9 June, www.theguardian.com/australia-news/2016/jun/09/we-vote-too-indigenous-groups-warn-both-parties-they-want-action.

Davis M (2015). Gesture politics: Recognition alone won't fix Indigenous affairs. *The Monthly*, December–January, www.themonthly.com.au/issue/2015/december/1448888400/megan-davis/gesture-politics.

Davis M (2016). Listening but not hearing: When process trumps substance. *Griffith Review* 51:73–87.

Department of Finance (2011). *Strategic review of Indigenous expenditure: Report to the Australian Government*, www.finance.gov.au/foi/disclosure-log/2011/foi_10-27_strategic_reviews.html.

Dodson P (2015). Tony Abbott's lifestyle comments highlight the lack of policy in Aboriginal affairs. *Age*, 13 March, www.theage.com.au/comment/tony-abbotts-lifestyle-comments-highlight-the-lack-of-policy-in-aboriginal-affairs-20150311-141u4s.

Everingham S (2015). Indigenous Affairs Minister faces angry protest in Alice Springs. *PM*, 30 March, www.abc.net.au/pm/content/2015/s4207607.htm.

FPARC (Finance and Public Administration References Committee) (2016). *Commonwealth Indigenous Advancement Strategy tendering processes*, Commonwealth of Australia, Canberra.

Goldberg DT (2002). *The racial state*, Blackwell, Massachusetts.

Goldberg DT (2009). *The threat of race: Reflections on racial neoliberalism*, Blackwell, Massachusetts.

Gooda M (2014). *Aboriginal and Torres Strait Islander Justice Commissioner: Social justice and native title report 2014*, Australian Human Rights Commission, Sydney.

Haughton J (2017). *Budget review 2017–18: Indigenous affairs—government priority areas*, Commonwealth of Australia, Canberra.

Henderson A (2015). Majority of grants from Indigenous Advancement Strategy first round given to non-Aboriginal groups. *ABC News*, 5 May, www.abc.net.au/news/2015-05-05/majority-of-indigenous-grants-go-to-non-aboriginal-organisations/6444534.

Holcombe SE & Sullivan P (2013). Australian Indigenous organisations. In Douglas Caulkins M & Jordan AT (eds), *A companion to organisational anthropology*, Blackwell, Massachusetts.

Howard-Wagner D (2015). Child wellbeing and protection as a regulatory system in the neoliberal age: Forms of Aboriginal agency and resistance engaged to confront the challenges for Aboriginal people and community-based Aboriginal organisations. *Australian Indigenous Law Review* 19(1):88–102.

Howard-Wagner D & Kelly B (2011). Containing Aboriginal mobility in the Northern Territory: From 'protectionism' to 'interventionism'. *Law, Text, Culture* 15(7):102–34.

Hudson S (2016). *Mapping the Indigenous program and funding maze*. Research Report 18, The Centre for Independent Studies.

Langton M (2016). Silent issues: The silence on Indigenous issues in the 2016 election. *Saturday Paper*, 11 June.

Lea T (2008). *Bureaucrats and bleeding hearts: Indigenous health in northern Australia*, UNSW Press, Sydney.

Lea T (2012). When looking for anarchy, look to the state: Fantasies of regulation in forcing disorder within the Australian Indigenous estate. *Critique of Anthropology* 32:109–24, doi.org/10.1177/0308275X12438251.

Liberal Party of Australia (2013). *Our plan: Real solutions for all Australians— The direction, values and policy priorities of the next Coalition Government.* Liberal Party of Australia, Canberra.

McCallum D (2011). Liberal forms of governing Australian Indigenous peoples. *Journal of Law and Society* 38(4):604–30, doi.org/10.1111/j.1467-6478.2011.00560.x.

Morgan M. (2015). Turnbull Government to retain similar policies to Abbott: Scullion. *NITV News*, 22 September, www.sbs.com.au/nitv/article/2015/09/21/turnbull-government-retain-similar-policies-abbott-scullion.

Murphy-Oates L (2016). NSW Indigenous legal line still facing funding uncertainty, says CEO. *NITV News*, 9 March, www.sbs.com.au/nitv/the-point-with-stan-grant/article/2016/03/09/nsw-indigenous-legal-line-still-facing-funding-uncertainty-says-ceo.

NCA (National Commission of Audit) (2014). *Towards responsible government: Phase one.* Commonwealth of Australia, Canberra.

Oscar J (2014). *Turning community action into national policy*, University of Sydney Charles Perkins Annual Oration, 30 October, Sydney.

Page A (2015). *The Australian settler state, Indigenous agency, and the Indigenous sector in the twenty first century. Proceedings of the Australian political science association conference*, University of Canberra, September, Canberra.

Pearson N (2016). Address to the National Press Club, 27 January, Canberra.

PMC (Australian Government Department of the Prime Minister & Cabinet) (2014a). *Indigenous Advancement Strategy guidelines 2014*, www.dpmc.gov.au/resource-centre/indigenous-affairs/indigenous-advancement-strategy-guidelines-july-2014.

PMC (2014b). *The indigenous advancement strategy*, www.dpmc.gov.au/indigenous-affairs/indigenous-advancement-strategy.

PMC (2014c). *Indigenous advancement strategy grant round reporting 2014*, www.pmc.gov.au/indigenous-affairs/grants-and-funding/ias-2014-grant-round-reporting.

PMC (2015). *Submission to the Senate Finance and Public Administration References Committee: Impact on service quality, efficiency and sustainability of recent Commonwealth Indigenous Advancement Strategy tendering processes by the Department of Prime Minister and Cabinet*, www.aph.gov. au/Parliamentary_Business/Committees/Senate/Finance_and_Public_ Administration/Commonwealth_Indigenous.

PMC (2016a). *IAS grant reporting (Excluding IAS 2014 grant round)*, www.dpmc. gov.au/indigenous-affairs/grants-and-funding/ias-grant-reporting.

PMC (2016b). *Indigenous Advancement Strategy grant guidelines March 2016— Amended May 2016*, www.dpmc.gov.au/resource-centre/indigenous-affairs/ indigenous-advancement-strategy-grant-guidelines-march-2016.

Productivity Commission (2010). *Contribution of the not-for-profit sector*, Commonwealth of Australia, Canberra.

Pusey M (1991). *Economic rationalism in Canberra: A nation-building state changes its mind*, Cambridge University Press, Cambridge.

The Redfern Statement (2016). res.cloudinary.com/www-changetherecord-org- au/image/upload/v1465428796/The_Redfern_Statement_-_9_June_2016_ FINAL_h7mvy9.pdf.

Rowse T (2012). *Rethinking social justice: From 'peoples' to 'populations'*, Aboriginal Studies Press, Canberra.

Russell L (2016). *2016–17 Budget: Indigenous affairs*. Menzies Centre for Health Policy, Sydney.

Sanders W (2002). *Towards an Indigenous order of Australian government: Rethinking self-determination as Indigenous affairs policy*, Discussion Paper 230, Centre for Aboriginal Economic Policy Research, The Australian National University, Canberra.

Sanders W (2014). *Experimental governance in Australian Indigenous affairs: From Coombs to Pearson via Rowse and the competing principles*. Discussion Paper 291, Centre for Aboriginal Economic Policy Research, The Australian National University, Canberra.

Scullion N (2014). *A new era of Indigenous grant funding commences*, media release, indigenous.gov.au, www.indigenous.gov.au/new-era-indigenous-grant- funding-commences.

Scullion N (2015). *$860 million investment through Indigenous Advancement Strategy grants round*, media release, www.indigenous.gov.au/news-and-media/announcements/minister-scullion-860-million-investment-through-indigenous-advancement.

Strakosch E (2015). *Neoliberal indigenous policy: Settler colonialism and the 'post-welfare' state*, Springer, New York, doi.org/10.1057/9781137405418.

Sullivan P (2009). Reciprocal accountability: Assessing the accountability environment in Australian Aboriginal affairs policy. *International Journal of Public Sector Management*, 22(1):57–71, doi.org/10.1108/09513550910922405.

Sullivan P (2011). *Belonging together: Dealing with the politics of disenchantment in Australian Indigenous policy*, Aboriginal Studies Press, Canberra.

Walter M & Andersen C (2013). *Indigenous statistics: A quantitative research methodology*. Left Coast Press, California.

Weber M (1949). *The methodology of the social sciences*, The Free Press, Glencoe, Illinois.

Wolfe P (2016). *Traces of history: Elementary structures of race*. Verso, London, doi.org/10.1111/1468-229X.12265.

11

The tyranny of neoliberal public management and the challenge for Aboriginal community organisations

Patrick Sullivan

Introduction

When we consider the relationship between indigenous peoples and the state, we tend to narrow down to the policies of the government of the day, as several of the chapters in this volume do. In these studies, the government stands as proxy for the state, even though we are aware that the state is much more pervasive than this. At its most abstract, it is an assemblage of coercive practices tending always to reinforce existing relations of power founded in control of the economy. These practices are instituted by the state's various organs—the judiciary, the police and defence forces, education and the parliament as a whole. None of them are without internal diversity and external rivalries, but they tend to reinforce each other nevertheless. Traditionally, liberal states have balanced what Strakosch calls 'social liberalism' (Strakosch 2015: 21), individual rights and responsibilities, with varying degrees of 'market liberalism', allowing the individuals and corporations that control commercial and industrial production to regulate their own markets. The innovation of neoliberalism is to extend market relations into the social sphere, first by imposing markets on civil society and then by regulating families and individuals as if life itself is a commercial activity, albeit one in which the majority of citizens have little or no market power. As Strakosch convincingly argues, the innovation of neoliberalism is that many citizens enter this pseudo-market as social debtors. While traditional liberal states guaranteed citizens entitlements, in neoliberal societies it is the state that is entitled, and liberal rights are extended or withdrawn according to the state's estimate of citizens' capacity to meet their obligations:

> the state itself has become morally authoritative and entitled. It makes demands of citizens—that they pay their dues, minimise their risk to society and mitigate their burden on the state through self-reliance. In this task, the neoliberal state joins them as partner and supervisor; it offers assistance through capacity building, but always with the threat of coercion if this capacity is not forthcoming (Strakosch 2015: 25).

Strakosch has analysed the ideology of regulating risk that normalises this intrusion of the state beyond the comfort zone of traditional liberals (Strakosch 2012).

Increasingly, each instance of the neoliberal state subscribes to the same technology of administration, first elaborated as 'new public management' (see Eckersley 2003, O'Flynn 2007), but now frequently simply described as neoliberal public management. This intensification of techniques of control beyond traditional bureaucratic practice into every facet of social life particularly impacts upon previously relatively autonomous, and largely self-governing, organisations such as Indigenous corporations, in ways that the chapters in this volume describe (e.g. Howard-Wagner, Humpage, Page, Bielefeld, McCormack). While case studies of the effects of neoliberal public management are important, equally important is the task of critically analysing contemporary public management as a coercive extension of the state, and considering alternatives. This chapter aims to do so broadly while tying this analysis to the position of Indigenous civil organisations in the Australian polity as a whole.

Neoliberal public management

In Australia, new public management (NPM), or neoliberal management theory, informed sweeping changes to the Australian Public Service from the mid-1980s to the mid-1990s (Eckersley 2003: 489–92, Nelson 2008: 76–105, Parliament of Australia 2010a). O'Flynn (2007, citing Kaboolian 1998) summarises the core principles of NPM as:

- Economic markets should be the model for relationships in the public sector
- Policy, implementation and delivery functions should be separated and constructed as a series of contracts
- A range of new administrative technologies should be introduced including performance-based contracting, competition, market incentives and deregulation (O'Flynn 2007: 357).

NPM was a bundle of reforms that intersected with a related trend in politics and public finance—neoliberalism, or market economics. It is common to call NPM 'neoliberal public management', and it is true that it shares many of neoliberalism's values and assumptions. The fundamental assumption is that markets are the fairest and most efficient way of distributing a society's resources. Fake markets are created within the bureaucracy, and by the bureaucracy for its dependent organisations, in order to introduce the magic of capitalism to its fundamentally different order of social activity. As Stoker (2006), summarising Moore's critique, puts it, private enterprise produces private value, public enterprise should produce public value. These are two fundamentally different results requiring fundamentally different processes of production. Contemporary bureaucrats and governments, however, profess to believe in the magical transfer of capitalist properties to public management activities because neoliberal public management delivers another benefit in the guise of efficiency—it tightens social control. Modern public sector management has rediscovered the original project of modern bureaucracy developed in the Anglosphere in the 1850s at the height of unfettered industrial capitalism and colonial expansion. Its present manifestation in strict performance measurement of identified contracted outputs, prospective risk management, itemised accountability for time and resources, and politically 'value neutral' research products and news sources sets a new benchmark in the struggle of high modernism against the human spirit.

Power (1997) has called this the 'audit society'. Citizens are increasingly required to itemise their lives, ascribe each item a value and account for themselves to an impersonal higher authority. The political nature of this accounting has not escaped criticism. Dean Neu, for example, identified the imposition of financial systems on developing countries as 'the software of colonialism' (Neu 2003). It is significant that bureaucracy as a technology of control was scientifically developed in the mid-19th century, the high point of European colonial control and unbridled industrial capitalism.

They are both expressions of the birth of modernity. Extending Neu's metaphor, accountability is one of the softwares of modernity, of which the hardware is the modern state, and the firmware, or operating system, the contemporary form of bureaucracy.[1] This has invaded every facet of life. Not only the workspace of commercial organisations and government departments, but increasingly non-government organisations (NGOs) and not-for-profits, and ever outwards embracing aspects of our personal and family lives. So, while this chapter is titled 'the tyranny of neoliberal public management', it is more broadly about 'the diffuse dictatorship of modernity'. It is not the dictatorship of a single despot, but of a managerial class as a whole enforcing, through its senior executives in the political sphere, the unseen requirements of global capital, parsed for the masses as 'economic necessity'.

---

1   I have been asked, not for the first time, to provide a foundation for the 'normative' tone of this chapter by reference to my previous supportive work. The ideas presented in this chapter have a long tail. In 1989, I submitted a PhD thesis examining the work of Aboriginal community-controlled organisations in the Kimberley (Sullivan 1991). Part of this, including a chapter on Aboriginal Affairs bureaucracy called 'Rational procedures and irrational results in Aboriginal administration', was subsequently published by the Australian Institute of Aboriginal and Torres Strait Islander Studies (AIATSIS) (Sullivan 1996). Neu's insight, and my critique of new public management, were first advanced at a seminar for the Centre for Aboriginal Economic Policy Research (CAEPR) in 2006, in a paper called 'Softwares of colonialism' (Sullivan 2006a). Refined and developed further, this paper, now called 'Softwares of modernity', was presented to a symposium on Ethnographic Research in the Social and Management Sciences at the School of Management, University of Liverpool (UK) in September 2006 (Sullivan 2006b). This paper was expanded and split to provide contributions to two international journals; one explored the theme of accountability, the other the culture of bureaucracy (Sullivan 2008, 2009) (one received the Outstanding Paper award for its year of publication from the journal editors and the other was in a collection deemed best collection of its year by the publishers). Penetration in Australia has been less marked. I wrote on the importance of the Aboriginal community sector, and the impact of new public management, in a published Working Paper for the Desert Knowledge Cooperative Research Centre in 2010 (Sullivan 2010), a paper that, re-worked, became a chapter in my 2011 book *Belonging together* (Sullivan 2011a). This book, tracing the changes in Aboriginal policy since the end of the Aboriginal and Torres Strait Islander Commission (ATSIC), perhaps gives the most extended empirical discussion of recent policy supporting the propositions advanced in this chapter. Subsequently, I explored the trajectory of managerialism and normalisation in public policy, introducing Moore's theory of public value, in an article for the *Asia Pacific Journal of Anthropology*, 'Disenchantment, normalisation and public value' (Sullivan 2013). I also examined alternative approaches to neoliberal public management, including public value, exploring the development of public administration as a field, and its impact on community sector organisations, in an extended essay for the Lowitja Institute in 2015 (Sullivan 2015).

The logic of neoliberal management and its effect on Aboriginal organisations

Highly technical 'scientific' public management is necessarily antagonistic to diversity. Correct management procedure stands above local and sectoral differences. One size must fit all, or the rational basis of the entire project is challenged. This apparently neutral uniformity of correct procedure disguises the relationships of economic power that it both serves and mimics, and it rides roughshod over local values. Coupled with a political program of normalisation in Aboriginal affairs in Australia (Sullivan 2013), contemporary public management has facilitated the destruction of the Aboriginal community–controlled service sector since the abolition of the Aboriginal and Torres Strait Islander Commission (ATSIC) in 2005. Technical management institutes a form of cultural chauvinism through the Australian public sector's inability to appreciate Aboriginal forms of management; its inability to take into account the value provided by culturally informed local third-sector organisations;[2] and its inability to hear local competence expressed in a dialect and idiom foreign to dominant public sector discourse.

In Australia, as in other modern societies, the Australian Government delivers many of its social, cultural and welfare services through the engagement of third-sector organisations.[3] Many of these organisations are working in the field of 'internal development', particularly the Aboriginal third sector that struggles with the kind of poverty and lack of infrastructure normally associated with underdeveloped countries. Good practice in development programs requires attention to the process of program delivery as much as the outcome or targets (Mosse 1998: 4–5). Similarly, in complex, uncertain and rapidly changing environments, contemporary management scholarship emphasises the need for 'experimentalist' organisations at the level of project implementation (Sabel 2004). Both approaches, starting with different aims and from different

---

2   Third sector is a common term for non-state, non-commercial organisations that provide quasi-governmental services. They are formally independent of government, comprising NGOs, charities and other not-for-profit and civil society entities.
3   It also meets these objectives by subsidies to state governments. These more commonly deliver services directly through their own agencies, but also engage third-sector organisations. The states have not been prominent in Aboriginal development since 1967, but are now, in this phase of normalisation, being required by the Commonwealth to take responsibility for the Aboriginal citizens in much the same way as for the rest of their population.

premises, therefore identify the need for significant local autonomy that recognises the diversity of program environments. Australia, in contrast, is still wedded to central planning, strict oversight of implementation, continual audit and interference and, throughout this, over-the-shoulder attention to political imperatives.

Data from interviews conducted with the CEOs and directors of 18 Aboriginal third-sector organisations in the Kimberley region of Western Australia in 2010[4] show a sector that is demoralised by this new regime. Some of the challenges they face include competition, often with compatriot organisations, over available funds to deliver services; limitation to narrow service provision roles rather than providing multifaceted community resources; short time frame, remotely conceived, highly fragmented, report-driven government programs; and high churn in government agencies, related to NPM public sector job flexibility, producing debilitating corporate amnesia in the agencies that plan and distribute development programs.

At least part of the fragmentation of this sector is due to Australian monoculturalism, which is deaf to cultural nuances, so that third-sector organisations' statements about their learning, governance and relation to others in the sector quite literally cannot be heard. As one Aboriginal CEO of a long-established Aboriginal resource agency told Sullivan:

> We broke into housing management four years ago and then that contract got taken off us. We used to manage [four communities] and they took that contract off us then said no, we're going to manage it ourselves and then just doubled the amount of funding available. Like up until the 31st December 2009, they gave us $4,000 per house to manage. Now when they're managing it, it's $8,000 a house ... Yeah they always had that luxury of going up to $8,000, it's just that they made us work for $4,000 a house, so that's $2,000 operational funding and $2,000 per house repairs and maintenance and then we had to collect at least $2,000 per house to subsidise the R & M budget. Repairs and Maintenance to the house. Repairs and Maintenance funding. And then like the following year you know they just doubled the funding, so it's again another case of you know making us sweat on a very restricted budget for a period of time and then all of a sudden, they do it or a non-indigenous contractor does it and the funding available blows out or doubles you know, like

---

4   Research undertaken in the Kimberley region by Sullivan in 2010 as a Senior Research Fellow at the Australian Institute of Aboriginal and Torres Strait Islander Studies. The data, which echoes Howard-Wagner (this volume, Chapter 12) for NSW, is largely unpublished, but see Sullivan (2011b).

that's racism or something isn't it? I'm sure it is. It's just not right and I've got so many instances of it … So you've got all this overload of State and Federal Governments just overloading them. [mimicking government liaison with the recipient communities] Oh yeah we're here to do this you know. [his organisation] did a shit job, so that's why we stopped their contract. And believe me they have been running us down and that's why they promoted the non-Indigenous contractors to step in, and they made them look great and everything got done in the community but they were doing it for treble the amount of money that we did it for and they made us look terrible by doing that … Of course I would have done that for $600,000 too instead of $180,000. I mean with $180,000 I had to employ a manager out there, operate a couple of vehicles, couple of staff houses, run the shed out there, the power house. We were used as scapegoats you know and one would have to wonder what the reasoning or motives were behind that. Is it part of a larger scheme to downgrade community control of resource agencies and the role they play or what? I mean it just makes me a bit suspicious about their motives (Author's transcript of interview 2010, identity withheld).

Instead of experience and capability, the inner-oriented public administrator sees only lack of capacity. Australia is a consciously homogenising nation with a relatively low tolerance of diversity. NPM managerialism therefore has a kind of 'naturalness' that suits Australian historical, administrative and cultural conditions. The intersection of NPM central control and Australian unease with local, regional and ethnic diversity currently impacts heavily on the Aboriginal component of the Australian third sector. The sector is subject to inappropriate regulation, takeover by state government agencies and open-market commercialisation of welfare/development service delivery functions (see Sullivan 2010, Sullivan 2011c: 8–9, Sullivan 2015). Aboriginal third-sector organisations are hampered in their ability to challenge this process by the inability of mainstream administrators to hear and credit the culturally inflected voices of Aboriginal management at the local level.

The Australian Government predominates in Australia because it has increasingly monopolised the capacity for revenue-raising throughout the country. The federal government provides few direct services. Its major service functions are those that are not easily outsourced—particularly defence and tertiary education that, in 2010, together accounted for 290,534 of the 367,845 people employed by the government. The remaining public servants either provide services within government itself or are desk-controllers of direct service providers in state government agencies and in the third sector (see Parliament of Australia 2010b: 7). While not being much of a service provider itself, the Australian Government controls services throughout Australia through commercial tendering, grants to state and local governments, and to third-sector organisations.

This fiscal bedrock of Australian society, largely unacknowledged by its citizens, is horizontal fiscal equalisation (see Yu et al. 2008: 50–1). It is the fiscal policy of the federal government that transfers central funds to the states to 'fill in the gaps' of fiscal capacity so that Australians experience broadly the same level of services and infrastructure across the country. It intersects with its demographic profile to underpin Australian monoculturalism. By far the largest proportion of Australian non-Indigenous people live in major cities or towns (about 88 per cent of the total population) (Australian Bureau of Statistics 2008: 9). These are usually situated on a river system close to the coast. A further 9.5 per cent live in outer regional areas (ibid.). Their expectation, largely fulfilled, is that their experience of one major city or regional centre will be very much the same as another as they travel about the country. This is quite a remarkable achievement in a country of such physical size. It does, however, encourage monoculturalism.

Monoculturalism is explicitly embraced by conservative liberalism, and it surfaces both in approaches to immigration and to Aboriginal affairs. It is well articulated by the most successful Australian prime minister of recent decades, John Howard, in a speech to The Margaret Thatcher Centre for Freedom in 2010. In this speech, he celebrated the common values of 'the Anglosphere', which he took to include Canada, the United States and New Zealand, all countries with significant indigenous populations:

> I think one of the errors that some sections of the English-speaking world have made in the past few decades has been to confuse multiracialism and multiculturalism. I am a passionate believer in multiracialism. I believe that societies are enriched if they draw, as my country has done, from all parts of the world on a non-discriminatory basis, and contribute, as the United States has done, to the building of a great society. But when a nation draws people from other parts of the world, it draws them because of the magnetism of its own culture and its own way of life, and the ideal, in my opinion, is to draw people from the four corners of the earth but to unite them behind the common values of the country which has made them welcome (Howard 2011: 5).

Howard speaks to the core values of 'old Australia', an Australia eager to rid itself of the international ignominy of race discrimination, but uncomfortable still with cultural diversity. This is both philosophical and emotional. On a philosophical level, it is indeed confronting to deal with competing systems of value, such as conceptions of right and wrong and the origins of social authority. However, the monoculturalism represented by politicians such as Howard is not simply a matter of intellectual struggle, but is also an appeal to cultural chauvinism. In the public service, this manifests as an inability to credit non-standard voices, and Aboriginal managers are deemed to 'lack capacity' simply because of the way they talk, behave and present themselves and the values of their communities.

The public value of Aboriginal organisations

The practices and ideologies described so far in this chapter support Strakosch's identification of lack of capacity and risk as the means by which the neoliberal state resiles from traditional liberal values that recognise citizen and minority rights. She identifies two distinct directions of neoliberal critique. One analyses neoliberalism as 'the decline of the state in favour of the market'; in other words, structural economic change (Strakosch 2015: 36). The other, Foucauldian, approach emphasises governmentality:

> the mobile technologies of government that activate and work through the calculative freedom of individuals. Such technologies include contractualism, privatisation, marketisation and the fostering of 'active' self-regulating citizenship (Strakosch 2015: 37).

In either case, in my view, the technology of neoliberal control is the same. It is the apparently neutral and scientific application of public management principles. This is therefore an arena where resistance and reform can potentially be mounted. One way to do this is to advance alternative approaches to public management in liberal societies. This is what Mark Moore does with his theory of public value (Moore 1995, 2013).

The concept of public value was advanced by Moore in the early 1980s when neoliberal public management first threatened to dominate the administrative apparatus of the Anglophone states. It has been refined since, and offers an alternative approach, now that neoliberal public management faces widespread public disillusion. Moore said that neoliberal public management mimics the production of private value in the commercial, market-oriented sector because of its perceived efficiency. One way that modern bureaucracies got this wrong, he believes, is by concentrating on the internal organisation of bureaucracies, introducing rigorous control, performance management and line accountability; whereas commercial organisations are typically less self-centred and are outwardly directed towards their customers and clients. Nevertheless, this form of rigorous governance is visited upon Aboriginal organisations by bureaucrats in the firm belief that it is more efficient. Moore nevertheless proposed that public value is fundamentally different to private value, and that it is wrong for public administrators to ignore these differences. One principal difference is that the process of producing a public good is itself intrinsic to its value, while the process of producing a private commodity for the commercial market is immaterial to its perceived value among the private organisations' customers. This opens up a second difference that was not explored by Moore. Public administrators should take into account a range of values desired by a range of publics, adapting their processes of value production, offering the possibility of putting Aboriginal values and Aboriginal publics at the forefront of Aboriginal policy once more.

Moore realised that public values are produced in the instrumental processes of governmental activity, not simply as an outcome. Citizens derive value by being treated in ways that acknowledge their rights, their dignity and their own culturally mediated understanding of civility. Neoliberal public administration, in contrast, mimics an economic market in which the goods or services provided are apparently divorced from the process that produces them. All that matters is that the process should be efficient. As a result, citizens may have become well-serviced but alienated from the administrative structures of government that ought to reflect their underlying sovereignty.

Moore's (1995) conception is dynamic. It involves negotiation between citizens, administrators and politicians in an active environment of desire for public benefit and the limiting of public harm. Moore tells the public servants of advanced democracies that they need to define public value in particular circumstances, build the operational capacity within and outside of the public service to deliver it and to do this within an accepted 'authorizing environment' (Benington & Moore 2011: 4). It is this idea of an 'authorizing environment' that delivers some tools to community-based service organisations to construct their counter arguments to bureaucrats whose only knowledge of public administration is passive absorption of

NPM. Although a public servant's mandate comes from the legislation informed by the values of the ruling party, this is not a guarantee that they are providing public value (Benington & Moore 2011: 6). Many community workers in Aboriginal development would argue that, in complex intercultural development programs, a simple mandate deriving from legislation is never sufficient. It is more common that:

> public policymaker and manager may have to create a network of partners and stakeholders, and to negotiate a coalition of different interests and agencies (from across public, private, voluntary and informal community sectors) to support them in achieving their goals (Benington & Moore 2011: 6).

Moore calls this the 'authorizing environment' within which public administrators can create value. Moore says the support of 'a coalition of stakeholders from the public, private and third sectors … is required to sustain the necessary strategic action' (Benington & Moore 2011: 4).

Moore's insistence that the role of the public manager is to encourage the creation of public value does not deny the importance of good management practice in organisations (Hood 1991, cited in Benington & Moore 2011: 10). However, management must be turned towards those things that the public as a whole values, and the public is more than a mob of individuals corralled into a consumer group. Much could be said about the constitution of the various publics (see Warner 2002), but here we can note that there are local Aboriginal publics with distinct values that can clearly be better represented when public managers are responsive to an authorising environment that includes their representative organisations and their significant spokespeople knowledgeable in lore and culture. This is an authorising environment that includes politicians and their programs, but also informs them both in a two-way process that requires workable trade-offs (Alford & O'Flynn 2009, cited in Benington & Moore 2011: 5).

Underpinning public value, according to Moore's original vision of the concept, is acknowledgement that benefits generally arise when governments, public servants and the public have a shared purpose. In the case of Aboriginal organisations and government, that shared vision has largely been absent or, at best, certainly not at the forefront of policy thinking, if it can ever be said to have existed in any influential sense. The Indigenous Advancement Strategy (see Page this volume, Chapter 10) and the current government's responses to the Community Development

Employment Projects program are two examples that vividly illustrate the lack of shared purpose, or shared conceptions of what constitutes public value to an Aboriginal public. Nevertheless, the concept of public value remains a form of contemporary nomenclature that offers an opportunity to make visible the full value of Aboriginal organisations to their publics in a manner intelligible to government, with potential to help restore a greater level of shared vision or, less ambitiously, to present a more realistic view of the valuable services these organisations provide. In short, it is an opportunity to develop a grounded counter-discourse that moves us away from punishment and disparagement.

Critics of increasing state control of every facet of daily life must become aware of, and be prepared to deploy, this significant counter-discourse in public sector management theory, fighting back with the argument that the task of public management is the creation of public value, and this is determined by local publics. This counter-discourse argues for the effectiveness of flexible pragmatic adaptive management at the local level (Sabel 2004), and for relational contracts that establish the terms of engagement rather than the precise product to be delivered (Mcneil 1978, Dwyer et al. 2009). These are alternative streams of public management theory that have at least as much coherence as neoliberal public management. They affect equally the way that civil society organisations themselves organise. No matter how much we attempt to resist the dehumanising effect of bureaucracy, we cannot escape the need to organise, and therefore to pursue appropriate forms of public management. Weber foresaw this double bind of bureaucracy (Jacoby 1973: 151–2). Modern bureaucracy is ruthlessly efficient, but efficiently organising against it effectively risks reproducing and perpetuating it. Resistance is important, but seeking out alternatives is also necessary. While a valid reaction to the totalising effect of bureaucracy is to subvert, undermine and resist, another is to reform, to humanise bureaucracy, so that it becomes adequate for the task of realising the values of citizens, not least Indigenous citizens holding values rooted in a society that long pre-dates their colonisation.

References

Alford J & O'Flynn J (2009). Making sense of public value: Concepts, critiques and emergent meanings. *International Journal of Public Administration*. 32:171–91.

Australian Bureau of Statistics (2008). *Australian social trends, 2008*, cat. no. 4102.0, Australian Bureau of Statistics, Canberra.

Benington J & Moore M (eds) (2011). *Public value: Theory and practice*, Palgrave Macmillan, Basingstoke, doi.org/10.1007/978-0-230-36431-8.

Dwyer JM, Lavoie J, O'Donnell K, Marlina U & Sullivan, P (2009). *The overburden report: Contracting for Aboriginal health services*, Cooperative Research Centre for Aboriginal Health, Darwin.

Eckersley R (2003). Politics and policy. In Dovers S & Wild River S (eds), *Managing Australia's environment*, Federation Press, Sydney.

Hood, C (2006). Gaming in targetworld: The targets approach to managing British public services. *Public Administration Review* 66(4):515–21. doi.org/10.1111/j.1540-6210.2006.00612.x.

Howard J (2011). *The anglosphere and the advance of freedom*, the Margaret Thatcher Freedom Lecture, 24 September 2010, the Heritage Foundation, Washington, www.heritage.org/report/the-anglosphere-and-the-advance-freedom.

Jacoby H (1973). *The bureaucratization of the world*, University of California Press, Berkeley.

Kaboolian L (1998). The new public management: Challenging the boundaries of the management vs administration debate, *Public Administration Review* 58(3):189–93.

Mcneil I (1978). Contract: Adjustment of long-term economic relations under classical, neo-classical and relational contract law. *North-western University Law Review* 72(6):854–905.

Moore MH (1995). *Creating public value: Strategic management in government*, Harvard University Press, Massachusetts.

Moore MH (2013). *Recognizing public value*, Harvard University Press, Massachusetts.

Mosse D (1998). Process-oriented approaches to development practice and social research. In Mosse D, Farrington J & Rew A (eds), *Development as process: Concepts and methods for working with complexity*, Routledge, London.

Nelson H (2008). Public employment in Australia: In competition with the market. In Hans-Ulrich D and Guy Peters B (eds), *The state at work, volume 1*, Edward Elgar, Cheltenham, doi.org/10.4337/9781848444942.00009.

Neu D (2003). Accounting for the banal: Financial techniques as softwares of colonialism. In Anshuman P (ed.), *Postcolonial theory and organisational analysis: A critical engagement*, Palgrave, NewYork.

O'Flynn J (2007). From new public management to public value: Paradigmatic change and managerial implications. *The Australian Journal of Public Administration* 66(3):357–8, doi.org/10.1111/j.1467-8500.2007.00545.x.

Parliament of Australia (2010a). *Chronology of changes in the Australian public service 1975–2010*, Background Note, Parliamentary Library, Department of Parliamentary Services, Canberra.

Parliament of Australia (2010b). *How many are employed in the commonwealth public sector?* Background Note, Parliamentary Library, Department of Parliamentary Services, Canberra.

Power M (1997). *The audit society: Rituals of verification*, Oxford University Press, Oxford.

Sabel CF (2004). Beyond principal-agent governance: Experimentalist organizations, learning and accountability. In Engelen E & Sie Dhian Ho M (eds), *De Staat van de Democratie. Democratie voorbij de Staat [The state of democracy. Democracy beyond the state]*. WRR Verkenning 3 Amsterdam: Amsterdam University Press.

Stoker G (2006). Public value management: A new narrative for networked governance? *American Review of Public Administration* 1(3):41–57, doi.org/10.1177/0275074005282583.

Strakosch E (2012). Colonial risk management. *Borderlands* 11(1), www.border lands.net.au./vol11no1_2012/strakosch_risk.htm

Strakosch E (2015). *Neoliberal Indigenous policy: Settler colonialism and the 'post-welfare' state*, Palgrave Macmillan, Hampshire, doi.org/10.1057/9781137405418.

Sullivan P (1991) [1989]. All free man now: Culture and post-colonialism in the Kimberley Division North-Western Australia. PhD thesis, The Australian National University, Canberra.

Sullivan P (1996). *All free man now: Culture, community and politics in the Kimberley Region North Western Australia*, Aboriginal Studies Press, Canberra.

Sullivan P (2006a). Softwares of colonialism: Contradictions of accountability in whole-of-government policy for indigenous affairs. Seminar presentation, 3 May, Centre for Aboriginal Economic Policy Research, The Australian National University, Canberra.

Sullivan P (2006b). Softwares of modernity: Accountability and the culture of bureaucracy in Australian Aboriginal affairs administration. Paper delivered to the symposium Current Developments in Ethnographic Research in the Social and Management Sciences, Liverpool University Management School, 13–14 September.

Sullivan P (2008). Bureaucratic process as Morris dance: An ethnographic approach to the culture of bureaucracy in Australian Aboriginal affairs administration. *Critical Perspectives on International Business* 4(2/3):127–41, doi.org/10.1108/17422040810869981.

Sullivan P (2009). Reciprocal accountability: Assessing the accountability environment in Australian Aboriginal affairs policy. *International Journal of Public Sector Management* 22(1):57–71, doi.org/10.1108/09513550910922405.

Sullivan P (2010). *The Aboriginal community sector and the effective delivery of services: Acknowledging the role of Indigenous sector organisations*, Working Paper 73, Desert Knowledge Cooperative Research Centre, Alice Springs.

Sullivan P (2011a). *Belonging together: Dealing with the politics of disenchantment in Australian Aboriginal policy*, Aboriginal Studies Press, Canberra.

Sullivan P (2011b) Third sector Aboriginal organisations in Australia and the new wave of normalisation. Paper delivered to stream Shaping the Spaces Between State and Market: Critical Perspectives on the 'Third Sector', 7th International Critical Management Studies Conference, Naples, Italy, 11–13 July.

Sullivan P (2011c). *The policy goal of normalisation, the national Indigenous reform agreement and Indigenous national partnership agreements*, Working Paper 76, Desert Knowledge Cooperative Research Centre, Alice Springs. www.nintione.com.au/resource/NintiOneWorkingPaper_76_PolicyGoalof Normalisation.pdf.

Sullivan P (2013). Disenchantment, normalisation and public value: Taking the long view in Australian Indigenous affairs. *The Asia Pacific Journal of Anthropology* 14(4):353–69, doi.org/10.1080/14442213.2013.804871.

Sullivan P (2015). *A reciprocal relationship: Accountability for public value in the Aboriginal community sector*, Lowitja Institute, Melbourne.

Warner M (2002). Publics and counterpublics (abbreviated version). *Quarterly Journal of Speech*, 88(4):413–25.

Yu P, Duncan E & Gray B (2008). *Report of the Northern Territory Emergency Response Review Board*, Commonwealth of Australia, Canberra.

Aboriginal organisations, self-determination and the neoliberal age: A case study of how the 'game has changed' for Aboriginal organisations in Newcastle

Deirdre Howard-Wagner

Introduction

Non-Indigenous bureaucratic structures have been forced upon different traditional organisational structures.

For example, when we talk to the housing service in a community, we need to understand that it may be controlled by one family group that doesn't necessarily speak with or for the others in the community.

Equally whoever runs it speaks with the self-interest that all service providers bring in discussions with governments. That problem is not particular to Indigenous Australia.

Large portions of communities weren't being heard; they weren't getting a chance to have their say …

Where specialist Indigenous services are required, they must be the best possible services we can offer. This raises another contentious issue. The history of these services is that they've been provided through

> Indigenous organisations. Some do a tremendous job but there has been waste, there has been corruption and that means service provision hasn't been what it should be. If we continue to regard these organisations as untouchable and unaccountable we are failing our Indigenous citizens yet again. The proposition I'm putting is simple. If you're funded to deliver a service, you should deliver it. If you don't, we'll get someone else to do it (Vanstone 2005).

On reading the above speech, what first caught my attention is how indicative it was of the discursive calculations and strategies used in the neoliberal age to justify intervention in the lives and affairs of Aboriginal people, Aboriginal organisations and Aboriginal communities in Australia (Howard-Wagner 2009, 2010). It smoothed the way for the imposition of a particular set of reforms to legislation and policy in relation to Aboriginal corporations, Aboriginal service delivery and Aboriginal political representation. One year earlier, the Australian Government had tried to mainstream Aboriginal legal services, which had been created in the early 1970s, putting this service out to tender among corporate law firms. One month later, the Aboriginal and Torres Strait Islander Commission (ATSIC) was abolished. Four months later, the Australian federal government of the day introduced the Corporations (Aboriginal and Torres Strait Islander) Bill 2005 into federal parliament. The Bill was to replace the *Aboriginal Councils and Associations Act 1976* (Cwth). It was designed to fix the so-called problems with Aboriginal organisations. Aboriginal organisations were progressively affected too by the further marketisation of a newly defined social service sector. Aboriginal organisations were no longer to be subsidised by the state. They were no longer to be given special treatment. This placed many existing urban Aboriginal organisations in funding competition with secular and religious non-government organisations. They were also subject to a whole new set of regulatory arrangements that dictated the way this newly defined social service sector did business with government. As Sanders notes, the new mainstreaming at a government department level has seen very different Indigenous-specific programs inherited from ATSIC turned into much more standardised versions of general government programs (Sanders 2014). This new mainstreaming has also entailed the standardisation of Indigenous-specific programs into one-size-fits-all programs and the standardisation of Aboriginal service delivery, so much so that specialised Aboriginal organisations become redundant and what becomes important is value for money. This is where mainstreaming meets a market rationality. The new mainstreaming differs in that it is not about mainstream services operating alongside Aboriginal services, as a form of complementary service delivery, which was the case in the ATSIC years, but the new mainstreaming is an apparatus or a technology of neoliberal governance.

Further reforms were to come in the state of New South Wales (NSW), diminishing the capacity of many Aboriginal organisations. This would ultimately be followed with a new federal Indigenous affairs funding scheme in 2014, known as the Indigenous Advancement Strategy (IAS), which would see 65 per cent of federal funding for Aboriginal and Torres Strait Islander service delivery go to large, mainstream not-for-profit organisations and the commercial sector, and only 21 per cent go to community-based Aboriginal organisations. While in principle the IAS enables Aboriginal organisations to apply for grants for community need–based programs, it has proven problematic not only in this context but nationally. Its narrow mandate, its blanket competitive process, its failure to fund successful Aboriginal organisations despite evidence-based data demonstrating success in the area, and its failure to support community-based Aboriginal organisations to meet the needs of Aboriginal people on the ground, are just some of the local criticisms of the IAS in the greater Newcastle region. These further reforms saw some community-based Aboriginal organisations go into administration. Others stopped operating (e.g. the Hunter Aboriginal Children's Service) and their services were mainstreamed (e.g. the Aboriginal Medical Centre in Western Sydney). Others started to change the way they did business in order to diminish the new stranglehold governments had on them and to reclaim their autonomy and independence and capacity to continue on with their social and cultural development agendas.

While this chapter discusses briefly the regulatory technologies governing Aboriginal organisations in the neoliberal age, it does not give detailed consideration to the political moment described above. Instead, it situates this political moment historically, returning to the moment urban Aboriginal organisations were formed in the Australian city of Newcastle. Aboriginal activists who formed Aboriginal organisations in Newcastle were not only 'very active in the pursuit of government support' but also became 'skilled grant-getters and grant-users' (Sullivan 2015: 7). This shows how they 'understood the rules of the game as it played out in their local areas and became adept at using them' (Sullivan 2015: 7). They were highly effective in leveraging grants from NSW government departments and the federal Department of Aboriginal Affairs, and later ATSIC, to freely pursue Aboriginal social and cultural development locally, which also led to positive economic outcomes through the creation of important Aboriginal social infrastructure. This led to the creation of various Aboriginal services and programs. This too significantly contributed to addressing the socio-economic disadvantage local Aboriginal people experience. Aboriginal people in Newcastle had found a mechanism for exercising their rights to self-determination and autonomy in matters relating to their internal and local affairs through the creation of autonomous Aboriginal organisations. Urban Aboriginal organisations have thus gone on to play a distinctive role in society in relation to urban Aboriginal peoples and their rights to self-determination and community development in Newcastle. They have proven essential to advocacy, the maintenance of community development and the creation of new social infrastructure, with their success resulting in both economic and social outcomes. Government grants provided a means for financing their autonomous functions.

Game changes

The political moment I describe at the beginning of this paper is when the 'rules of the game suddenly changed' (Sullivan 2015: 7). This chapter provides insights into how the regulatory technologies of neoliberal governance weakened Aboriginal autonomy and self-determination. That is, how changes to funding arrangements severely restricted the means for financing their autonomous functions, reducing the capacity of community-based Aboriginal organisations to meet the needs of local Aboriginal people. It also explains that, while all grasp the rules of the neoliberal game and adapt, it is not about adapting to the new rules of the game. It is about finding strategies to respond to this invasive system, which attempts to colonise the Aboriginal domain, as well as to its racialised effects and its undermining of Indigenous rights (Howard-Wagner 2006, 2016, 2017a). I argue elsewhere that there has been a transformation in state governance wherein neoliberal rationalities and technologies have been applied to the governance of Indigenous affairs (Howard-Wagner 2006). Via an analysis of the neoliberal rationalities and technologies governing Indigenous affairs, certain points are established (Foucault & Ewald 2003: 140–1). These are the systems of differentiations; the types of objectives; instrumental modes; forms of institutionalisation; and the degrees of political rationalities (ibid.). The subjective processes, ethical projects and moral logics of neoliberalism in relation to the governing of Indigenous affairs are also considered in this body of work. However, I argue that it is also important to acknowledge the sites of agency and resistance that come from such responses. For example, how the reactions and strategies of those who manage Aboriginal organisations evidence the critical or reflexive vigilance of Aboriginal agency and resistance in the neoliberal age (Howard-Wagner 2006, 2016). Aboriginal agency and resistance is, for example, expressed as endeavours to pursue innovative funding solutions that will change the funding dynamic with the state, subsidise organisational initiatives, or lead to funding self-sufficiency, which are adopted creatively to bring about social change. So, in this chapter, I suggest the issue is not that Aboriginal organisations in Newcastle embody the economic agenda of the neoliberal state, which arguably they do not (a point Bargh also makes in Chapter 16), but rather that while all are highly successful organisations, there are Aboriginal organisations that have greater capacity than others to acquire assets and pursue an economic development agenda to subsidise social and cultural development.

The disciplinary turn and its deeply racialised effects

Also, while the rationalities and technologies governing Aboriginal organisations in the neoliberal age are not unique to Aboriginal organisations, or not-for-profit organisations in Australia (Dean 2004, Howard-Wagner 2006, Sullivan 2009, 2015), the insidious racialised effects and how this new regime undermines the rights of Indigenous people is troubling (Howard-Wagner 2006, 2009, 2017a). Maria Bargh makes this point too in Chapter 16. Elsewhere, I examine how the disciplinary turn embodied in the processes and practices of governing through neoliberal paternalism has deeply racialised effects (Howard-Wagner 2006, 2010, 2017a). I show the convergence between neoliberalism and what Lawrence Mead (1997) first termed the 'new paternalism' as a form of public administration with a directive and supervisory approach to disadvantaged populations in the neoliberal age, which are considered as lacking self-discipline and personal responsibility (Mead 1997, Howard-Wagner 2006, 2010). This form of conditionality that governs social service contracts and the way the not-for-profit sector does business with the state in the neoliberal age, like welfare conditionality, has the fundamental aim of not only changing social behaviour (e.g. the 'the making of parenting payments conditional on school attendance and regular health checks', Howard-Wagner 2006, 2010), but also changes the conditions under which the state provides and manages social service delivery. In this collection, Shelley Bielefeld explains 'conditionality' in more depth in the context of the cashless welfare card (see Chapter 8). Elsewhere, too, I define the neoliberal age and discuss how these new regulatory arrangements constrain the capacity of community-based Aboriginal organisations, requiring them to meet new accreditation standards and attend leadership and governance workshops, while their performance is regulated and monitored through a new contractualism (Howard-Wagner 2016). Patrick Sullivan also describes the effect of the new public management (NPM), or neoliberal public management, on Indigenous corporations in the neoliberal age (see Chapter 10).

Methodology

This chapter is informed by the findings of a recent four-year study in the Australian city of Newcastle of Aboriginal success in addressing Aboriginal disadvantage and improving Aboriginal wellbeing.[1] The study builds on a three-year sociological ethnography of the progressing of Indigenous rights in the neoliberal age conducted from 2000 to 2003. This research was designed to develop a collaborative approach between Aboriginal organisations in Newcastle, government program managers and administrators, and the researcher, and to promote research that meets community-based, policy and scholarly concerns. The research aim was to not only provide an account of an urban Aboriginal community's success in addressing Aboriginal disadvantage and improving Aboriginal wellbeing, but also to tell the story behind this success. Those contributing to this research included 14 Aboriginal organisations, seven government departments and eight mainstream non-government organisations in the greater Newcastle region. The findings come from lengthy discussions with local Aboriginal people in the design phase of the study; 71 in-depth interviews (some group interviews and some repeated) conducted with Aboriginal and non-Aboriginal people working in Aboriginal service delivery and policy positions in local,

---

1   This chapter is generated from research undertaken by the author as part of an Australian Research Council Early Career Research project titled 'Indigenous societies, governance and wellbeing: A study of Indigenous community success in addressing disadvantage and promoting wellbeing' (DE120100798).

state and federal government organisations, Aboriginal organisations and mainstream not-for-profit organisations in Newcastle; historical documents and oral histories; a discussion circle with Aboriginal elders; several informal in-depth discussions; successive follow-up interviews; observations; two community forums to discuss the findings of the research; and collaborator and participant feedback on a lengthy report of the research findings. Triangulated, the texts, interview narratives and life histories tell a story of multidimensional Aboriginal success (individual, organisational and community) in Newcastle—time and again. They also provide important knowledge about the current challenges facing the local Aboriginal community and people.[2]

Indigenous policy in the recognition and social development era

The adoption of the federal policy of self-determination and decentralised governance by the Whitlam Government in the 1970s, and the Aboriginal development approach of the day was directed at supporting the creation of 'autonomous de-colonised self-governing [Aboriginal] entities' so that Aboriginal people could manage 'their lives in culturally appropriate ways' (Moran 2012: 1). While dropping self-determination as a federal policy agenda, the Fraser Government continued with a broad policy of Indigenous self-management and self-sufficiency. Its passing of the *Aboriginal Councils and Associations Act 1976* (Cwth) furthered this policy agenda, allowing for the formal establishment of Aboriginal governance and autonomous self-governing community organisations. The original intent of the Act was to 'enable Aboriginal communities to develop legally recognisable bodies that reflect their own culture and do not require them to subjugate this culture to overriding Western European legal concepts' (Viner 1976). Arguably, too, the state was responding to the agency, activism and agenda set by Aboriginal people. Statutory recognition

---

2   I wish to thank those who gave their voice to the argument presented in this chapter, as well as their comment and feedback on the research findings, its argument and its situating of the research. Many involved in this research have been de-identified, even though they agreed to being identified, and the data has been coded thematically in terms of looking for patterns and themes. Furthermore, while based on comprehensive in-depth interviews with Aboriginal people who were generous and willingly engaged and assisted with this study, by way of respect, I wish to note that this chapter does not 'speak for' nor does it represent an Aboriginal voice or claim an Indigenous authority. The writing of this chapter involves a non-Indigenous researcher imposing their theoretical and analytical understanding onto data that was collected from in-depth interviews with Aboriginal people.

generally was by no means perfect. It did see the rise of urban Aboriginal corporations, which relied heavily on government grants as not-for-profit organisations, but used government grants to create Aboriginal social infrastructure to support urban Aboriginal people in localities around NSW, for example. As Fletcher notes, the 'importance of developments flowing from this period should not be underestimated' (Fletcher 1994: 7). This concerned:

> the impetus given to Aboriginal communities to incorporate as community organisations for the conduct of their own affairs ... [and] it is largely through the growth of [Indigenous] autonomous community organisations and the pressure they have exerted for change that [Indigenous] aspirations for self-determination continued to be advanced (Fletcher 1994: 7).

This era had its critiques. For example, Perkins argued that Aboriginal organisations 'became preoccupied with following the agendas established by others' (Perkins 1994: 34).

Rowse, and many others (Page this volume, Chapter 10), have argued that this saw the rise of an 'Indigenous sector', which Rowse argues was an important product of the self-determination era (Rowse 2005). The Indigenous sector is a shorthand term not only for the Aboriginal incorporated councils, employers and job placement agencies, Indigenous health services, legal services, housing associations and schools and sporting clubs, but also for this 'sector's' relationship to government (Rowse 2005). Arguably, the formation of Aboriginal organisations was something far more complex, and Rowse gets at this in terms of his analysis of the dual political and service delivery function of Aboriginal organisations. Much too has been written about the function of Aboriginal organisations (e.g. Smith 2002, 2008, Martin 2003, Sullivan 2015), and even their risk to informal Indigenous social practices through the juridification of social relations (Martin 2003).

The passing of the *Aboriginal Councils and Associations Act* did not suddenly see Aboriginal councils and associations form. Aboriginal activism in urban areas in NSW had already led to the establishment of an Aboriginal legal service in Redfern (1970) and Newcastle (1974), an Aboriginal medical service in Redfern (1971), and the establishment of the Awabakal Newcastle Aboriginal Co-operative (the Awabakal Co-op) in Newcastle (1975), for example. There was also the Aboriginal Christian Co-operative Movement, which lead to the establishment of various cooperatives on missions in NSW and Queensland, as well as the Tranby Aboriginal Cooperative College in Glebe in 1958 (Loos & Keast 1992). There were also the political Aboriginal associations formed earlier to progress the rights of Aboriginal people, such as the Aborigines Protection Association, an all-Aboriginal body formed in 1937 with the three aims of full citizenship rights for Aboriginal Australians, Aboriginal representation in parliament and abolition of the NSW Aborigines' Protection Board.

Consistent with Fletcher's argument, I argue here and elsewhere that urban community-based Aboriginal organisations in particular have been essential to urban Aboriginal self-determination in Newcastle, and elsewhere, in terms of Aboriginal community development, including the building and maintenance of Aboriginal social infrastructure and the taking of service delivery into urban Aboriginal peoples' own hands (Howard-Wagner 2017b). Importantly then, urban community-based Aboriginal organisations in Newcastle are not simply a sector or a service provider. Rather, they symbolise autonomy and control and are at the heart of, and central to, urban Aboriginal community building and development in this city. As one local Aboriginal person notes, it is about 'being equal to the white people and running [Aboriginal country, organisations, programs and services] the way we want to' (interview 64).

Aboriginal people were not establishing enterprises, but rather Aboriginal and non-Aboriginal activists were engaged in establishing new forms of community-controlled cooperatives, associations and services in the urban areas of NSW, for example. These initial Aboriginal organisations were not established from government funding, but from donations. The incorporation of the Awabakal Co-op reflects its emergence from the endeavours of local activism and its communal intent. It was established in 1975 from donations from local Aboriginal and non-Aboriginal people, replacing the Newcastle Aboriginal Advancement Society, and first registered as a Community Advancement Cooperative Society in 1977 under the *Charitable Collections Act 1934* (NSW) (Heath 1998: 66). The term cooperative was used to reflect the fact that the organisation was a cooperative or an autonomous association of Aboriginal people united voluntarily to meet their common economic, social, and cultural needs and aspirations through a jointly owned and democratically controlled community collective. As Heath notes:

> The decision to register under the Cooperative Societies Act was based on the feeling that the spirit of cooperative societies better reflected philosophies of traditional [Aboriginal] societies than that of other incorporated bodies which basically reflect competition (Heath 1998: 66).

It was established:

> to provide empowerment to the Aboriginal communities of the Hunter through the delivery of health and social services, in a practice consistent with and relevant to community needs, while maintaining respect for our cultural diversity (interview 59).

As such, the community development activities of the Awabakal Co-op were mostly cultural and social economy activities.

Like Aboriginal Friendship Centres in Canada and Indian Centres in the United States, the Awabakal Co-op was set up by a group of local Aboriginal activists, who had migrated to Newcastle in the 1950s and 1960s, with the assistance of non-Aboriginal people from the Newcastle Trades Hall Council, to support the increasing number of Aboriginal people migrating to Newcastle in the 1970s from rural areas in western and north-western NSW. Its formal incorporation and governance structures not only reflected the fact that it was formed out of Aboriginal activism but was also a communal entity, rather than serving the purposes of a select few Indigenous family groups. It was a cooperative owned and operated by local Aboriginal people and, as such, was membership-based. It also put in place the formalised Western structures of incorporated associations, including a separation of powers between the elected board of directors and the chairperson, and annual general meetings. Initially, the Awabakal Co-op was a 'hub' (Jonas 1991) or 'incubator' (Smith 2008) for other Aboriginal organisations, such as Yarnteen, because governments would only invest in new programs if they were under the umbrella of the Awabakal Co-op (Jonas 1991). It went on to become 'a leading example of Aboriginal community power in Australia' (Awabakal Ltd 2016). Aboriginal people in Newcastle did not have statutory property rights, and their revenue-raising capacity for community social and cultural development was highly restricted (Dodson & Smith 2003). The only viable funding option was to seek out government support.

Aboriginal organisation building in Newcastle was not economically driven, but rather served a civil society function. It was about Aboriginal control, autonomy and self-determination. Yarnteen's vision, for example, was to become a 'full free agent in our own development' (Jonas 1991: 12). Organisation building offered a mechanism for achieving a separate Indigenous domain in that it offered a way of circumventing mainstream social, educational, employment, housing and health services, building Aboriginal social infrastructure, providing culturally centred programs and services, and 'doing business the Aboriginal way' (interview 53). It was also a means for revitalising local Aboriginal culture, knowledge and language, as well as improving the wellbeing of local Aboriginal people. Local Aboriginal people created 'a really good base here … a social base within our community. There are some very big, dominant, longstanding organisations that the community respond to and have very significant cultural processes' (interview 58).

Over the next 30 years, Aboriginal people went on to create what Arthur (1994) terms a 'loose confederation' of culturally centred community-based Aboriginal organisations in Newcastle. They were a loose confederation not primarily because of the association between programs or services, but because of the association between key Aboriginal people who played a role in the setting up and development of Aboriginal organisations, like Awabakal Co-op, Yarnteen Ltd, Wandiyali Aboriginal and Torres Strait Islander Corporation, Miromaa Aboriginal Language and Technology Centre and the Awabakal Local Aboriginal Land Council. While a key group of Aboriginal people started these organisations, and they and their families are associated with Aboriginal organisations locally, they have not (contra Vanstone 2005) historically been the antithesis of accountability, transparency and equity (Smith 2008: 206). Nor have select local Aboriginal families been employed by these organisations or been the only ones to have access the Aboriginal social infrastructure, programs and services they provide. Contrary to Perkins' argument, despite their dependency on government funding and its coercive effects in other contexts, community-based Aboriginal organisations in Newcastle maintained their creativeness and innovation from the 1970s through to the early 21st century (Perkins 1994: 35).

By the early 21st century, Aboriginal organisations offered medical and dental services, transport services for elders, services for the disabled, childcare services, preschools, social and public housing programs, youth and family programs, language and cultural programs, and employment and training services. They were closing the gap through the establishment of much-needed culturally centred Aboriginal social infrastructure for Aboriginal people living in the region as far north as Karuah to the north of

Maitland and as far west as Toronto on the western side of Lake Macquarie. The creation of urban Aboriginal social infrastructure in Newcastle has been a pathway to economic empowerment for local Aboriginal people. It has created jobs, encouraged social inclusion, improved access to facilities, services and programs, improved socio-economic outcomes and health and wellbeing, and increased social mobility.

According to data from the first three Australian Bureau of Statistics census periods in the 21st century (2001, 2006 and 2011), the Indigenous population in Newcastle has fared better than the Indigenous populations in NSW, more generally, in comparison to 23 urban NSW localities with populations of 2,000 or more. It also fares better than the national Indigenous population across a range of indicators. The Newcastle Indigenous population has the second-lowest unemployment rate in 2011 at 13.4 per cent, and the second smallest gap (10 per cent) in unemployment rates between Indigenous (13.4 per cent) and non-Indigenous populations (3.4 per cent) compared with the other 23 urban localities. The Newcastle Indigenous population has the second-highest median personal income at AU$411 per week. It also has the second-highest median household income at AU$1,044 per week. The Newcastle Indigenous population has the third-highest rate of year 12 completions at 31.6 per cent. It also has the second-highest rate of tertiary (university or other) completion at 13.7 per cent. The socio-economic outcome is an Aboriginal community that 'sits at the top of the bottom of the socio-economic pile' (interview 58). What the interviewee means by this is that Newcastle stands out as a locality that is successfully reducing Indigenous unemployment and additionally closing the unemployment and education gap between Indigenous and non-Indigenous peoples.

Other events too played a critical role in the development of Aboriginal organisations in Newcastle. As Will Sanders notes in Chapter 6, ATSIC and the Community Development Employment Projects (CDEP) program played a critical function in this regard (see below). ATSIC had a significant effect on the formation and development of Yarnteen Ltd. What is more, from 1994 to 2002, Yarnteen CDEP was the largest CDEP program in NSW with over 250 participants. Yarnteen has not only contributed to improved social wellbeing among local Aboriginal people, but also has a successful track record in enterprise development.

One of the best projects that ever came about was CDEP. Initially Yarnteen wasn't interested because a section of our board felt that it was just another prop. Not really in it, but once we investigated it and Yarnteen took it on because we could see that there was so much flexibility, there was capital input. There was money towards each—for participants to just work two days for the goal.

My role back then was employment manager. I could have a young person come in say I'd like to be a florist. So, I can take that two-day incentive or that two day's work for dole, I'd use that as incentive to an employer. I'd say to that employer, let's build a training plan, you've got to add at least a third day and a training plan and it's got to be a pathway with an outcome for this person. We'd be like—we'd be the employer. We'd pay their wages, we'd bill the employers. So, we had programs like that happening everywhere. We had projects with John Hunter Hospital, maintenance with parks, Housing Commission, cleaning out of the houses. We had a landscape company, building company. We had over 240 participants at any one time. We didn't ignore our other organisations in the area. We would have agreements and partnerships with land councils where they might take six people from their community to be on a project.

The CDEP also gave capital expenditure so we were able to go, well this is what equipment is needed for that particular business opportunity so we'll invest in that. I guess it was really a great—used correctly CDEP was an excellent program and it was the thing that made the difference for Yarnteen in going forward and being wise about, from there, having opportunity to be a part of the normal business opportunities available. Banking loans to purchase premises, to house these programs and building up an asset base … Yamuloong was built and people got their trades so started to do first year trades, do landscaping and seeding of indigenous plants.

We ran kitchens where they were doing hospitality, catering and product—we had business … [a] practice firm. … one of the practice firm ideas was all around bush tucker. So, the participants would come in and learn about business plans and how do you establish a business …

We're always seeing new governments, new policy, new … When the CDEP closed it was disappointing because we could see the great success and the opportunity. … We were particularly, I guess … smart in the good times so we were quite well established and we were able to continue to operate … (interview former CEO Yarnteen).

Yet, the game slowly changed at the turn of the 21st century. A notable change came around 2005, when ATSIC was abolished followed by CDEP.

> What's happened in the last ten years is we lost ATSIC, CDEP as well ... (interview 53).

The idea of NPM as a neoliberal project is important to understanding this game change. There has been a change in the relationship between the state and Aboriginal peoples and a rethinking of Indigenous rights (Howard-Wagner 2017a). Mainstreaming can be understood in the context of its rationale, which contends that the social service delivery needs of Aboriginal peoples are easily met by mainstream not-for-profits or the corporate sector. NPM has been accompanied by new paternalistic top-down Indigenous policies and approaches, facilitating pathways to individual development and individual entrepreneurship at the federal level, focusing on Indigenous jobs, land and economy, and increasing business and employment opportunities for the individual, obscuring the diverse approaches of participatory or Indigenous-driven development (Hunt 2013, Howard-Wagner 2016, 2017b).

NPM's consequent sociological effect is that its modalities have reduced the function of Aboriginal organisations to service delivery organisations. Aboriginal organisations, which formerly operated like community cooperatives and had a far more societal function in relation to community development and self-determination, now operate in a competitive social service market, competing with mainstream not-for-profits, and each other, for funding. A market that is nonetheless false and does not attribute a true economic, social or public value to the social service that is provided.

Many interviewees talked about the various policy and regulatory changes since the *Corporations (Aboriginal and Torres Strait Islander) Act 2006* (CATSI Act), which promoted good corporate governance and management, and the establishment of Office of the Registrar of Indigenous Corporations (2007 – present), through to the IAS (2014 – present).

They talked about how the new regulations now unnecessarily govern the way they do business, as well as how policies and funding arrangements constrain their capacity to act autonomously in meeting the needs of local Aboriginal people as defined by local Aboriginal people.

I know when they did mainstream, the Aboriginal programs and asked for tenders across the community that diluted ownership of our own programs. I think we've got to be letting Aboriginal people have that, I guess, place where they're able to bring the services to their own people and not dilute it across a whole range of different service providers who may not have the connection to community or the real understanding of the needs. So, it's really important that Aboriginal community based organisations have those programs (interview 50).

Many noted how this, coupled with the demands of new contractual and funding arrangements, is changing and limiting the way Aboriginal organisations operate.

Huge personal pressure. Huge organisational pressure to be still doing that and the stresses, which of course come with it. It actually makes our time really hard to be involved with or to go out and keep those relationships or whatever they are, strong and to even grow them. Right at this moment I have zero time as an example, to be able to go out there and be knocking on the Land Council's door and sitting down and having meetings with them and giving them an overview of what we're up to. How can we support your work or support your members as such and your role you're playing with your community? I don't have the time to go down to Awabakal Co-op where it's a staff member here to talk with the preschool to try and build up that relationship with the teachers there, with the kids. It could be introducing language into their programs or talk to the medical staff within their programs, about using language and identity as a means of mental healing and so forth there and strengthening identity and self-esteem.

… They're the things that we like to do. They're the things which we also do see [as] part of our wider service and agenda. But we'd love to be able to do that. But it's as hard … Not just us, but other organisations, for them to be able to do that. The climate politically, and the funding, which is also attached to that. It's just really hard … (interview 53).

Interviewees talked about the courses senior position holders are sent on to ensure they engage in 'good governance' practices, manage risk and improve standards and efficiency, and the processes their organisations have to go through to meet new forms of accreditation required to deliver housing, child wellbeing and family services, for example.

While their accounts detail the effects of the marketisation of social services, they also reveal how the new forms of contractualism, the new paternalism and conditionality impact on their capacity to 'do business the Aboriginal way' (interview 53). They talked about how this game changed in terms of, for example:

> Advocacy's been lost through changes to contracts ... every time recently there's been critical [issues] in the Aboriginal space ... It's eerily silent and that really bothers me (interview 58)

> ... one-size-fits-all programs, which don't work (interview 55)

> ... chasing the resources and doing the paperwork, which doesn't leave time for the important stuff (interview 58)

> ... hindering their capacity for innovation and entrepreneurship (interview 56)

> ... limit[ing] the time we have for collaborating with other organisations (interview 61)

> ... stopping our momentum in addressing Aboriginal disadvantage (interview 58).

Those who had been sent to mandatory governance training as part of their contractual arrangements with funding bodies accepted that this was part of the way 'governments now do business' (interview 66), but also noted that governments often failed to recognise the importance of Aboriginal culture and obligations to community as central to the governance and success of local Aboriginal organisations (see Howard-Wagner 2016). Many also commented to the effect that 'good [Aboriginal] governance is also being inclusive of community and being— ensuring service provision to the community ... That shared vision ...' (interview 55).

This is coupled with the fact that Aboriginal organisations are accountable not to just one funding body, but several.

> It's crazy. It is crazy and then you've got all your accreditations on top. So, you're not just reporting to funding bodies, every service has an accrediting body so you have to be compliant with all of that. So, we have four different bodies that we have to be accredited to so, yeah, it's mad. It is mad! (interview 10)

The present moment underscores the precarity community-based Aboriginal organisations face while remaining in a relationship of funding dependency with governments. This is reflected in the following statements:

> The problem that we've had to date with social development is we have a strong dependency on government to deliver the social services … (interview 66)

> I think while we still have that reliance, or that prevalence to focus on funding, to determine our affairs, so we're going to consistently have an issue where we will have that dictated to us (interview former CEO Awabakal Ltd).

It is a relationship in which the state holds the power, and it can change the game at any moment.

Today, too, interviewees no longer talk about self-determination in terms of autonomous self-governing entities, but also 'self-determination is about being financially sustainable and viable' (interview 61) and 'economic development is just a means to an end … that will allow us to do what we want to do culturally, and do what we want to do socially' (interview 66). Yet, there are Aboriginal organisations that will remain dependent on government funding because of the types of social services they provide. And, while others already have soundly managed income-generating assets and/or social enterprises and subsidise social programs through income generated from these assets and enterprises, such as Miromaa selling its language database nationally and internationally, they are far from achieving funding sustainability. They face the challenge of getting 'governments to see some value in what you do' (interview 60) or 'moving away from a government funded model to a purchasing model and insisting that the government is then purchasing these services off you' (interview CEO Awabakal).

For others like Yarnteen Ltd and Awabakal Co-op, this is not about creating social and economic enterprises or acquiring assets, as that has been very much a part of their business operations for decades, but about moving towards greater self-sufficiency. Awabakal Co-op is no longer a cooperative. In 2014, it became Awabakal Limited and registered as a not-for-profit public company limited by guarantee. It has a new constitution and its principal purposes have broadened to reflect its new economic development agenda, which sits alongside its original objectives to provide services to Aboriginal people in the Newcastle area as well as strengthen and foster the development of Aboriginal identity and culture in the Newcastle area (Section 6, Awabakal Ltd Constitution).

Conclusion

In conclusion, in their efforts to end this new relationship of dependency with the state in the neoliberal age, do Aboriginal organisations in Newcastle create the very model that governments ultimately encourage— entrepreneurial, autonomous organisations with increased participation in the mainstream economy? Arguably, the answer is no. The development of social and economic enterprises and acquisition of assets among Aboriginal organisations in Newcastle is not new nor is their participation in the mainstream economy. This is demonstrated in the case study of how Yarnteen leveraged CDEP to create capital, social enterprises and build its business—the 'good times' allowed it to keep going in the 'hard times'. Also, while Aboriginal organisations in Newcastle have adapted to this new regime, their core business, the way Aboriginal organisations do business culturally, and the types of services Aboriginal organisations deliver, has not changed. Aboriginal autonomy remains their core objective. What has changed is the rules of the game, their relationship with the state and the means by which Aboriginal organisations in Newcastle are funded. If urban Aboriginal organisations have the capacity to not only acquire land but also to use it for development, carry out agricultural, pastoral, fishing, forestry, mining and other primary producing activities, process, manufacture or distribute products, increase their assets, create more enterprises and get governments to purchase the services they provide to local Aboriginal people, the ground shifts in terms of their dependency on the state. Self-sufficiency improves the capacity of Aboriginal organisations in Newcastle to achieve what they originally set out to achieve. This may be seen as co-opting or embodying the very economic agenda that many critique is associated with the neoliberal game change, but a more complex reading of the situation reveals how its involves resisting the rules of the game, modifying them to one's own end, and finding new ways to pursue urban Aboriginal self-determination. It is too early to determine success. Whether the new regime provides Aboriginal organisations in Newcastle a new means for achieving recognition from below and access to the decision-making power they once had is yet to be seen; Maria Bargh (Chapter 16) argues that it has for Māori tribal (*iwi*) enterprises.

Also, as Dominic O'Sullivan argues in Chapter 13, is it 'more instructive to consider what [Indigenous peoples] want from economic and political activity and the ways in which [Indigenous peoples] are agents in managing neoliberalism's constraints and pursuing its possibilities'? What's more, as Will Sanders argues in Chapter 6, '[f]raming and labelling are important, and it may be that insisting that this is still the age of decolonisation, as well as neoliberalism, is a way to keep alive ideas about the recognition of Indigenous rights'.

Acknowledgement

This research described in this paper has been funded by an Australian Research Council DECRA Fellowship (DE120100798).

References

Arthur B (1994). *The same but different: Indigenous socio-economic variation*, Australian Institute of Aboriginal and Torres Strait Islander Studies, Canberra.

Awabakal Ltd (2016). Website, www.awabakal.org/.

Dean M (2004). *Governmentality: Power and rule in modern society*, SAGE Publications, London.

Dodson & Smith D (2003). *Governance for sustainable development: Strategic issues and principles for Indigenous Australian communities*. Centre for Aboriginal Economic Policy Research, The Australian National University, Canberra.

Fletcher C (1994). *Aboriginal self-determination in Australia*, Aboriginal Studies Press, Canberra.

Foucault M & Ewald F (2003). *'Society must be defended': Lectures at the collège de France, 1975–1976 (Vol. 1)*, Picador, New York.

Heath J (1998). Muloobinbah: The contributions of Aboriginal people to the resources of the Hunter region. In Hunter C (ed.), *Riverchange*, Newcastle Region Public Library, Newcastle.

Howard-Wagner D (2006). Post Indigenous rights: The political rationalities and technologies governing federal Indigenous affairs in Australia in the contemporary period. PhD thesis, University of Newcastle, Australia.

Howard-Wagner D (2009). Whiteness, power relations, resistance and the 'practical' recognition of Indigenous rights in Newcastle. *Theory in Action* 2(1), doi.org/10.3798/tia.1937-0237.08028.

Howard-Wagner D (2010). The state's Intervention in Indigenous affairs in the Northern Territory: Governing the Indigenous population through violence, abuse and neglect. In Browne C & McGill J (eds), *Violence in France and Australia: Disorder in the postcolonial welfare state*, Sydney University Press, Sydney.

Howard-Wagner D (2016). Child wellbeing and protection as a regulatory system in the neoliberal age: Forms of Aboriginal agency and resistance engaged to confront the challenges for Aboriginal people and community-based Aboriginal organisations. *Australian Indigenous Law Review* 19(1):88–102.

Howard-Wagner D (2017a). Governance of Indigenous policy in the neoliberal age: Indigenous disadvantage and the intersecting of paternalism and neoliberalism as a racial project. *Ethnic and Racial Studies* 41(7):1332–51, doi.org/10.1080/01419870.2017.1287415.

Howard-Wagner D (2017b). *Successful urban Aboriginal-driven community development: A place-based case study of Newcastle*. Discussion Paper 293, Centre for Aboriginal Economic Policy Research, The Australian National University, Canberra.

Hunt J (2013). *Engaging with Indigenous Australia—Exploring the conditions for effective relationships with Aboriginal and Torres Strait Islander communities*, Issues paper no. 5, produced for the Closing the Gap Clearinghouse.

Jonas W (1991). *Awabakal, Bahtabah, Biripi, Worimi: Four successful Aboriginal organisations*. University of Newcastle, Newcastle.

Loos N & Keast R (1992). The radical promise: The Aboriginal Christian cooperative movement. *Australian Historical Studies* 25(99):286–301, doi.org/10.1080/10314619208595911.

Martin DF (2003). *Rethinking the design of Indigenous organisations: The need for strategic engagement*. Discussion Paper 248, Centre for Aboriginal Economic Policy Research, The Australian National University, Canberra.

Mead LM (1997). The rise of paternalism. In Mead LM (ed.), *The new paternalism: Supervisory approaches to poverty*, The Brookings Institution, Washington DC.

Moran M (2012). The 30 year cycle: Indigenous policy and the tide of public opinion. *The Conversation*, 6 July 2012, theconversation.com/the-30-year-cycle-indigenous-policy-and-the-tide-of-public-opinion-8114.

Perkins C (1994). Self-determination and managing the future. In Fletcher C (ed.), *Aboriginal self-determination in Australia*, Aboriginal Studies Press, Canberra.

Rowse T (2005). The Indigenous sector. In Austin-Broos D & Macdonald G (eds), *Culture, economy and governance in Aboriginal Australia (proceedings of a workshop of the Academy of Social Sciences)*, Sydney University Press, Sydney.

Sanders W (2014). *Experimental governance in Australian Indigenous affairs: From Coombs to Pearson via Rowse and the competing principles.* Discussion Paper 291, Centre for Aboriginal Economic Policy Research, The Australian National University, Canberra.

Smith D (2002). *Jurisdictional devolution: Towards an effective model for Indigenous community self determination.* Discussion Paper 233, Centre for Aboriginal Economic Policy Research, The Australian National University, Canberra.

Smith D (2008). The business of governing: Institutional capital in an urban enterprise. In Hunt J, Smith D, Garling S & Sanders W (eds), *Contested governance: Culture power and institutions in Indigenous Australia*, ANU E Press, Canberra.

Sullivan P (2009). Reciprocal accountability: Assessing the accountability environment in Australian Aboriginal affairs policy. *International Journal of Public Sector Management* 22(1):57–72, doi.org/10.1108/09513550910922405.

Sullivan P (2015). *A reciprocal relationship: Accountability for public value in the Aboriginal community sector*, Working/Technical Paper, Lowitja Institute, Carlton, Victoria.

Vanstone A (2005). Address to National Press Club, 23 February, Canberra.

Viner I (1976). Second reading speech, Aboriginal Land Rights (Northern Territory) Bill 1976, House of Representatives, Hansard, 4 June, 3081–4.

PART 3

The dynamic relationship Māori
have had with simultaneously
resisting, manipulating and working
with neoliberalism in New Zealand

13

Māori, the state and self-determination in the neoliberal age

Dominic O'Sullivan

Introduction

Māori pursue their claim to 'sovereign and economic independence' (O'Sullivan & Dana 2008: 364) in a neoliberal age of paradoxical influences. Neoliberal reforms to the public sector, beginning in the mid-1980s, have had significant yet inconsistent influence on Māori legal, political, economic and cultural opportunities. On the one hand, unemployment levels rose significantly as, for example, large state sector Māori employers were corporatised; while trade liberalisation compromised manufacturing's competitiveness. By 1992, Māori unemployment was 25 per cent, in contrast with a national rate of 10 per cent (Mitchell 2009). In 2018, the Māori labour force is growing and the unemployment rate has reduced to 12.2 per cent. While this is more than twice the national rate of 5.2 per cent, it is partly explained by a disproportionately young Māori population (Statistics New Zealand 2016). On the other hand, under the Treaty of Waitangi, Māori could advantageously challenge the terms of the privatisation of state assets.

Policy measures to reduce the size of the state have created opportunities for Māori to increase their collective wealth. They have contributed to the Māori asset base increasing from NZ$9.4 billion in 2001 to NZ$36.9 billion in 2010 to explain the rhetorical presumption that 'Māori business is New Zealand business' (Westpac New Zealand 2014). At the same time, the neoliberal 'small state' philosophy has created opportunities for Māori to take greater responsibility for their own delivery of public services which has, in turn, enhanced self-determination.

The neoliberal constraints on Māori wellbeing that this chapter describes are significant, and the opportunities that it describes are not panaceas for just policy outcomes, but they are grounded in new relationships between Māori and the state where agency is privileged over subservience and perpetual victimhood. While I sympathise with the critique that Bell offers in this volume, I take a more positive position than that where the 'New Zealand state is not a fit subject for recognition politics' (Bell this volume, Chapter 4). Although it was not the state's intent for neoliberalism to facilitate 'recognition politics', such is the effect of the new Treaty jurisprudence emerging from Māori challenges to the privatisation of state assets, and judicial insistence that Māori occupy a distinct position within the modern state. Bell's concern is for political relationships of recognition *within* the state. These are significant, but so too are the relationships that self-determination presumes Māori will pursue beyond the state. It is these extra-state relationships that neoliberalism fosters in ways that were not previously available to Māori on a significant scale.

This chapter begins by explaining the neoliberal paradox that distinguishes contemporary Māori politics and policy. It then sets out some of the ways in which Māori economic entities position themselves to pursue collective interests and thus challenge the constraints of a neoliberal order while simultaneously pursuing its possibilities. Māori participation in the commercial fishing industry is discussed as an example. The chapter then discusses the opportunities for self-determination that Māori have found through neoliberalism's devolution of state functions and responsibilities to non-government entities. The opportunities that the Tūhoe tribe of the central North Island is pursuing are presented as one important example. However, further political and constitutional transformations are sought by, for example, the Iwi Chairs' Forum, and its broader aspirations are also discussed in this chapter. The chapter is ultimately concerned with neoliberalism as a context that is reshaping Māori relationships with the state, as well as Māori positions within the state.

The neoliberal paradox

Neoliberal values and practices simultaneously reinforce and confront colonial legacy; 'a dualism of political space in which settler space is governed by liberal principles and native space is governed through conquest and occupation' (Dahl 2016: 4). Neoliberalism's focus on capital accumulation can be at the expense of cultural considerations and, in some jurisdictions, indigenous livelihoods (Friedman 1999, Kelsey 2005a, 2005b, Stewart-Harawira 2005, Fenelon & Hall 2008). Yet, Fenelon and Hall argue that 'by their very continued existence [indigenous peoples] … pose a major challenge to neoliberal capitalism on the ground, politically and ideologically' (2008: 1872). For Lauderdale, globalisation causes 'cultural assimilation', which, in turn, undermines local and global democracy (2008: 1837). Stewart-Harawira argues that this is compounded by the 'co-optation of tribal elites within a Western paradigm of corporatisation and co-modification' (2005: 179). Friedman's position is similar: there is a Māori tribal 'movement from cultural identity to tribal property' focused on 'genealogical rights to means of production' (1999: 9). In short, material accumulation and cultural identity are incompatible. However, it is also true that indigenous experiences are sometimes uncritically co-opted into non-indigenous campaigns of resistance to neoliberal imperatives. The outcome is to understate the absolute importance that Māori attach to material prosperity through participation in labour and commodity markets. It is, then, a neo-colonial dismissal of Māori agency to argue that the state has used the Treaty of Waitangi and settlements of its breaches to redefine 'tino rangatiratanga [self-determination] to mean commercialised self-governance; and a central illusion of an autonomous Māori economy floating free of its New Zealand counterpart' (Kelsey 2005a: 82). Instead, the Treaty affirms tribal independence or even nationhood. Māori politics' distinguishing concern since 1840 has remained the protection of that nationhood within the New Zealand state. Yet, it is recognised that self-determination requires engagement with others, and that Māori economic opportunities do not, in fact, 'float free' of the Māori economy's 'New Zealand counterpart'.

It is also significant that Māori claims on the state transcend social democratic or egalitarian imperatives to address material disadvantage. These claims are grounded in rights of prior occupancy, relating especially to language, culture and natural resources. Substantive opportunities for participatory parity in the public life of the state is a further consideration.

As Bell notes, in this volume, Treaty settlements offer relatively limited financial compensation, but, together with the development of a comprehensive Treaty jurisprudence, they were sufficient to give some *iwi* (tribes) the economic importance to add to their moral and democratic claims to political voice.

Ironically, as Humpage observes, also in this volume, public dissatisfaction with neoliberal economic policies during the 1980s was the catalyst for the adoption of a proportional representation electoral system, which, in turn, increased Māori parliamentary membership to a proportionate share. However, as a further illustration of the philosophical inconsistencies that pervade Māori public policy, the question of guaranteed Māori representations on local authorities is sharply contested. Humpage shows the paradox through the Whānau Ora social policy and the work of the Ministerial Committee on Poverty, which both 'challenge *and* extend a neoliberal agenda' (Humpage this volume, Chapter 14).

Critiques of neoliberalism can overstate the tensions between cultural and economic aspirations; Māori thought positions the two as inextricably connected and is more likely to reflect Lauderdale's observation of a people not 'interested in reforming the world [capitalist] system … [but] more interested in autonomy and collective determination' (2008: 1837). In 2016, culture continues to distinguish attitudes to Māori economic development where 'characteristics inherent in how Māori view the world … [are] important in assessing and proposing Māori economic development policy' (NZIER 2003).

Coleman et al. dismiss Māori economic agency when they describe the contemporary Māori economy as a 'transformation of Māori from members of a tribal-based, communal culture at the beginning of the nineteenth century to members of an individualistic capitalistic culture at the end of the twentieth century' (2005: 17). Rata similarly sets aside agency when she proposes that 'tribal capitalism' shows how 'a local movement can become reorganised into the global system' to create 'doubly oppressive social and economic structures: the oppressive political and social relations of traditional societies in conjunction with the exploitative economic relations inherent to capitalism' (2003: 44). However, Bargh's introduction to the Māori economy, in this volume, describes quite a different set of relationships, assets and activities. As Bargh argues, it is an oversimplification to suggest that Māori are 'only either champions or victims of neoliberal policies and practices'. It is more instructive to consider what they want from economic and political activity, and the ways in which Māori are agents in managing neoliberalism's constraints and pursuing its possibilities. For example, Māori agency is evident in the non-market opportunities that Bargh shows Māori pursuing, as well as in the ascription of 'legal personhood' to a mountain as part of the Tūhoe Treaty settlement (Bargh this volume, Chapter 16). However, it is true that:

> If Māori do not feel secure about their culture, commercialisation will be seen as a threat, and will be resisted. In this sense, grievances and insecurity spill over into a self-imposed limit on economic development (NZIER 2003: 18).

Iwi Authority Annual Reports, strategy papers and the work of national policy bodies such as the Federation of Māori Authorities (FOMA) show that Māori attention to neoliberal opportunities is, in fact, extensive (FOMA 2015). It is in this context that, in 2014, the Iwi Chairs' Forum sought a NZ$1 billion public contribution to the development of 'underperforming' Māori land. The request appealed to restitutive justice, but was also pragmatically responsive to the Ministry of Primary Industries' projection of an NZ$8 billion benefit, over 10 years, from the full utilisation of Māori land. The Ministry has projected a further benefit of the creation of 3,600 new jobs (Iwi Chairs' Forum 2014).

'Binary understandings of indigenous peoples as either ecological natives or colonised subjects are simplistic and inadequate' (Bargh 2012: 281). For example, in the context of contemporary Treaty of Waitangi claims to water rights:

> it is necessary to avoid a sharp contrast between custom and commodity, between a spiritual conception of water and the commercial exploitation of water, or between pre-industrial or 'indigenous' conceptualisations of the commons and the seemingly irreversible global trend towards privatisation of the public domain (van Meijl 2015: 220).

Māori identity can be important to the ways in which economic aspirations are pursued. Identity can also contextualise the opportunities that are available to Māori.

Neoliberalism and collective economic development

The *iwi* is especially well placed to enhance group identity and use collective resources to integrate cultural and economic imperatives. Smith et al.'s (2015) study of four *iwis*' economic aspirations found that cultural values are paramount, but not exclusive, in framing Māori responses to neoliberal thought: 'financial gains and individual benefits should not outweigh those of the collective' (ibid., 93), which means that the individual liberal view that individual rights take precedence over the collective' is based on a false dichotomy. For indigenous peoples, corporate rights are necessarily preliminary to personal liberty. For the entities of Smith et al.'s study:

> economic development is a component of a broader, integrated system of strategic thought, activity and kaupapa [philosophy], undertaken by the tribe in order for it to enhance and distribute mana [authority] and matauranga [knowledge]. It provides for social meaning and cohesion, identity, understanding of relationships ... amongst ourselves, but also between all people ... It provides for an understanding of benefits and burdens as part of a collective way of life ... it builds sustainable hapu communities and addresses the gaps and underlying unity structures, so that present and future generations enjoy oranga whanui [collective well-being], access to power influence and choice of their way of life (R. Gage, personal communication, 3 August 2011, cited in Smith et al. 2015: 77).

The *iwi*'s long-term focus challenges neoliberal capitalism but not in ways that understate the modern *iwi*'s certain and unapologetic pursuit of material wellbeing. The *iwi*'s permanency, geo-political attachment and trans-generational approach to investment gives it stability. Its purpose is not constrained by the immediate needs and expectations of private shareholders. Its trans-generational time horizon gives it a unique approach to economic growth. For example, one Māori Incorporation adopts a:

> 100 year strategic plan that builds on the [more than 100-year-old] founding principles: to retain ownership, tread lightly upon the land, engage with the local community and ensure our mokopuna's mokopuna [grandchildren's grandchildren] live a healthier, wealthier life (Westpac New Zealand 2014).

Māori participation in the commercial fishing industry demonstrates a particular form of engagement with global capitalism, which McCormack describes, in this volume, as a 'neoliberal "opening of spaces"'. However, she also explains the cultural contradictions in the commodification of fisheries, and notes that the integration of returned assets into capitalist markets can 'lead to new and more permanent forms of loss' (McCormack 2016). However, the fisheries example does illustrate, again, the ways in which Treaty settlements are helping to assert a culturally framed commercial identity focused on the 'reinvention of the relationship between "coloniser and colonised"' (Johnson 2008) to recognise that:

> Indigenous peoples have the right to maintain and strengthen their distinct political, legal, economic, social and cultural institutions, while retaining their right to participate fully, if they so choose, in the political, economic, social and cultural life of the State (United Nations Declaration on the Rights of Indigenous Peoples: Article 5).[1]

It was from this same perspective that, in 1992, Māori responded to a government proposal to bring market discipline to fisheries management through tradeable quota. Māori raised a number of questions about ownership of the fisheries that challenged government presumptions of resource ownership: Who actually owns the fisheries? Whose are they to sell or allocate to private commercial interests? Was the proposal a 'commodification of the common heritage' (Frame 1999: 23) that extinguished a Māori property right? Certainly, a case was made to the Waitangi Tribunal that the Quota Management System (QMS) was 'a transfer by the Crown of fishing rights that the Muriwhenua people have not relinquished' (De Alessi 2012: 401).

The claim was upheld. The settlement that was negotiated to allow the QMS to proceed was the establishment of a Māori Fisheries Commission, Te Ohu Kaimoana, that was allocated 10 per cent of the inshore fishery.

> [T]he introduction of a property rights systems for fisheries not only gave rise to the largest indigenous rights claim in the country's history, it also provided the means for indigenous rights to be recognised, ensuring the sustainable utilization of fisheries, while providing for indigenous rights holders to realise their own … social and economic aspirations (Hooper 2000: 18).

---

1   For the full text of the United Nations Declaration on the Rights of Indigenous Peoples, see www.un.org/development/desa/indigenouspeoples/declaration-on-the-rights-of-indigenous-peoples.html.

A further claim to the Tribunal was that earlier actions of the Crown had impeded the Māori fishing industry's commercial development and that further redress was justified. The settlement of that claim and further commercial growth meant that by 2015 the Commission held net assets to the value of NZ$227 million, while the *iwi*-owned Aotearoa Fisheries Ltd recorded a NZ$22 million profit for the year ended September 2014 (Aotearoa Fisheries Limited 2015).

Māori fishing has become a significant contributor to the New Zealand economy. However, in 2016, the government proposed creating a 620,000 km^2 marine sanctuary around the Kermadec Islands, which Māori have challenged as inconsistent with the original settlement on the grounds that it would extinguish a property right that cannot ordinarily occur without compensation.

The government itself was divided on the issue. The senior Coalition partner, the National Party, was committed to the sanctuary, with the Māori Party being concerned to protect fishing rights, while also objecting to the precedent that would be set if a condition of a Treaty settlement were set aside. The Prime Minister's announcement that the proposal would not, for the moment, be pursued illustrated the contemporary significance of the Māori democratic position *within* the state. That position has evolved with the gradual increase in the relative Māori population status, increasing collective and personal wealth and significant increases in the proportion of Māori Members of Parliament, due to the changes to the electoral system introduced in 1996: 'We are not about to go and do something that is going to cause the Māori party to walk away. If we have to wait a while we have to wait a while' (Key, cited in Jones & Trevett 2016). There is, however, the possibility that the sanctuary could proceed with appropriate compensation negotiated between the government and Te Ohu Kaimoana, especially as for Te Ohu Kaimoana the point is more one of principle than potential financial loss. Te Ohu Kaimoana holds 15 per cent of the proposed sanctuary's quota, valued at approximately NZ$65,000 a year (Gillspie 2016). The issue is one of equally respecting the property rights that underlie neoliberal economic imperatives.

Devolution and Māori self-determination

The neoliberal political imperative to reduce the size of the state also influences contemporary Māori policy possibilities. Supporting policy measures have created opportunities for Māori to increase their collective wealth, and participate in culturally framed health and education delivery, for example. Māori claims against the privatisation of state assets, on the grounds that natural resources such as land, fisheries, water and the radio spectrum are not always and necessarily the Crown's to sell, have been used to rebalance relative political authority and pursue those opportunities for self-determination that neoliberalism's smaller state presents. In these ways, it may be that indigeneity provides a significant challenge to neoliberal imperatives. Indeed, the contemporary tribe is especially well placed to enhance group identity and use collective resources to integrate cultural and economic imperatives. It is deliberately focused on transcending colonial subjecthood, using the opportunities and resisting, rather than being defined by, the constraints of neoliberalism.

The proposition that public decisions and policymaking best occur at the closest possible point to policy delivery is consistent with King Tawhiao's[2] still influential account of self-determination: 'Maku ano e hanga toku whare—I will build my own house'—a principle that is foundational to Tawhiao's Waikato *iwi*'s contemporary development strategies (Waikato-Tainui 2015). The same principles inform the Tūhoe people's negotiations with the Crown to assume responsibility for housing, schools, health care and welfare benefits in its tribal area. Tūhoe is motivated by a belief that 'we can design a system where there is a transition from benefits to wages and salaries' (Kruger, cited in Collins 2015). The Crown and Tūhoe would share the savings, creating a financial incentive for both parties. The policy question raised in the government-commissioned report on the proposal's feasibility, *Decentralising welfare—Te mana o tuhoe* is:

> If you take a portion of core Government service and devolve to any group how might you do that in a way that incentivises the agent to achieve positive outcomes while protecting Government exposure to risk … ? (Moore et al. 2014: 7)

---

2   Tawhiao was the third Māori King, he reigned between 1860 and 1894.

The presumption is that Tūhoe 'could get better results … because of the knowledge, proximity and influence with the potential beneficiaries' (ibid.: 33).

The proposal is politically and constitutionally difficult as Tūhoe and the Crown seek alignment between the aspiration to self-determination and the neoliberal principle of devolution to address a policy problem where the lifetime costs of welfare for the 29 per cent of the Tūhoe population in receipt of benefits is NZ$78.1 billion. This includes 4,000 16- and 17-year-olds for whom the lifetime cost is NZ$1 billion (Moore et al. 2014). Tūhoe welfare dependency is the outcome of profound policy failure, including, especially, the impact on employment levels of the corporatisation of the state forestry industry during the 1980s and 1990s. Neoliberalism contributed to a serious policy problem, but now finds itself at the centre of Tūhoe-initiated solutions.

Decentralising welfare notes the aspiration to 'become independent of the Government, generate its own revenue and become self-sustaining' (Moore et al. 2014: v). In particular, 'Tūhoe consider youth parenting and unemployment as an area where they could improve social outcomes for both current and future generations—a concept entirely consistent with mana motuhake [self-determination]' (Moore et al. 2014: 10).

The proposal's success is dependent on a series of complex variables, including the capacity to develop functioning and culturally responsive education and labour markets as poor schooling outcomes and a small local labour market have been further contributors to Tūhoe dependence. The Tūhoe intent is to redirect welfare expenditure to labour market development and to support 'changing a mindset in Tuhoe around being beneficiaries of the state' (Kruger, cited in Moore et al. 2014: 42).

The Tūhoe intention is a dramatic reconfiguration of the relationship between itself and the state. Relationships with the state are an ongoing concern for Māori politics and, in 2010, as a mark of the political significance of the growth in collective Māori wealth, the national Iwi Chairs' Forum established an Independent Working Group on Constitutional Transformation. Its purpose was to develop models of constitutional inclusivity with reference to the Declaration of Independence (1835), the Treaty of Waitangi (1840) and 'other international human rights instruments' (Independent Working Group on Constitutional Transformation 2016: 7). The working group's establishment was the product of self-determination outside the state. Its report was supported by a United Nations' fund established to facilitate the implementation of the Declaration on the Rights of Indigenous Peoples (UNDRIP) to 'express the wish for Māori to make decisions for Māori' (Independent Working Group on Constitutional Transformation 2016: 8). The working group's report, *Matike Mai Aotearoa*, is representative of a broad body of contemporary Māori political thought, helping to clarify questions of what Māori mean by self-determination and showing that Mörkenstam is correct to argue that self-determination's recognition at international law does challenge 'the traditional nation-state centred understandings of political rights and democracy' (2015: 634), which, in turn, challenges the idea of sovereignty as the concern of states alone.

The report is likely to attract criticism. However, in the present context, it is not the merits of its substantive recommendations that are important, but that neoliberal developments over the past 30 years have reconfigured Māori relationships with the state, and positions within the state, to create greater opportunities for collective deliberation in constitutional and political discourse.

Questions about the potential Māori position within the state, in the neoliberal age, are also raised by the Waitangi Tribunal's (2014) finding that in acquiescing to the Treaty of Waitangi, Māori chiefs did not cede sovereignty to the British Crown. The New Zealand Government contests the finding, but, for the Māori claimants, a long-held position is affirmed. From either perspective, questions of what sovereignty means are important to the Tūhoe aspiration described above and to how one might evaluate *Matike Mai*. The finding suggests that state sovereignty is not the all-encompassing power that Hobbes imagined (1988). Nor is it the 'unconstrained' concern of biculturalism's 'Pakeha' Crown (O'Sullivan 2007).

Māori are not entirely excluded from national sovereignty. However, the extent to which they are included, and in which ways, are matters of ongoing political contest. The contest is not always distinguished by what Macedo (1997) calls the liberal virtue of public reasonableness. Yet, the Tribunal finding adds to the moral persuasiveness of arguments for substantive and meaningful shares in national sovereignty. It shows the importance of conceptual clarity on the meaning of sovereignty; a meaning that is morally just, pragmatic and relevant to contemporary Māori claims on the state. However, at the very least, Māori claims to self-determination in the neoliberal age are supported by a construct that, at the very least, accommodates *particular* Māori claims, not as junior partners in a bicultural relationship, but as equal participants in a common body politic as holders of rights that are distinct from, but do not supersede, the rights that they enjoy individually in common with other citizens.

Conclusion

Neoliberal political and economic theories have contextualised Māori public policy over the last 30 years. The neoliberal age needs to work for Māori if it is to work for New Zealand. These theories' influences are both transformative and paradoxical. On the one hand, material and political inequality explains Friedman's argument that 'liberation from one form of oppression [colonialism] can lead to another integrative process and new forms of class differentiation' (1999: 1), causing 'socio-economic depression and further cultural suppression' (Fenelon & Hall 2008: 1874). On the other hand, political reforms intended to support neoliberal economic aspirations created opportunities to reconfigure the nature of national sovereignty and to begin a new Treaty of Waitangi jurisprudence that has altered the ways in which Crown and Māori entities engage. Opportunities were also created for extra-state economic opportunities that Māori actively pursue as self-determination. Critiques of neoliberal philosophy are, then, wrong to cast Māori as perpetual victims (MacDonald & Muldoon 2006), bereft of agency and devoid of thought about the aspirations they wish to pursue and how they will use traditional tribal structures to support these aspirations.

The possibilities for Māori self-determination are broad and multifaceted. They exist beyond the neoliberal paradigm, as much as they exist within it. The common ground is the cultural purpose that is associated with economic activity. While there are arguments for further and more substantive forms of recognition, for more far-reaching expressions of belonging together differently (Maaka & Fleras 2005), it remains that the neoliberal age has gone a significant way towards explaining contemporary opportunities for self-determination; opportunities of an order not otherwise seen since British settlement.

References

Aotearoa Fisheries Limited (2015). *Annual report*, Aotearoa Fisheries Limited, Auckland.

Bargh M (2012). Rethinking and re-shaping indigenous economies: Māori geothermal energy enterprises. *Journal of Enterprising Communities: People and Places in the Global Economy* 6(3):271–83, doi.org/10.1108/17506201211258423.

Coleman A, Dixon S & Mare D (2005). *Māori economic development—Glimpses from statistical sources.* Motu Economic and Policy Research, Wellington.

Collins, S (2015). Tuhoe takes its own path, *New Zealand Herald*, 18 November, www.nzherald.co.nz/maori/news/article.cfm?c_id=252&objectid=11546915.

Dahl A (2016). Nullifying settler democracy: William Apess and the paradox of settler sovereignty. *Polity* 48(2):279–304, doi.org/10.1057/pol.2016.2.

De Alessi M (2012). The political economy of fishing rights and claims: The Māori experience in New Zealand. *Journal of Agrarian Change* 12(2–3):390–412, doi.org/10.1111/j.1471-0366.2011.00346.x.

Fenelon JV & Hall TD (2008). Revitalization and indigenous resistance to globalization and neoliberalism. *American Behavioral Scientist* 51(12):1867–901, doi.org/10.1177/0002764208318938.

FOMA (Federation of Māori Authorities) (2015). *Annual report 2015.* Available: docs.wixstatic.com/ugd/e53368_1d2e844394b54214a1225d7c9791d60c.pdf.

Frame A (1999). Property and the Treaty of Waitangi: A tragedy of the commodities? In McLean J (ed.), *Property and the constitution: A practical guide to company investigations*, Hart Publishing, Oxford.

Friedman J (1999). Indigenous struggles and the discreet charm of the bourgeoisie. *The Australian Journal of Anthropology* 10(1):1–14, doi.org/10.1111/j.1835-9310.1999.tb00009.x.

Gillspie A (2016). Co-operation key to making Kermadecs our Galapagos. *New Zealand Herald*, 20 September, www.nzherald.co.nz/nz/news/article.cfm?c_id=1&objectid=11712888.

Hobbes T (1988) [1651]. *Leviathan*, Oxford University Press, Oxford.

Hooper M (2000). Maori power. In Kumar KG (ed.), *Sizing up: Property rights and fisheries management. A collection of articles from SAMUDRA report*, International Collective in Support of Fishworkers, Chennai.

Independent Working Group on Constitutional Transformation (2016). *The report of Matike Mai Aotearoa*, www.converge.org.nz/pma/Matike MaiAotearoaReport.pdf.

Iwi Chairs' Forum (2014). *Iwi collective proposals: Briefing for the Deputy Prime Minister, Minister of Housing and Minister for the Environment.*

Johnson JT (2008). Indigeneity's challenges to the white settler-state: Creating a thirdspace for dynamic citizenship. *Alternatives* 33:29–52, doi.org/ 10.1177/030437540803300103.

Jones N & Trevett C (2016). PM John Key: Kermadec sanctuary will be put on ice if no agreement with Maori Party. *Northland Age*, 20 September, www.nzherald. co.nz/northland-age/news/article.cfm?c_id=1503402&objectid=11713179.

Kelsey J (2005a). Māori, te Tiriti, and globalisation: The invisible hand of the colonial state. In Belgrave M, Kawharu M & Williams D (eds), *Waitangi revisited: Perspectives on the Treaty of Waitangi*. Oxford University Press, Melbourne.

Kelsey J (2005b). World trade and small nations in the South Pacific region. *Kansas Journal of Law and Public Policy* 14(2):247–306.

Lauderdale P (2008). Indigenous peoples in the face of globalization. *American Behavioral Scientist* 51(12):1836–43, doi.org/10.1177/0002764208318934.

Maaka R & Fleras A (2005). *The politics of indigeneity: Challenging the state in Canada and Aotearoa New Zealand*, University of Otago Press, Dunedin.

MacDonald L & Muldoon P (2006). Globalisation, neoliberalism and the struggle for indigenous citizenship. *Australian Journal of Political Science* 41(2):209–23, doi.org/10.1080/10361140600672477.

Macedo S (1997). In defense of liberal public reason: Are slavery and abortion hard cases? *American Journal of Jurisprudence* 42(1):1–29, doi.org/10.1093/ ajj/42.1.1.

McCormack, F (2016). Indigenous claims: Hearings, settlements, and neoliberal silencing. *PoLAR: Political and Legal Anthropology Review* 39(2):226–43.

Mitchell L (2009). *Māori and welfare*. New Zealand Business Roundtable, Wellington.

Moore D, Scott G, Drew R, Smith J & Whelen C (2014). *Decentralising welfare—Te mana motuhake o tuhoe, report to the ministry of social development*, www.msd.govt.nz/documents/about-msd-and-our-work/publications-resources/research/decentralising-welfare-te-mana-motuhake-o-tuhoe/decentralising-welfare-te-mana-motuhake-o-tuhoe.pdf.

Mörkenstam U (2015). Recognition as if sovereigns? A procedural understanding of indigenous self-determination. *Citizenship Studies* 19(6–7):634–48, doi.org/10.1080/13621025.2015.1010486.

NZIER (New Zealand Institute of Economic Research) (2003). *Māori economic development: Te ōhanga whanaketanga Māori*, Wellington.

O'Sullivan D (2007). *Beyond biculturalism*. Huia Publishers, Wellington.

O'Sullivan J & Dana T (2008). Redefining Māori economic development. *International Journal of Social Economics* 35(5):364–79, doi.org/10.1108/03068290810861611.

Rata E (2003). Late capitalism and ethnic revivalism. *Anthropological Theory* 3(1):43–63, doi.org/10.1177/1463499603003001751.

Smith G, Tinirau R, Gillies A & Warriner V (2015). *He mangopare amohia: Strategies for Māori economic development*, Te Whare Wananga o Awanuiarangi, Whakatane.

Statistics New Zealand (2016). *Maori population estimates*. www.stats.govt.nz/browse_for_stats/population/estimates_and_projections/maori-population-estimates-info-releases.aspx.

Stewart-Harawira M (2005). *The new imperial order: Indigenous responses to globalization*. Zed Books, London.

van Meijl T (2015). The Waikato river: Changing properties of a living Māori ancestor. *Oceania* 85(2):219–37, doi.org/10.1002/ocea.5086.

Waikato-Tainui (2015). *Whakatupuranga Waikato-Tainui 2050*, www.tgh.co.nz/wp-content/uploads/WhakatupurangaWT20501.pdf.

Waitangi Tribunal (2014). *Te Paparahi o te Raki reports*, www.waitangitribunal.govt.nz/inquiries/district-inquiries/te-paparahi-o-te-raki-northland/.

Westpac New Zealand (2014). *Māori business is New Zealand business*, 6 October, www.westpac.co.nz/rednews/business/maori-business-is-new-zealand-business/.

14

Indigenous peoples embedded in neoliberal governance: Has the Māori Party achieved its social policy goals in New Zealand?

Louise Humpage

Introduction

The re-election of conservative governments in many countries in the 2010s suggests that neoliberalism has become normalised and neoliberal values represent 'a common sense of the times' (Peck & Tickell 2002: 381). Yet, indigenous protest movements and political agency exemplify the kind of ongoing 'resistances, refusals, and blockages' that Clarke (2004: 44) believes hinder the smooth running of global neoliberalisation. Despite considerable policy coherence under neoliberal governance, the nuanced, dynamic concept of neoliberal*isation* highlights that differing forms of neoliberal*ism* exist across temporal phases and geographical spaces (Peck & Tickell 2002). As other chapters in this volume illustrate, neoliberalism has inhibited indigenous wellbeing and rights *and* provided important opportunities for indigenous peoples in varied ways across the world.

In New Zealand, for instance, public disgruntlement with neoliberal policies was one factor behind the adoption of a mixed-member proportional (MMP) representation system, which, in turn, saw an increase in the number of electorate seats made available to indigenous Māori in the New Zealand Parliament. Labour MP Tariana Turia caused a by-election in one of these seats in 2004 when refusing to vote for her own government's legislation placing the foreshore and seabed into public ownership, thus denying Māori tribes an opportunity to seek judicial recognition of their continued ownership of this important resource. Her new Māori Party went on to win four Māori electorate seats in the 2008 election. Although the conservative National Party held sufficient general electorates under MMP to govern alone in 2008, it negotiated supply and confidence agreements with smaller parties. This included the Māori Party, challenging an historical alliance between Māori electorates and the Labour Party (Bargh 2015). The relationship continued until the 2017 election, when a Labour–New Zealand First Government came to power (Election Aotearoa 2017).

The Māori Party combines 'a drive towards rangatiratanga [self-determination], *and* an attempt to address the socio-economic needs of Māori' (Smith 2010: 215, emphasis added). Relatively poor levels of health, education, housing and income/wealth among Māori compared to non-Māori New Zealanders (Marriott & Sim 2014) explain why social policy is central to the Māori Party's political platform. Consequently, this chapter focuses on analysis of two key social policy initiatives— Whānau Ora and the Ministerial Committee on Poverty—resulting from Māori Party–National Party relationship accords. At the time of writing, both continued under the new government. Yet some critics claim the Māori Party's relationship with National favoured tribal elites at the expense of the poor (Sykes 2010, Harawira 2011, see also Bargh, Chapter 16, and McCormack, Chapter 15, this volume). Others view Māori Party support or silence on neoliberal/neoconservative agendas— such as the weakening of environmental regulations in return for greater consultation/representation rights for *iwi*—as evidence the Māori Party 'sold out' to neoliberalism (Sachdeva 2015, see McCormack this volume, Chapter 15). This chapter considers how each policy challenges *and* extends a neoliberal agenda, arguing that the Māori Party *began* to achieve its goals in social policy but political constraints inhibited this new opportunity for an indigenous party to make a significant and lasting difference in the social policy arena and, potentially, to hinder the smooth running of neoliberalism.

New Zealand's unique political context

Specific indigenous representation in parliament has existed since Māori electorate seats were established in 1867, providing unique opportunities for Māori to shape New Zealand politics. Forming part of a ruling government offered the Māori Party unprecedented leverage compared to earlier dedicated Māori political parties (Bargh 2015). Supply and confidence agreements require the Māori Party to support the National Party's position in all matters subject to confidence and supply votes in the House of Representatives, as well as on any budgetary or procedural votes needed to pass Bills in parliament. But, in return, the Māori Party gained:

- the right to be consulted on major legislative, budget and policy issues to which the Māori Party is likely to be sensitive

- several key ministerial or associate ministerial positions outside of Cabinet for the Māori Party co-leaders

- progress on Māori Party policies, including the replacement of the *Foreshore and Seabed Act 2004*, which was the catalyst for the establishment of the party; an agreement there would be no attempt to remove nor entrench the Māori electorate seats; a constitutional review; the signing of the United Nations Declaration on the Rights of Indigenous Peoples (UNDRIP); and funds to improve Māori electoral participation (NP & MP 2008, 2011, 2014, English 2016).

Although these policy gains would likely have remained unfulfilled without the Māori Party's influence, critics (Sykes 2010, Harawira 2011) rightly argue that the policy gains were limited and did not fundamentally change Māori lives. The Māori Party claims that it voted against National more than it voted with it. But there are also significant overlaps between National's neoliberal agenda and the economic interests of tribes and Māori businesses with significant assets (see Bargh this volume, Chapter 16), as well as articulated beliefs that the welfare system is part of the 'problem' for Māori, requiring both greater individual and familial responsibility and decentralised models of funding (Turia 2006).

Nonetheless, some members of National's core constituency actively resist recognition of either indigenous rights or the rights associated with the 1840 Treaty of Waitangi, New Zealand's 'founding document'. The National Party itself tends to acknowledge the Treaty's Article 2, which articulates the right to self-determination when considering resource claim settlements, but not in social policy where it prioritises Article 3's promise of equal citizenship rights (Humpage 2005, see O'Sullivan this volume, Chapter 13). We might therefore expect many National voters to feel uncomfortable about their party's formal relationship with the Māori Party, whose *kaupapa* (agenda or philosophy) is based on nine key principles summarised in the left-hand column of Table 14.1. Referring to this *kaupapa*, Turia (cited by Leahy 2015: 357) has highlighted: 'The Māori Party does not intend to operate like any other political party. The tikanga Māori [Māori custom] nature of the party is an essential part of the justification for its existence'.

Scholars (Peck & Tickell 2002, Clarke 2004, Humpage 2015) caution against homogenising the 'actually existing' neoliberalism that has emerged in differing geographical and temporal contexts, while O'Sullivan in this volume notes how it is easy to overstate the tensions between indigenous cultural and economic aspirations. Nonetheless, brevity requires Table 14.1's rather simplistic summary of relevant key principles associated with both the Māori Party and neoliberalism. Tensions clearly exist between these principles, notably around individual versus collective responsibility and the narrow economic focus of neoliberalism compared to the holistic focus of Māoridom. But there are also *parallels* between neoliberal desires to increase choice/competition and reduce the size of government and Māori calls for self-determination, providing the Māori Party with spaces for policy negotiation. In assessing whether the Māori Party achieved its social policy goals, this chapter examines the two key social policy initiatives that the Māori Party named as priorities in relationship accords, considering how well the twin drive towards *rangatiratanga* and socio-economic parity, as well as the Māori Party's broader *kaupapa*, was achieved and to what degree these challenged or embedded neoliberalism.

Table 14.1: Māori and neoliberal principles

Māori	Neoliberal
Mana whenua Defines Māori by the land occupied by right of ancestral claim and is essential for Māori wellbeing.	**Laissez faire** The market is the fundamental structure for production and distribution; state intervention limited to ensuring laws governing the market are applied equally.
Kaitiakitanga Spiritual and cultural guardianship of the physical world, involving active exercise of responsibility in a manner beneficial to resources and the future welfare of the people.	**Property rights** Individual ownership rights to the proceeds generated by property and control over a resource or good.

Māori	Neoliberal
Te reo rangatira The Māori language 'is the cornerstone of all that is Māori … [and] is the medium through which Māori explain the world'.	**Economic efficiency** Targeting spending cuts and other interventions reduce government expenditure; bureaucratic waste and inefficiency require 'performance management' and 'actuarial' models of assessing financial risk.
Mana tupuna/whakapapa Defines 'who we are, from whom we descend, and what our obligations are to those who come after us. This is achieved through the recital of whakapapa' (genealogy).	
Rangatiratanga Attributes of a *rangatira* (chief or leader), including humility, leadership by example, generosity, altruism, diplomacy and knowledge of benefit to the people.	**Small government** Decisions should be made at level closest to those affected to be effective and not necessarily best provided by government.
Manaakitanga Acknowledging the *mana* (prestige or power) of others as having equal or greater importance than one's own, through the expression of *aroha* (love or concern), hospitality, generosity and mutual respect.	**Choice and competition** Needed to ensure individual freedom and self-interest, leading to privatisation of many previously government-owned resources and services.
Kotahitanga Unity of purpose and direction, demonstrated through the achievement of harmony and moving as one and encouraging all to make a contribution, to have their say and then, together, to reach a consensus.	
Whānaungatanga Underpins the social organisation of *whānau* (extended family), *hapū* (sub-tribe) and *iwi* (tribe) and includes rights and reciprocal obligations consistent with being part of a collective.	**Individual responsibility** Citizens framed as responsible for ensuring their own wellbeing (and for poor social outcomes).
Wairuatanga Belief that there is a spiritual existence alongside the physical, affirmed through knowledge and understanding of Māori ancestors or gods and necessary for achieving wellness.	

Source: Quotes from the Māori Party (2013: 2–6), see also Humpage (2015).

Whānau Ora

Following a Taskforce on Whānau-Centred Initiatives (2010) proposed in the 2008 relationship accord, the Māori Party secured funding for a new Whānau Ora strategy. This provided inclusive services to families in need in a way that empowers them as a whole, rather than focusing separately on individual family members and their problems. *Whānau ora* is loosely translated as 'family wellbeing', but, unlike nuclear family-focused programs implemented elsewhere, *whānau* refers to *multi-generational* family groups made up of many households, supported and strengthened by a wider network of relatives. 'Wellbeing' also encompasses the physical, mental, spiritual *and* cultural health of Māori (Māori Party 2014). In many ways, Whānau Ora 'simply formalised the manner in which many Māori health providers … have been operating since their inception in the early 1990s' (Boulton et al. 2013: 27), but its national and international significance lies in the acknowledgement that *whānau* as a collective hold both rights and obligations through broad, interdependent relationships with tribal and other Māori organisations (Māori Party 2013). Whānau Ora also endorsed 'a group capacity for self-determination' that moves beyond the individualised notions of empowerment evident in mainstream policies (Taskforce on Whānau-Centred Initiatives 2010: 30).

As the first Minister for Whānau Ora, Turia led the strategy that was jointly implemented by the Ministry of Māori Development (TPK 2015) and the Ministries of Social Development and Health with multiple government agencies required to work together to assist families. 'Joined-up government' is trending internationally but here is aligned with a Māori world view that social issues are interconnected and must be addressed holistically. The first phase of the strategy involved three initiatives:

- **Whānau plans:** By 2015, almost two-thirds of *whānau* engaged with Whānau Ora had been funded to develop plans of action, with most meeting their goals and producing other benefits such as reconnecting *whānau* members or identifying skills and expertise already within *whānau* (Auditor-General 2015, TPK 2015). The plans thus supported self-determination at the *whānau* level; some also preserved *whānau* histories, cultural traditions and/or traditional lands, or established/maintained connections to family lands and *whānau*/tribal groupings (Māori Party 2013).

- **Provider collectives and navigators:** Funding encouraged providers to form collectives to deliver coordinated services addressing both individuals and *whānau* needs and to employ 'navigators' who work intensively with 15 or more *whānau* each year, assisting families to access the varied services offered by government (Auditor-General 2015). By 2014, 32 collectives represented more than 180 independent Māori, Pasifika, health and social services providers as well as tribal organisations (Turia 2014). Navigators had worked with 58 per cent of families engaged with Whānau Ora and '[t]hose whānau who were engaged with more services and programmes experienced more improvements' (TPK 2015: 43), resulting in increasing funding in 2014 and 2016 (Auditor-General 2015, English 2016).

- **Integrated contracting and government agency support:** Improvements in the efficiency of contract management aimed to provide the time available for building provider capability to deliver *whānau*-centred services (Auditor-General 2015).

The Auditor-General's (2015: 4) report on the first four years of the strategy described Whānau Ora as 'an opportunity for providers of health and social services in the community to operate differently and to support families in deciding their best way forward'. It challenged neoliberal individualism by incorporating a collective focus that acknowledges the negative impact neoliberal reforms have had on Māori families. Te Puni Kōkiri's (TPK 2015) analysis of provider reports and *whānau* plans suggests that culturally specific *whānau* plans and the integrated service knowledge of navigators are helping families, with 60–75 per cent reporting improved safety, access to services, happiness, motivation, positive *whānau* relationships, mutual respect, parenting/caregiving confidence, skills and education/training. Around half of evaluated *whānau* saw improvements in early education use, healthy housing situation, eating/exercise, cultural confidence and *whakapapa* knowledge. The latter two items indicate Whānau Ora may facilitate cultural revival, although Boulton and Gifford's (2014: 9) analysis of 46 *whānau* interviews suggest this is not yet central to everyday Māori understandings of *whānau ora*.

More fundamentally, requiring *whānau* to apply for funding via a legal entity responsible for any resulting contract indicates that Whānau Ora, like previous capacity-building initiatives, embedded Māori within Western models of governance (Humpage 2005). Only 34 per cent of provider collectives described government agencies as becoming more responsive to *whānau*-centred approaches and the Auditor-General (2015: 5) noted 'the providers are mainly required by their contracts with government agencies to deliver services to individuals … The signals currently sent by different parts of government are, at best, mixed'. Dormer's (2014) interviews with government officials and Whānau Ora providers further suggested that the silo mentality associated with neoliberal contracting-out processes and performance management models was not overcome.

Boulton et al. (2013: 28) note:

> [e]arlier research with Māori health providers indicates that local or regional difference is rarely reflected in contracts, and that in circumstances where it is, these differences are not translated into performance measures that are meaningful to either the provider or the community they service.

Yet attempts to develop outcome indicators regionally were inconsistent and contributed to a lack of clear, generic outcomes that enabled an assessment of whether the strategy made a significant difference to Māori lives nationally. Most outcome indicators also remained focused on individuals, not *whānau* collectively (Auditor-General 2015, Boulton et al. 2013). These concerns, along with delays in *whānau* and providers getting funding and almost a third of total spending going on administration (Auditor-General 2015), saw the National and Māori parties commit to an engagement strategy with *whānau*, tribal and Māori organisations in 2014 to improve understanding of how policies are impacting on local communities (Bedwell 2014).

But such problems also justify further 'privatisation' of service delivery and responsibility. While the Taskforce (2010) proposed a standalone commissioning agency as the second and final phase of Whānau Ora, enabling greater Māori control over decision-making and governance of the Māori social service sector, *three* agencies were established: one each for the North and South islands and one for Pasifika peoples across the country. The commissioning agencies sought applications from and entered into contracts for funding from any community-based organisation in any sector (Auditor-General 2015), using funds transferred from Ministry of Social Development programs aligned with the Whānau Ora approach (Tolley & Flavell 2016). Although offering greater Māori control over government funding, commissioning agencies also trialled payments-by-results mechanisms that have been widely criticised internationally (see Gustafsson-Wright et al. 2015) and are part of the National Government's experimentation with funding models that are 'a step toward smaller government and a society in which individuals look to themselves and services provided by market-like forces rather than government intervention' (Dormer 2014: 843). This clearly sat in tension with the collective Māori values and aspirations articulated by the strategy and the Māori Party.

The strategy's intended focus on Māori self-determination was also diminished by the shift to include Pasifka peoples, which reflects former prime minister John Key's view that Whānau Ora should be used by all New Zealanders, as well as their similarly poor socio-economic outcomes (Marriott & Sim 2014). While this inclusive approach arguably reflects the principle of *manaakitanga* (Dormer 2014), it also means that Māori made up only 64 per cent of the 9,408 *whānau* comprising 49,625 individuals who had benefited from Whānau Ora by June 2014. TPK's (2015: 90) analysis concluded that '[a] strengths-based approach without an emphasis on rangatiratanga does not generate whānau independence and leadership'. Thus, the *whānau* focus may be easily translated to other New Zealanders, but this comes at the risk of diminishing the potential to transform state–Māori relationships either through service delivery or the new funding mechanisms.

Ministerial Committee on Poverty

It is doubtful if Whānau Ora's work to reverse negative social outcomes will be successful long-term unless there are improvements in the disproportionately poor material circumstances many Māori face (Marriott & Sim 2014). Frustrated by progress in this area, the Māori Party negotiated a new Ministerial Committee on Poverty in 2011 to 'bring a greater focus to, and improve co-ordination of, government activity aimed at alleviating the effects of poverty in Aotearoa/New Zealand' (NP & MP 2011: 2). Co-chaired by the deputy prime minister and Minister of Finance and Turia, the quarterly committee brought together the Ministers of Health, Education, Tertiary Education, Skills and Employment, Social Development, Social Housing, Māori Affairs and Whānau Ora (NP & MP 2011).

However, alongside reviewing 'the effectiveness of current approaches and responses against a backdrop of Better Public Services and getting value for money for taxpayers', the Committee prioritises the neoliberal view that '[w]ork is the primary route out of poverty … and educational achievement is the platform for creating opportunity' and mobility (Department of Prime Minister and Cabinet 2016). Thus, it frames individuals, rather than structural inequalities, as the 'problem'. The Committee's achievements were also rather ad hoc; although not intended to lead to culturally specific initiatives, those with particular benefit for Māori included:

- **A new free home insulation program:** Targeted around 46,000 low-income households containing children, the elderly and people with pre-existing health conditions by matching government investment with funding from landlords, trusts and other third parties.

- **NZ$21.6 million over four years to expand rheumatic fever prevention beyond school-based programs, as well as the extension of free general practitioner visits and prescriptions to under-13-year-olds:** Both likely significantly impacted Māori families, who are disproportionately affected by rheumatic fever due to over-crowding, as well as other poverty-related diseases (Leahy 2015, Marriott & Sim 2014).

- **NZ$790 million hardship fund to increase the incomes of benefit recipients with children by NZ$25 per week:** The was the first core benefit increase since 1972. Fox (2015) estimated that 310,000 families and 570,000 children—including 100,000 Māori families with 89,000 children—would benefit from this and smaller increases for working families from 2016. In return, however, sole parent benefit recipients faced work obligations when their child turns three (up from age five). Focusing only on benefit recipients with children is also less effective in reducing poverty than Māori Party (2008, 2011, 2014) proposals to increase core benefit levels across the board; introduce a universal child benefit and an official poverty line and target for eliminating child poverty by 2020; eliminate tax on the first NZ$25,000 of income; reintroduce a universal living allowance for tertiary students and abolish tertiary tuition fees; and invest in a model of reciprocal and collective development based on food security. This suggests the hardship fund was a major compromise for the Māori Party.

- **New trades training and employment programs:** These included targeting rural unemployed youth for employment opportunities on local projects of up to six months paid at minimum wage; 3,000 zero-fee Māori and Pasifika trade training placements each year for four years (with plans to double this number to 6,000); and 350 cadetships for unemployed Māori involving at least six months' paid employment and mentoring from employers (Leahy 2015). Such initiatives aimed to better incorporate Māori into the neoliberal labour market and were inadequate, given TPK's (2015) research found 29 per cent of Whānau Ora provider collectives indicated their outcomes were limited by poor employment or education opportunities. Budget 2016 funding for a new microfinance program to improve financial independence for *whānau*—including *whānau*-led small and medium enterprises—while more adequate than other measures, still regarded inclusion in the capitalist economy as the key solution to Māori poverty (English 2016).

Although not directly associated with the Committee, it is important to acknowledge that a new Māori Housing Strategy and a Māori Housing Network in 2015 both facilitated greater roles for *iwi* and other Māori organisations in building and managing social housing to better meet Māori needs, while the Māori and Pacific Health Innovation Funds aimed to support communities to find their own health solutions (Flavell 2014, Māori Party 2014). However, like Whānau Ora, these were part of National's broader plans to decentralise and privatise social service provision (Flavell 2014, English 2016).

Such limited gains saw Turia (in Radio New Zealand 2014) criticise government ministers for failing to fully support the Ministerial Committee on Poverty. The Māori Party negotiated the Committee's continuity and a role on it for non-ministerial Māori Party MP, Marama Fox, in 2014, alongside an agreement that TPK should urgently refocus on strategic policy advice improving Māori employment and training, housing and education outcomes alongside continued work on a Māori Economic Strategy (NP & MP 2014). But a lack of progress on poverty was a major reason that MP Hone Harawira left the Māori Party in 2011 to form the Mana Party, which specifically addresses poverty among Māori and non-Māori. This public disharmony not only threatened the principle of *kotahitanga*—the idea that the Māori Party works for unity among Māori people, respecting and enhancing the status of all involved—but highlights both the limits of the Māori Party's influence on National and significant overlaps in its neoconservative agendas when it comes to work and welfare (Māori Party 2013). Although incorporation into the Western capitalist economy can benefit Māori (see Bargh this volume, Chapter 16), the collective focus of Whānau Ora was notably absent. Ultimately, it is unlikely the Ministerial Committee on Poverty fundamentally improved the material circumstances of Māori by offering greater control over their economic lives. Poverty rates among both the whole population and children remained remarkably high and steady—with Māori disproportionately likely to be affected—across the National-led government's time in power from 2008 (Perry 2016).

Conclusion: Success within the boundaries of neoliberalism

The Māori Party negotiated some significant and innovative social policy initiatives, supporting Smith's (2010: 215) argument that: 'In terms of representation and power, the Māori Party have achieved more than any other Māori electoral group'. As with any party, it has not been able to implement all of its policy goals, but evidence suggests that Whānau Ora and the Ministerial Committee on Poverty would not exist without the Māori Party's formal relationship with National and the former is showing signs of making a real difference to Māori lives. The first section of Table 14.2 summarises how these initiatives, particularly Whānau Ora, challenged the normalising effects of neoliberalism. The Māori Party also reshaped the state–Māori relationship by rejecting traditional adversarial-style politics and emphasising *manaakitanga* or maintaining honest and respectful relationships with all parties, while its consultation with Māori Party members prior to each relationship accord challenges the common criticism that 'consultation' under neoliberalism is an empty promise (Humpage 2005).

Table 14.2: Māori Party policy challenged *and* extended neoliberalism

	Whānau Ora	Ministerial Committee on Poverty
Challenged neoliberalism		
Embedded Māori principles in mainstream policy	✓	✗
Recognised there is not only one cultural 'norm'	✓	✓
Moved away from sole focus on individual responsibility	✓	✓
Attempted to deal with impact of neoliberal reforms on family functioning/cultural preservation, etc.	✓	✓
Implemented *rangatiratanga* by recognising the leadership and authority of *iwi, hapū* and *whānau*	✓	✗
Attempted to move away from 'silo-based' funding and policymaking	✓	✓
Extended neoliberalism		
Extended neoliberal 'contracting out' processes, embedding Māori organisations further into a government-funded and led system	✓	✓

	Whānau Ora	Ministerial Committee on Poverty
Embedded Māori into a 'performance management' model of governance	✓	✓
Potentially shifted blame for poor outcomes onto Māori	✓	✓
Embedded Māori into neoliberal labour market/ economy	✓	✓

Source: Author's summary.

Nonetheless, *manaakitanga* arguably constrained the Māori Party from achieving greater success in social policy. Voters might have simply been *unaware* of Māori Party achievements, since National took much of the credit and the Green and Labour parties often supported (and sometimes claimed as their own) Māori Party initiatives, but electoral results—particularly in 2017 when the Māori Party failed to hold even one Māori electorate seat—suggest that Māori voters were critical of the compromises the Māori Party made to maintain a good relationship with National. These include claims (summarised in the second column of Table 14.2) from working-class Māori that the party was beholden to National and driven by tribal elites. This is because it supported a neoliberal agenda through supply and confidence votes, exploited opportunities to win gains for Māori by endorsing policies extending commodification, privatisation and marketisation (Harawira 2011, for alternative views see McCormack and Bargh this volume, Chapters 15 and 16 respectively) and/or potentially devolved responsibility and blame for continued poor outcomes onto Māori. In the 2014 election, when the Māori Party held only one Māori electorate and had only two MPs in parliament (Bargh 2015), Flavell (cited by Bedwell 2014) reported consultations where '[o]ur people said it's vital for the Māori Party to be in Government so we can help reset the current landscape and deliver more tangible gains for Māori'. But 2017 demonstrated that most Māori are not voting for the Māori Party or its candidates. Notably, however, this was not the result of National broadening its political base, as it had hoped, because Labour won all seven Māori electorates (Election Aotearoa 2017).

The Māori Party's achievements indicate that supply and confidence relationships can bring important, incremental gains—including internationally significant policies that embed indigenous cultural values and governance within mainstream social policy frameworks—benefiting indigenous peoples. But such relationships also require compromises that further embed neoliberalism. By tying them to indigenous agendas and politics, it is possible that this may also make it less likely that some indigenous peoples will challenge neoliberal principles and policies in the future. This does not bode well for greater recognition of indigenous/ Treaty rights and the material disadvantage faced by Māori. Although many Māori voted for the Labour and New Zealand First parties who, in 2017, claimed that neoliberalism had 'failed' (Election Aotearoa 2017), it remains uncertain as to whether they together will represent a significant challenge to the neoliberalism agendas that detrimentally impact many Māori New Zealanders or if they will extend or constrain the innovative social policies initiated by the Māori Party.

References

Auditor-General (2015). *Whānau Ora: The first four years*, Office of the Auditor-General, Wellington.

Bargh M (2015). The Māori seats. In Hayward J (ed.), *New Zealand government and politics*, 6th edition, Oxford, Melbourne.

Bedwell Q (2014). *Agreement between the Māori Party and National Party welcomed*, www.maoriparty.org/agreement_the_Maori_party_and_national.

Boulton A & Gifford H (2014). Whānau Ora; He whakaaro ā whānau: Māori family views of family wellbeing. *The International Indigenous Policy Journal* 5(1):1–16, doi.org/10.18584/iipj.2014.5.1.1.

Boulton A, Tamehana J & Brannelly T (2013). Whānau-centred health and social service delivery in New Zealand: The challenges to, and opportunities for, innovation. *MAI Journal* 2(1):18–32.

Clarke J (2004). Dissolving the public realm: The logics and limits of neoliberalism. *Journal of Social Policy* 33(1):27–48, doi.org/10.1017/S0047279403007244.

Department of Prime Minister and Cabinet (2016). *Ministerial Committee on Poverty*, www.dpmc.govt.nz/dpmc/publications/mcop.

Dormer D (2014). Whānau Ora and the collaborative turn. *International Journal of Public Administration* 37(12):835–45, doi.org/10.1080/01900692.2014.917101.

Election Aotearoa (2017). *Election Aotearoa*, www.maoritelevision.com/election.

English B (2016). *Summary of initiatives in Budget 2016*, www.treasury.govt.nz/budget/2016/summary-initiatives/b16-sum-initiatives.pdf.

Flavell TU (2014). Last speech in the 50th Parliament, *Scoop*, 31 July, www.scoop.co.nz/stories/PA1408/S00006/maori-party-last-speech-in-the-50th-parliament.htm.

Fox M (2015). Māori Party delivers for vulnerable whānau. *Scoop*, 21 May, www.scoop.co.nz/stories/PA1505/S00361/maori-party-delivers-for-vulnerable-whanau.htm.

Gustafsson-Wright E, Gardiner S & Putcha V (2015). *The potential and limitations of impact bonds: Lessons from the first five years of experience worldwide*, Brookings Institution, Washington DC.

Harawira H (2011). Hone Harawira's statement on his caucus suspension, *New Zealand Herald,* 8 February, www.nzherald.co.nz/nz/news/article.cfm?c_id=1&objectid=10704905.

Humpage L (2005). Experimenting with a 'whole of government' approach: Indigenous capacity building in New Zealand and Australia. *Policy Studies* 26(1):47–66, doi.org/10.1080/01442870500041744.

Humpage L (2015). *Policy change, public attitudes and social citizenship: Does neoliberalism matter?* The Policy Press, Bristol.

Leahy H (2015). *Crossing the floor*, Huia, Wellington.

Māori Party (2008). *Policy priorities: He aha te mea nui?—he tangata*, Māori Party, Wellington.

Māori Party (2011). *Our whānau: Our future*, Māori Party, Wellington.

Māori Party (2013). *Māori Party constitution*, Māori Party, Wellington.

Māori Party (2014). *Māori Party policy manifesto*, Māori Party, Wellington.

Marriott L & Sim D (2014). *Indicators of inequality for Māori and Pacific people*. Business school working paper in public finance 09/2014, Victoria University of Wellington, Wellington.

NP & MP (National Party & Māori Party) (2008). *Relationship and confidence and supply agreement between the National Party and the Māori Party*, National Party & Māori Party Wellington.

NP & MP (2011). *Relationship accord and confidence and supply agreement with the Māori Party*, National Party & Māori Party, Wellington.

NP & MP (2014). *Relationship accord and confidence and supply agreement with the Māori Party*, National Party & Māori Party, Wellington.

Peck J & Tickell A (2002). Neoliberalizing space. *Antipode* 34(3):380–404, doi. org/10.1111/1467-8330.00247.

Perry B (2016). *Household incomes in New Zealand: Trends in indicators of inequality and hardship 1982 to 2015*, Ministry of Social Development, Wellington.

Radio New Zealand (2014). *Poverty committee not fully supported—Turia*, 20 April, www.radionz.co.nz/news/political/242116/poverty-committee-not-fully-supported-turia.

Sachdeva S (2015). Maori Party: Quiet achievers want to raise profile in 2016, *Stuff.co.nz*, 8 December, www.stuff.co.nz/national/politics/75133560/Maori-Party-Quiet-achievers-want-to-raise-profile-in-2016.

Smith K (2010). Māori political parties. In Mulholland M and Tawhai V (eds), *Weeping waters: The Treaty of Waitangi and constitutional change*, Huia, Wellington.

Sykes A (2010). The politics of the brown table. *Scoop*, 19 October, www.scoop. co.nz/stories/PO1010/S00199/the-politics-of-the-brown-table.htm.

Taskforce on Whānau-Centred Initiatives (2010). *Whānau Ora: Report of the Taskforce on Whānau-Centred Initiatives*, Ministry of Social Development, Wellington.

Tolley A & Flavell TU (2016). *Funding and programmes for whānau-centred services transferred to Whānau Ora*, media release, www.beehive.govt.nz/release/funding-and-programmes-wh%C4%81nau-centred-services-transferred-wh%C4%81nau-ora.

TPK (Te Puni Kōkiri) (2015). *Understanding whānau-centred approaches: Analysis of Phase One Whānau Ora research and monitoring results*, Te Puni Kōkiri, Wellington.

Turia T (2006). Speech to ACT National Conference, *Scoop*, 27 March, www.scoop.co.nz/stories/PA0603/S00443/turia-speech-to-act-national-conference.htm.

Turia T (2014). *Whānau Ora achievements report July 2014*, Office of the Minister Responsible for Whānau Ora, Wellington.

15

Indigenous settlements and market environmentalism: An untimely coincidence?

Fiona McCormack

Introduction

This chapter considers the entanglement of indigeneity and neoliberalism in Aotearoa/New Zealand in the context of fisheries. A relationship, I argue, that is mediated by market environmentalism. This is given substance in two Acts: The *Treaty of Waitangi (Fisheries Claims) Settlement Act 1992*, which resolved commercial claims against the Crown, and the complementary *Fisheries (Kaimoana Customary Fishing) Regulations 1998*, which legislated for customary fishing activities. The settlement was made feasible by the implementation of new forms of enclosures in the seascape—that is, individualised property rights, ITQs (individual transferable quota).

In this neoliberal 'opening of spaces', indigenous fisheries were repatriated as private, tradeable commodities. It is important to note, nevertheless, that Māori acceptance of quota as a way to resolve colonial alienations was an attempt to make the best of a major Treaty of Waitangi breach; the implementation of New Zealand's Quota Management System (QMS) was, in fact, by 1986 a fait accompli. There is, however, a major paradox in this settlement. Although Māori own about 33 per cent of the quota in an industry internationally hailed as successful (Seafood New Zealand n.d.) and three of the five companies in New Zealand (which supply 80 per cent of the catch) are Māori-owned, an ongoing sense of alienation exists from what is perceived of as an ancestral resource. I will address this contradiction in two ways. First, as Kingfisher and Maskovsky (2008) suggest, indigeneity may be just as likely to appropriate neoliberalism for its own ends as the other way round. This 'opening of spaces', incongruously, may strengthen the capacity of the state to shape and neutralise opposition. Treaty settlement processes are an example of this double-edged articulation of neoliberalism with indigeneity. Second, the use of market-based instruments, such as ITQs, is premised on a radical restructuring of human and natural worlds. This reassigns value to that generated through future trading and recreates the ontology of natural resources, making this exchangeable with wealth creation in society.

The two strands of my argument can be synthesised as follows: the resolution of Māori indigenous claims to fisheries, a neoliberal possibility, coincided with the implementation of a fisheries management regime wherein fishing rights are privatised and value arises out of market trading as opposed to harvesting fish. This articulation helps explicate the dissatisfaction many Māori currently express over fisheries: the quota system is perceived as 'broken', as 'stifling *kaitiakitanga* [guardianship]' and as a system wherein Māori, for the most part, perform as 'quota flickers'.[1] Given that settlements are deemed 'full and final', this discontent is effectively silenced.

The empirical evidence in this chapter is drawn broadly from my research into Māori fisheries and indigenous claims over the last 15 years. This is buttressed by my more recent comparative research into ITQ systems in Iceland and Ireland and fisheries governance in Hawai'i, the latter having no ITQ system.

The chapter is divided into three parts. The first describes the historic context surrounding the pan-Māori settlement of claims to fisheries in 1992. It highlights the interplay of privatising fishing rights and the use of quota as property to repatriate indigenous loss, and considers the resultant dichotomisation of Māori fishing interests into commercial and customary spheres. Rather than resolving colonial grievances, I suggest

---

1   These quotes come from interviews conducted with Māori from three different *iwi* in 2017 as part of my 'Iwi Settlement Quota: Opportunities and Constraints' research project.

that the settlement has resulted in a new round of alienations, an argument I illustrate with ethnography drawn from a recent Waitangi Tribunal claim. The second section focuses critically on ITQs, the technology that connects fisheries, indigeneity and market environmentalism. It ties ITQs into the Blue Economy, an emergent meta-ideology, which seeks to identify a new wave of growth opportunities in marine and coastal ecosystems. It also considers the rise of a virtual market in fishing quota. The third section argues that the discourse of sustainability surrounding rights-based fisheries ignores, to a large extent, traditional ecological knowledge. Where indigeneity is included in ITQ systems, it is in terms of securing access to fishing rights, now recreated as quota property.

Treaty of Waitangi fisheries settlement

There is a long history of Māori opposition to the loss of their property and resources, and this is particularly the case in terms of tribal fishing rights (Bargh 2016). A sophisticated customary marine tenure system existed precolonisation, one in which boundaries demarcated tribal *rohe moana* (seascape), and *kaitiakitanga* practices (resource guardianship) included the establishment of *rahui*—that is, the placing of a *tapu* (taboo) on a seascape for conservational or political purposes, or following a death by drowning (Metge 1989). *Kaimoana* (seafood) was variously shared or traded depending on kinship connections and the desire to create alliances with other tribes (Ropiha 1992). Trade also occurred internationally; Māori were actively engaged in trading fish and agricultural produce both before and immediately after the signing of the Treaty of Waitangi in 1840 (Petrie 2002), and owned boats capable of sailing to Australia on a frequent basis for commercial purposes—cured fish was among the products exchanged (Waitangi Tribunal 1988: 44–66). The cultural significance of fishing also finds expression in Tangaroa, the god of the sea, and in numerous legends pertaining to ancestral activities in the seascape (see Ellison, cited in Sykes 2004, Mead & Grove 1981, 2001).

These ownership practices, which intertwine land and sea in the same property construct, are replicated across the Pacific (Johannes 1981, Clarke 1990, Hviding 1996). In New Zealand, this linkage was inconsistent with colonial property ideologies whereby boundaries are drawn around where land meets the sea, the former being designated as susceptible to private property divisions and the latter subject to Crown ownership (Mulrennan

& Scott 2000). The initial opposition of Māori to ITQs made explicit the irony of this most recent enclosure. It was couched in terms of: first, on colonisation, you denied that we had tribal property rights in the sea and claimed that it was public property, then you privatise it, exclude us from these rights and assume that we never had any commercial interests in fisheries. ITQs thus give to Pākehā (New Zealand Europeans) the full, exclusive and undisturbed possession of the property right in fishing that the Crown has already guaranteed to Māori in the 1840 Treaty of Waitangi.

Māori common property constructs in fisheries were for the first time recognised as aboriginal title rights in a seminal case (*Te Weehi*) in 1986.[2] This recognition correlated with two important reports issued by the Waitangi Tribunal following the Muriwhenua and Ngāi Tahu claims,[3] and claims lodged in the High Court challenging the ITQ system. Taken together, these led to an unprecedented recognition of Māori ownership rights, in addition to evidencing an established precolonial trade in *kaimoana*.

In 1987 a High Court injunction was granted against the further issuing of ITQs, and government was forced into a round of negotiations with Māori litigants as an alternative to further litigation (David Williams QC, pers. comm., 2016). This resulted in the *Māori Fisheries Act 1989* (considered an interim settlement), significant for marking the moment when the Crown finally recognised that Māori have a commercial, and not just a cultural or ceremonial interest, in fisheries. Almost simultaneously, however, this recognition was undermined. This was achieved in the Act by making a legislative distinction between commercial and customary fishing rights, a distinction later formally incorporated into the *Treaty of Waitangi (Fisheries Claims) Settlement Act 1992* and the *Fisheries (Kaimoana Customary Fishing) Regulations 1998*. The dichotomy importantly revitalised the stalled extension of ITQs by divvying up Māori fisheries interests into capitalist and non-capitalist concerns,

---

2   A landmark case that established that traditional Māori fishing rights could override European laws. *Te Weehi v Regional Fisheries Officer* [1986] 1 NZLR 680, 691–2.
3   Ngāi Tahu and Muriwhenua are tribes in the tip of the North and South islands in New Zealand. Both groups lodged fisheries claims with the Waitangi Tribunal in the 1980s. The Tribunal hearings and subsequent reports emphasise the extent of Māori fishing activities and their commercial worth, and government failure to protect them.

commercial and subsistence interests, and private or pseudo-communal property institutions. It also identified appropriate levels of Māori society to engage with each—*iwi* (tribe) or *hapū* (sub-tribe).

ITQs synthesised Māori interests with the fisheries quota system by becoming the property right through which the 'commercial' claims were resolved. Customary practices became a separate 'non-economic' domain, primarily concerned with conservation and noteworthy for making illegal any material exchange. While an arduous application process allows for the gathering of seafood for ceremonial purposes, restricted to *hui* (meetings) and *tangi* (funerals), the regulations prohibit the exchange, barter or sale of fish—that is, they remove any semblance of trade.

Three further points about Treaty of Waitangi settlements are relevant here. First, in repatriation processes one particular form of kin entity is favoured over others. A prerequisite for settlements to proceed is that claimants 'establish a large natural group', as a means to streamline the negotiations. This prejudices smaller kin groups and ignores commentary that the basis of Māori society is *hapū* rather than *iwi* (see Ballara 1998). Claimants must also have a 'mandate' to enter into negotiations; a requirement that is complicated by the large natural group prerequisite and the fact that traditional common property rights were non-exclusive and fluid. In the post-settlement stage, there is a need to develop specific management structures, Mandated Iwi Organisations (MIOs), to handle settlement assets (New Zealand Parliament 2006). MIOs are closely aligned with maximising the chances of a successful transfer to market capitalism. Rumbles (1999) writes that these pre- and post-settlement stipulations effectively rationalise Māori social relations; Māori who undertake Treaty of Waitangi settlement processes are forced to adopt forms of organisation that are rooted in Western legal traditions (Jackson 1995).

Second, although embedded in the history and political economy of contemporary New Zealand, contrary perceptions of the Tribunal cloud the functioning of (Pākehā) civil society. Newly elected governments invariably invoke a shift in the Tribunal's financial fortunes, political and moral status, and predicted life span. The current national government, for instance, advocates direct and speedy negotiations with mandated claimant groups through the Office of Treaty Settlements (OTS).[4] This undermines

---

4   A Labour–New Zealand First coalition government (a minority government reliant on the support of the Green Party) was elected in late September 2017. To date they appear to have taken a more cautionary approach to treaty settlements.

not only the Tribunal but, importantly, the production of tribal history undertaken by and on behalf of Māori *iwi* and *hapū* groups; histories that crucially empower the revitalisation of group identity and provide an invaluable archival oral history resource.

Third, all settlements are categorically full and final, an insistence that generates social silencing. Silences, for instance, are created within the settlement process, as a result of the rationalisation of claimant groups, and as an outcome of the economies of previous settlements. The fisheries settlement, for example, silenced future claims to the seascape and discontent with the current regime. This silencing was explicit in the 2014 West Coast Harbour hearings I attended. These represented the collective claims of *hapū* and *iwi* from three coastal areas—Aotea, Whaingaroa and Kawhia—and are part of the Rohe Pōtae Tribunal Inquiry. Claims in the inquiry referred to historic and contemporary issues: for instance, land that was confiscated or otherwise alienated, sacred sites that were desecrated and *marae* (meeting house complexes) that were destroyed. Yet, the 'elephant in the room' was fisheries. Māori were concerned about the conservation of existing resources and, especially, the demise of a once-thriving local commercial fishery. In the fisheries settlement, Waikato-Tainui Fisheries Ltd, the MIO of the region's largest *iwi*, was granted the quota that they now lease as a package, typically to large consolidated and non-local companies, the dividends from which partly trickle down to beneficiary *marae*. It was the incongruity of living by the sea, high rates of local unemployment, the inability to generate an income from an ancestral resource and fishing practices and policies that were perceived to be culturally irreverent and environmentally destructive that most frustrated local Māori. Tex Rickard, for instance (from Ngāti Porou on the east coast of the North Island of New Zealand, though longtime resident in Whaingaroa and husband to the late Eva Rickard of Tainui *hapū*), described the sea in Whaingaroa as formerly 'the people's food basket, the mainstay of local diets'. The pre-quota local commercial fisheries venture, Hartstone fisheries, he explained, had encouraged Māori employment; the company had also gifted much fish to local Māori families. Hartstone fisheries was sold simultaneously with the implementation of the quota system. The food basket, he decried, was now depleted. A result of the marketisation of fisheries and the imposition of national regulations that were unable to comprehend variations in local ecosystems.

These issues were continually raised in the pre-hearing *hui*. The claimants' lawyers, while sympathetic, and professing to 'trying to figure out what angle to take',[5] were equally clear that, as dictated by existing legislation, no reference to fisheries could be made in the hearings. A silencing that obscures the existence of a pronounced and ongoing alienation. Tensions also existed over who had the *mana* (authority/power) to claim the harbours. Waikato-Tainui *iwi* argued that these fell within their tribal *rohe* and comprised part of their unresolved claims. Further, that the existence of a proven negotiation and a commercial body made it the most suitable, and resourced, 'large natural' body to engage with the Crown and to receive settlement assets. Their preference was to proceed to the OTS stage, thereby bypassing the Tribunal hearings. Coastal harbour *hapū* and *iwi* claimants largely disputed this and argued that the harbour claims emerged from customary interests, alternative *whakapapa* (genealogies) and their identity as sea people as opposed to the *iwi*'s identification with the Waikato River.[6] Crucially, they rejected Waikato-Tainui's claim because they perceived the *iwi* to have mishandled fisheries and to have excluded them from the distribution of productive rights (McCormack 2016a).

Fisheries governance through market environmentalism

ITQs are the technology that connect fisheries, indigeneity and market environmentalism. They are promoted as the 'purest' example of a payment for ecosystem services in marine environments and considered a poster child for the Blue Economy. While less popularised than its sibling the Green Economy, the Blue Economy emerged out of the Rio +20 conference in 2012. The United Nations' Food and Agriculture Organization (FAO) solidified the idea with the launching of its Blue Growth Initiative in 2013, wherein Blue Growth is defined as:

> the sustainable growth and development emanating from economic activities in the oceans, wetlands and coastal zones, that minimize environmental degradation, biodiversity loss and unsustainable use of living aquatic resources, and maximize economic and social benefits (FAO 2015: 8).

---

5 Three lawyers were present from Aurere Law in Rotorua.
6 These issues were discussed at *hui* I attended in Whaingaroa and Kawhai.

The initiative addresses four key components: capture fisheries, aquaculture, livelihood and food systems (that is, access to markets and value chains), and *economic growth from ecosystem services*. Maria Bargh argues that the Blue Economy framework (as promoted by 'serial entrepreneur' Gunter Pauli (2010)) operates from a particular 'cultural genealogy' that 'places a focus on individual entrepreneurs and innovations rather than collectives and communal-owned operations per se' (Bargh 2014: 467). An overt future orientation displaces historical practices and traditional knowledge. Arguably, the Blue Economy accentuates the centuries-long process of enclosures in the world's fisheries by identifying a new wave of 'growth opportunities' in marine and coastal ecosystems.

Although not initially framed as a market-based mechanism to achieve environmental goals, privatisation policies in fisheries, such as ITQs, have been rebranded to meet these new prerogatives. In the context of the Blue Economy, ITQs have been incorporated as an exemplary ecosystem tool showcasing the opportunities such conversions enable. This inclusion ties ITQs into an emergent meta-ideology and implies not only a 'greening' of inherent conflicts but also a newly invigorated drive to extend their global reach (see Longo et al. 2015).

A succinct account of ITQs can be made by unpacking the acronym: thus 'I' refers to enclosures, 'T' market exchange and 'Q' the point where the science of measuring fish stocks merges with the political objective of generating wealth (see also Gibbs 2009). Where ITQs prevail, fishing effort[7] is limited by the establishment of a total allowable catch (TAC). This is then divided into quota shares and distributed to various owners. Typically, when the system is first introduced, quota is freely gifted according to fishing history and/or the amount of wealth invested in the fishery. Subsequently, quota is distributed via 'the market', where it can be bought, sold and/or leased, often with the help of quota brokers and online trading systems. Owning quota guarantees a share of the TAC, and the more quota owned the larger the share. This assurance is assumed to incentivise sustainable fishing practices, reduce the danger of

---

7   A measure of the amount of fishing. More specifically, the amount of fishing gear of a specific type used on the fishing grounds over a given unit of time, e.g. hours trawled per day, number of hooks set per day, and so on.

overcapitalisation and solve the problem of fishermen racing.[8] The fishery, it is proposed, becomes economically efficient as less efficient operators leave the fishery, selling their quota to their more efficient counterparts. Excess capacity is thus reduced and there is an assumed increase in economic rents from a previously underproductive common property resource (see Costello et al. 2010).

ITQ fisheries are a becoming increasingly hegemonic on a global scale. That countries as spatially and culturally distinct as South Africa, Australia, Mexico and the Cook Islands have implemented ITQs and others such as Russia, Japan and Norway are moving in this direction is suggestive of two main possibilities: ITQs are able to reverse the notorious sustainability crisis in the world's fisheries; and the economic thesis on which the system is based is everywhere applicable, being compatible with local biophysical and cultural contexts, existent economic forms and human values. Neither supposition is correct. I suggest, rather, that ITQs are rooted in fantastical imaginings about the superiority of private property rights in generating good governance and economic efficiency; and that faith in the universality of 'the market' as the optimal space through which to distribute fishing rights is radically misplaced.

A shift to market environmentalism is apparent in the replacement of government regulatory standards with voluntary schemes, the growth of market-based mechanisms such as pollution permit trading schemes, the substitution of taxpayer-subsidised public good services, such as water, with full-cost consumer pricing and the growth in cost–benefit evaluations of environmental policies—the last of which created the demand for monetary valuation schemes, such as wetland banking, carbon trading and biodiversity offsets (Kallis et al. 2013). The construction of the environment as a package of ecosystem services to be assigned a monetary valuation, and to which an appropriate market-based tool can correct degradation, powerfully privileges market rationality over any other human–environment relationship. It also neatly sidesteps the critique of capitalism, and in particular its manifestation under neoliberalism, as itself heavily implicated in environmental destruction (Castree 2008, Sullivan 2013). Capitalism as a system is inherently driven to expand,

---

8   A race for fish is assumed to occur in the absence of individual property rights. It implies that in a common property resource fishermen will increase their effort and invest in larger boats and new technologies in order to harvest today what will not be available tomorrow. It is associated with Hardin's (2009) tragedy of the commons thesis.

to invent new outlooks for accumulation, rendering apparently natural the internalisation into capital of previously uncommodified aspects of nature and society (Escobar 1996). As Eriksen (2016) so poignantly asks, can the world capitalist system and the 'system earth' accommodate this accelerating relational, institutional and ecological 'overheating'?

There is an obvious conceptual convergence between neoliberalism as a political-economic system and market environmentalism as a specific means through which it is actualised in nature. ITQ systems signify an early example of this union and connect a new wave of concern for the environment with the ideology of neo-classical economics; that is, the assumption that sustainability will emerge through the incentivised bargaining of those with private property allocations.

Once privatised, quota has the propensity to become activated in markets and, while there is no logical relationship between quota as property rights and free market trading, there is an assumed innate trajectory. This tendency, captured in the T (transferability) of ITQs, is perhaps its most potent characteristic. A potency that helps explicate the disjuncture between Māori property in fishing rights and the demise of fishing livelihoods. The devolution of quota to *iwi* began in 2004 with the implementation of the Māori Fisheries Act. The Act set out the legislative basis for a pan-*iwi* distribution of fisheries settlement assets—that is, the capital and quota centrally held by Te Ohu Kai Moana[9] up to that point. In order to qualify for fishing assets, *iwi* must set up an MIO and one or more asset-holding companies. There are currently 57 recognised MIOs, inclusive of four collective groupings of *iwi* (Te Ohu Kaimoana n.d.). MIO entities blend a corporate structure with a charitable trust fund complex.

Iwi Settlement Quota (ISQ) is unique: it can be conceived of as a repatriation of Māori commercial fishing rights long alienated by successive colonial governments—ISQ is thus a Treaty right. This is evidenced in the technical nomenclature used to describe ISQ: quota shares that derive from the settlement are abbreviated as SET, a reference to their Treaty settlement origins. Only quota allocated to *iwi* under the fisheries settlement can legally carry this title, all other quota is termed 'normal' quota (Iwi Collective Partnership n.d.). It is also distinctive in that it represents a Māori property right that preceded New Zealand's

---

9   The organisation set up to handle settlement assets following the 1992 commercial settlement.

QMS. Indeed, the settlement of Māori claims to commercial fisheries strengthened the overall character of quota as property in New Zealand's ITQ. ISQ also carry different legal restrictions and statutory provisions to non–*iwi*-owned quota, but also to other *iwi*-owned assets. This makes divestment, or sale, very difficult. For instance, 75 per cent of *iwi* members must agree to the sale of quota, and quota can only be sold to other *iwi* following a complicated legal process. Further, ISQ carry the mandate that wealth must be generated and subsequently distributed for the benefit of *iwi* members. No ISQ has been sold since allocation in 2004; quota is either fished or, more commonly, leased as an annual catch entitlement (ACE). There is an absence of Māori fishermen at all levels in the commercial industry (NZIER 2002, and from observation). Importantly, ISQ is entangled with ancestral rights and knowledge, contemporary identity and livelihood practices and accountability to future generations.

Since 2004, there has been an upsurge in the quota-leasing market. There are a number explanations for this. First, many *iwi* do not have the technology or capital to harvest, in particular, deep-sea fish. Second, the quota held for a particular species is often too small to sustain a local fishing venture and is leased to companies that then aggregate it. Third, *iwi*-owned quota packages often contain a disproportionate amount of high-volume species on the lower end of the commercially valuable spectrum; economic viability, thus, requires leasing. Fourth, while some Māori settlement quota is owned as part of a more diversified set of asset holdings, for many *iwi* fishing quota is their only significant asset. Thus reducing risks and reaping the highest profit from the least amount of capital input may be the only rational economic choice. Finally, more wealth can be generated from trading activities than chasing fish in the sea. Therefore, in many ways, transferability is not about fish in the sea. It concerns, rather, the emergence of virtual fish and the attendant relegation of labour as now inconsequential in generating wealth. It elevates the status of quota traders and brokers while devaluing the knowledge associated with harvesting.

In ITQ fisheries, a distinction can be made between quota holders, those who have the right to fish and/or to lease this right to others, and fishers who do the actual harvesting. If one considers the findings in other ITQ systems, such as British Columbia and Iceland, that ITQ holders made more money trading fishing rights than fishing (see Pinkerton & Edwards 2009, Einarsson 2011), it should not be surprising that this also applies in New Zealand. This is true not only in activities in the quota trading market (buying and selling quota), but is also reflected in the rewards that accrue to owners who lease their quota as distinct from fishing it. An illustration of the latter is provided in the case of the *pāua* (abalone) fishery. About 1,200 tonnes of *pāua* are caught commercially in New Zealand each year, the majority of which is exported; export earnings are about NZ$60 million a year. The value of *pāua* quota has risen considerably over time. The average price of quota increased by 63.5 per cent in the first six months of trading—from NZ$11 to NZ$17.99 per kilo. By 2003, the average price reached NZ$300 per kilo, 27 times the price at the start of *pāua* quota trading in 1988. Figures for the 2014–15 year put the dollar per kilo price of quota at NZ$338. The average ACE value is NZ$15.50 per kilo whereas the port price is NZ$16.50 per kilo; thus, after paying for the leasing arrangement, non–quota-owning harvesters receive NZ$1 per kilo of *pāua* sold (see Table 15.1). The ratio of the value of quota to the price of fish is approximately 23:1 (383:16.5) and the owner obtains 15-and-a-half times as much from leasing quota for one year (NZ$15.50) than the fisher gets from harvesting (NZ$1). Unsurprisingly, *pāua* quota holders describe their right as akin to having won the lottery.[10]

Table 15.1: *Pāua* value in the quota market in the 2014–15 fishing year

Quota/kilo	ACE/kilo	Port price/kilo	Port price−ACE
$388	$15.50	$16.50	$1

Source: Author's summary.

The tension between labour and ownership in these statistics is reflected in the distinction between production and quota trading. Production, including the vertical integration of companies and the sale of fish, is a historic process. It is arguably a real, or at least visible, market whereas the quota trading system is a virtual market in which the participants buy and sell 'fish' without ever having any need to have fish to sell (sellers) or ever wishing to own fish (buyers). Fish in this instance may be considered an example of Polanyian fictitious commodity production. Quota trading, however, may be a radically different type of fiction: while

---

10   The data in this section comes from FishServe as part of my research on Fishing Quota and Financialisation. Since the *Fisheries Act 1996*, many registry-based QMS services are devolved or contracted to Seafood New Zealand (the commercial industry organisation funded by quota owner levies), as an approved government provider. FishServe is the trading name of Commercial Fisheries Services, which is a wholly owned subsidiary of Seafood New Zealand.

there is a physical limit to the amount of fish that can be harvested, quota trading does not appear to be constrained by any obvious boundaries (McCormack 2016b).

Sustainability

Since the late 1980s, there have been endeavours to include indigenous knowledge, or traditional ecological knowledge, in sustainable development programs (Soini & Birkeland 2014). This progression is not mirrored in the sustainability projects in rights-based fisheries. Where culture, particularly indigenous culture, is recognised in ITQ systems, it seems to be in terms of negotiating access to fishing rights—that is, property (typically in terms of a community development quota), not in the acceptance of local and traditional knowledge as a valid basis for management decisions. In New Zealand, for instance, while Māori indigenous knowledge of fisheries is recognised in non-commercial customary regulations, largely in terms of conservational features, it plays no part in the sustainability of fisheries outside of this sphere (McCormack 2010). McCarthy et al. (2014) highlight the disparity between New Zealand's internationally acclaimed fisheries management strategy and the concerns of local, in particular Māori, stakeholders.[11] In their interviews with over 100 seaside inhabitants, they found very different assessments concerning the health of stocks from those reported by fisheries scientists and the commercial industry. They comment:

> The locals also draw attention to a much wider suite of social and cultural consequences from unsustainable fishing than just the economic consequences emphasised by commercial interests that dominate Ministry of Primary Industry[12] research and policy (McCarthy et al. 2014: 65).

Participation in the system leads to the double bind of generating wealth out of a natural resource while arguably contributing to its environmental demise. The parcelling out of a complex ecosystem as individual quota depicts fish as mere units of a resource in a spreadsheet. It recreates the

---

11 This research was based on quantitative interviews and aimed to investigate local perceptions of the state of New Zealand's inshore fisheries stocks and contrast this with New Zealand's international reputation concerning its fisheries.

12 Fisheries is governed in New Zealand by the Ministry of Primary Industries. Under the new Labour coalition government, the Ministry of Primary Industries has been broken into three parts: agriculture, fisheries and forestry.

ocean ecosystem as a partible complex of commodities, quota stocks, to be cherry-picked, high-graded in ITQ terms, for consumption, or discarded as valueless. ITQ systems, for instance, are acknowledged to encourage high-grading, dumping, poaching and misreporting (Simmons et al. 2015). Despite the mooted ability of private property rights to generate sustainable practices, there is little evidence in ITQ fisheries to support this claim. As Emma Cardwell (2016, pers. comm.) notes, stewardship over the environment is very different to stewardship over the right to fish—that is, the quota right. The first requires responsible ecological behaviour, the second only responsible financial behaviour.

Conclusion

Marx's description of 'primitive accumulation' captures a process that continues unabated today, though in perhaps more insidious forms than his portrayal of it as a history written in 'letters of blood and fire' (Büscher 2009). This analysis, like Harvey's (2005) more recent conception of 'accumulation by dispossession', refers to how enclosures, which mark a separation of producers from the means of production, create a pliant and abundant proletariat and the conditions necessary for the development of capitalism. In this way, nature is imported into production and opened up to the logic of capitalism. Neoliberalisation, however, extends the reaches of classical primitive accumulation in contradictory ways. While privatisation implies the transference of resources and property from state to private ownership, for instance in fisheries, from 'the public' to quota holders, the process may not end at this point. In the context of natural resources, there may also be a provision to secure rights for the poor, as for example the community development quota assigned to indigenous groups in New Zealand, though also Western Alaska and, more recently, fishing communities in Iceland. However, as Harvey (2005) notes, this opens the door for subsequent appropriations. This can happen through outright violent dispossession, a delegitimisation of the new resource owners through legislation and, critically, 'through the market' whereby 'those who have valuable assets, but are earning incomes too low to permit social reproduction, inevitably have to sell them' (Fairhead et al. 2012: 243). Veracini adds to Harvey's list of contradictions with the concept of 'accumulation without reproduction', wherein, while work is required, this is increasingly within a 'political economy of promise', and as 'nonremunerated forms of labour and "voluntary servitudes" multiply, wages are less and less meant to recreate us as labour' (2015: 92).

In New Zealand, ITQ enclosures have led to further dispossessions. On a national scale, this means that fish, a commons resource, are now the private property of individuals, though, more often, corporations. As Lloyd and Wolfe point out, under the new mode of neoliberal accumulation, 'the state's role is being redrawn to furnish a conduit for the more rapid distribution of what were once public goods into the hands of corporations' (2016: 109). Dispossessions also include a disenfranchisement of small-scale and part-time Māori fishers; a delegitimising of the new resource owners through legislation, for instance, the corporate entities mandated to receive and manage quota; and the removal of exchange from customary regulations. Dispossessions, however, occur critically, through the market. Not so much in terms of the sale of quota—as in order to do so 75 per cent of *iwi* members must agree—but in terms of leasing, a divestment not of property per se, but of reproductive labour rights and of the relationships coastal tribes have with their fisheries.

A number of commentators argue that Treaty settlements are themselves facilitating a gradual transformation of tribal hierarchies into class distinctions (see, for instance, Rata 2011). While not disagreeing with the observation that new indigenous hierarchies have arisen, and that these may articulate with the appropriation and control of material resources by a select few, I root the source of these new relations within a broader political-economic framework. The settlement of Māori fisheries rights coincided with the marketisation of fisheries, a process that has increasingly influenced the production and exchange of fish, coerced the behaviour of actors within the sector to an important degree, and elevated the status of traders and brokers while devaluing the knowledge associated with harvesting, the result being the transformation of nature into a financial derivative. Quota trading works through a radical disembedding: in this instance, disembedding the economic issue from the historical question of how to manage fisheries in a way that sustains coastal communities and the ecosystems on which they depend.

References

Ballara A (1998). *Iwi: The dynamics of Māori tribal organisation from c. 1769 to c. 1945*, Victoria University Press, Wellington.

Bargh B (2016). *The struggle for Māori fishing rights: Te ika a Māori*, Huia, New Zealand.

Bargh M (2014). A blue economy for Aotearoa New Zealand? *Environment, development and sustainability* 16(3):459–70, doi.org/10.1007/s10668-013-9487-4.

Büscher B (2009). Letters of gold: Enabling primitive accumulation through neoliberal conservation. *Human Geography* 2(3):91–3.

Castree N (2008). Neoliberalising nature: The logics of deregulation and reregulation. *Environment and Planning A: Economy and Space* 40(1):131–52, doi.org/10.1068/a3999.

Clarke W (1990). Learning from the past: Traditional knowledge and sustainable development. *The Contemporary Pacific* 2(2):233–51.

Costello C, Lynham J, Lester SE & Gaines SD (2010). Economic incentives and global fisheries sustainability. *Resource* 2:1–393, doi.org/10.1146/annurev.resource.012809.103923.

Einarsson N (2011). Culture, conflict and crises in the Icelandic fisheries: An anthropological study of people, policy and marine resources in the North Atlantic arctic. PhD thesis. Uppsala Universitet.

Eriksen TH (2016). Overheating: The world since 1991. *History and Anthropology* 27(5):469–87, doi.org/10.1080/02757206.2016.1218865.

Escobar A (1996). Constructing nature: Elements for a post-structural political ecology. In Peet R (ed.), *Liberation ecology*, Routledge, New York.

Fairhead J, Leach M & Scoones I (2012). Green grabbing: A new appropriation of nature? *Journal of Peasant Studies* 39(2):237–61, doi.org/10.1080/03066150.2012.671770.

FAO (Food and Agriculture Organization) (2015). *FAO contribution to part 1 of the report of the secretary-general on oceans and the law of the sea*, www.un.org/depts/los/general_assembly/contributions_2015/FAO.pdf.

Gibbs M (2009). Individual transferable quotas and ecosystem-based fisheries management: It's all in the T. *Fish and Fisheries* 10(4):470–4, doi.org/10.1111/j.1467-2979.2009.00343.x.

Hardin G (2009). The tragedy of the commons. *Journal of Natural Resources Policy Research* 1(3):243–53, doi.org/10.1080/19390450903037302.

Harvey D (2005). *Spaces of neoliberalization: Towards a theory of uneven geographical development*, vol. 8, Franz Steiner Verlag.

Hviding E (1996). *Guardians of Marovo Lagoon: Practice, place, and politics in maritime Melanesia*, University of Hawai'i Press, Honolulu.

Iwi Collective Partnership (n.d.). *The inconvenient truth of Maori fisheries*, www. iwicollective.co.nz/the-inconvenient-truth-of-maori-fisheries/.

Jackson M (1995). Justice and political power: Reasserting Māori legal process. In Hazlehurst K (ed.), *Legal pluralism and the colonial legacy: Indigenous experiences of justice in Canada, Australia, and New Zealand*, Avebury, Aldershot.

Johannes R (1981). *Words of the lagoon: Fishing and marine lore in Palau District of Micronesia*, University of California Press, Berkeley.

Kallis G, Gómez-Baggethun E & Zografos C (2013). To value or not to value? That is not the question. *Ecological Economics* 94:97–105, doi.org/10.1016/j. ecolecon.2013.07.002.

Kingfisher C & Maskovsky J (2008). Introduction the limits of neoliberalism. *Critique of Anthropology* 28(2):115–26, doi.org/10.1177/0308275X08090544.

Lloyd D, & Wolfe P (2016). Settler colonial logics and the neoliberal regime. *Settler Colonial Studies* 6(2):109–18, doi.org/10.1080/2201473X.2015. 1035361.

Longo SB, Clausen R & Clark B (2015). *The tragedy of the commodity: Oceans, fisheries, and aquaculture*, Rutgers University Press, New Jersey.

McCarthy A, Hepburn C, Scott N, Schweikert K, Turner R & Moller H (2014). Local people see and care most? Severe depletion of inshore fisheries and its consequences for Māori communities in New Zealand. *Aquatic Conservation: Marine and Freshwater Ecosystems* 24(3):369–90, doi.org/10.1002/aqc.2378.

McCormack F (2010). Fish is my daily bread: Owning and transacting in Maori fisheries. *Anthropological Forum* 20(1):19–39, doi.org/10.1080/ 00664670903524194.

McCormack F (2016a). Indigenous claims: Hearings, settlements, and neoliberal silencing. *PoLAR: Political and Legal Anthropology Review* 39(2):226–43, doi.org/10.1111/plar.12191.

McCormack F (2016b). Quota systems: Repositioning value in New Zealand, Icelandic and Irish fisheries. In Angosto-Ferrandez L and Presterudstuen G (eds), *Anthropologies of value: Cultures of accumulation across the global north and south,* Pluto Press, doi.org/10.2307/j.ctt1dwstjr.14.

Mead S & Grove N (1981). *Ngā Pēpeha a ngā tīpuna: He Whakairiwhare Na. 2.* Department of Māori, Victoria University, Wellington.

Mead S & Grove N (2001). *Ngā Pēpeha a ngā tīpuna: The Sayings of the Ancestors.* Victoria University Press, Wellington.

Metge J (1989). *Evidence of Alice Joan Metge in respect of Te Wharo Oneroa A Tohe.* Submission to the Waitangi Tribunal Muriwhenua Land Report 1992, Wai 45 H/C 20.

Mulrennan M & Scott S (2000). Indigenous rights in saltwater environments. *Development and Change* 31(3):681–708, doi.org/10.1111/1467-7660.00172.

NZIER (New Zealand Institute of Economic Research) (2002). *Preserving fisheries quota for Maori,* Report to the Treaty of Waitangi Fisheries Commission, teohu. maori.nz/te_ohu/archive/allocation/Preserving%20fisheries%20quota%20 for%20Maori.pdf.

New Zealand Parliament (2006). *Treaty of Waitangi settlement process,* www. parliament.nz/resource/0000021392.

Pauli G (2010). *The Blue Economy: 10 years, 100 innovations, 100 million jobs,* Paradigm Publishers, Taos.

Petrie H (2002). Colonisation and the involution of the Maori economy. Paper presented at the XIII World Conference of Economic History, Buenos Aires, July.

Pinkerton E & Edwards DN (2009). The elephant in the room: The hidden costs of leasing individual transferable fishing quotas. *Marine Policy* 33(4):707–13, doi.org/10.1016/j.marpol.2009.02.004.

Rata E (2011). Discursive strategies of the Māori tribal elite. *Critique of Anthropology* 31(4):359–80, doi.org/10.1177/0308275X11420116.

Ropiha J (1992). Alienation of Māori fisheries in Mahia Peninsula 1920–1990. MA thesis, University of Auckland.

Rumbles W (1999). Treaty of Waitangi settlement process: New relationship or new mask. Paper presented at the Compr(om)ising Post/colonialism(s): Challenging Narratives and Practices Conference, Wollongong, Australia, 10–13 February.

Seafood New Zealand (n.d). *Key facts*, www.seafood.co.nz/our-seas/key-facts/.

Simmons G, Bremner G, Stringer C, Torkington B, Teh L, Zylich K, Zeller D, Pauly D & Whittaker H (2015). *Preliminary reconstruction of marine fisheries catches for New Zealand (1950–2010)*, University Of British Columbia, Vancouver.

Soini K & Birkeland I (2014). Exploring the scientific discourse on cultural sustainability. *Geoforum* 51:213–23, doi.org/10.1016/j.geoforum.2013.12.001.

Sullivan S (2013). Banking nature? The spectacular financialisation of environmental conservation. *Antipode* 45(1):198–217, doi.org/10.1111/j.1467-8330.2012.00989.x.

Sykes A (2004). *Opening submission foreshore and seabed Wai 1071*, Claim to the Waitangi Tribunal, Wellington, New Zealand.

Te Ohu Kaimoana (n.d.). *Did you know/Iwi ika—supporting iwi fisheries*, www.iwiika.maori.nz/ahc/did-you-know.htm.

Veracini, L (2015). *The settler colonial present*, Springer, doi.org/10.1057/9781137372475.

Waitangi Tribunal (1988). *Muriwhenua fishing claims report (Wai 22)*, New Zealand Department of Justice, Wellington.

16

Māori political and economic recognition in a diverse economy

Maria Bargh

Introduction

The relationship between Māori and the state in Aotearoa/New Zealand has been radically reshaped in the past 20 years. In some respects, Māori tribal (*iwi*) enterprises now have more recognition from the Crown, primarily as economic actors, and more access to decision-making power than they have had since the 1820s, when *iwi* had complete *tino rangatiratanga* (sovereignty) in Aotearoa/New Zealand. In particular, many *iwi* enterprises that have completed Treaty of Waitangi settlements[1] and have re-established a strong economic base are receiving greater recognition from Crown agencies. The Māori Party, formed in 2004, has been instrumental in assisting the Iwi Chairs' Forum (a national grouping of the leaders of tribal enterprises) access ministers and key policymakers, symbolic of the manner in which economic recognition has also led to forms of political recognition.

In other respects, however, the Crown persists with policies, predominantly neoliberal policies, that continue to restrict and marginalise Māori political and economic organisational forms and rights. In this chapter,

---

1 These are negotiated settlements between Māori and the Crown in part as reparation for Crown breaches of Te Tiriti o Waitangi 1840.

I am defining neoliberal policies as those that include reducing the size of the state, promoting forms of trade that have few barriers to the movement of goods and finance, and are premised on the belief that the market is the best mechanism to regulate all forms of human behaviour as people are predominantly self-maximising and selfish individuals (Bargh 2007).

The situation is not as simple as it may appear, however. There is not simply a group of elite Māori recognised by the Crown as economic actors, indoctrinated in neoliberal thought and a marginalised underclass of Māori resistance. In this chapter, I examine the multiple roles that Māori enterprises inhabit and suggest that expanding the way these roles are defined assists in avoiding simplistic conceptualisations of Māori enterprises, and Māori, as only either champions or victims of neoliberal policies and practices. I end by suggesting that, in order to avoid assuming neoliberal policies consume all other forms of labour and enterprises in economies, critiques of neoliberal policies and practices must be accompanied by an exploration of those areas of a diverse economy that are forging other alternative neoliberal or non-neoliberal worlds.

Increasing recognition of Māori enterprises and economy

When considering the topic of 'recognition' it is important to note that Māori *hapū* and *iwi* have long been recognised by and recognise the political and legal status and institutions of other *hapū* and *iwi*, as well as other indigenous nations in the Pacific (Petrie 2006). When considering the recognition of Māori by non-indigenous actors, one of the earliest forms of informal recognition for particularly the northern tribes in New Zealand came in a letter from King William IV in 1832, read out by James Busby, the first appointed British Resident of New Zealand (Waitangi Tribunal 2014). In the letter, King William IV proposed that, in exchange for Māori protecting the British Resident, they would receive benefits from the 'friendship and alliance with Great Britain' (Waitangi Tribunal 2014: 114). Formal recognition of Māori sovereignty came in the 1835 Declaration of Independence and Te Tiriti o Waitangi 1840 (Mutu 2010).

In the subsequent century and a half after 1840, the Crown breached Te Tiriti o Waitangi in a variety of ways through their actions and inaction. Māori used numerous political and legal avenues in attempts to have these breaches rectified, and eventually in the 1970s significant progress was achieved with the establishment of the Waitangi Tribunal to hear cases brought by Māori about Treaty breaches. The Crown also established a direct negotiations process in the mid-1990s to ensure further control over the process and to speed up the 'full and final' settlements of historical Treaty breaches (Durie 1999).

The Crown's Treaty of Waitangi settlement process has led a number of government agencies to pay close attention to the governance structures of *iwi* enterprises. Two agencies have a significant role in the assessment and structuring of *iwi* governance structures. The first is the Office of Treaty Settlements (OTS), which is based within the Ministry of Justice and takes a leading role in direct negotiations on behalf of the Crown. The second is the Māori Fisheries Commission (Te Ohu Kaimoana), which was created originally by the *Treaty of Waitangi (Fisheries Claims) Settlement Act 1992* and modified with the *Māori Fisheries Act 2004*.[2] In particular, the OTS and Te Ohu Kaimoana have sought to ensure that *iwi* enterprises have governance structures that they view as appropriate to manage returned financial and commercial assets. Those enterprises recognised and deemed appropriate to the Crown are commonly referred to as 'post-settlement governance entities' and those recognised by Te Ohu Kaimoana as 'mandated *iwi* organisations'. Post-settlement governance entities and mandated *iwi* organisations follow specific processes relating to mandating, representation, governance and accountability that are prescribed by the OTS and Te Ohu Kaimoana (OTS 2015, Te Ohu Kaimoana n.d.). Those enterprises that follow these prescriptions are subsequently formally recognised by the Crown (Cowie 2012). Those *iwi* enterprises that do not follow these prescriptions do not receive recognition, as was the experience in 1998, for example, when the *iwi* of Whakatohea declined their settlement (Graham 1998, Vertongen 2012). The Waitangi Tribunal has reported other occasions where *iwi* groups have been excluded from negotiations because the OTS picked other 'favourites' (Waitangi Tribunal 2007).

---

2   For the full text of the *Treaty of Waitangi (Fisheries Claims) Settlement Act 1992*, see www. legislation.govt.nz/act/public/1992/0121/latest/DLM281433.html. For the full text of the *Māori Fisheries Act 2004*, see www.legislation.govt.nz/act/public/2004/0078/latest/DLM311464.html.

Around 50 *iwi* have had legislation pass through parliament to bring their Deeds of Settlement with the Crown into effect. This is an ever-changing figure, as new settlements are reached and other settlements relating to specific resources (such as rivers) are additional to this number. At least 10 of the post-settlement governance entities resulting from these 50 settlements have been operating for more than 10 years, including the two financially largest settlements of Ngāi Tahu and Waikato-Tainui.

Crown and Māori attention has turned therefore to not only recognising but also to assessing the performance and activities of the post-settlement governance entities, and there has been a proliferation of theses and government, scholarly and popular reports about the potential of Māori enterprises and the 'Māori economy' (Mataira 2000, Warriner 2009, Hudson 2014, Spiller et al. 2015, Prendergast-Tarena 2015).

In 2003, a report commissioned by Te Puni Kōkiri (the Ministry of Māori Development), *Māori economic development*, encouraged government and readers in general to consider the Māori economy in new ways, as full of potential and a success rather than as a drain on the New Zealand economy. The report argued further that Māori culture was a significant feature of the Māori economy and could support the profitability and success of Māori businesses (NZIER 2003). Subsequent media coverage about the report encouraged the general public to consider a similar re-evaluation (James 2003).

In 2009, the Māori Economic Taskforce was established by the Minister of Māori Affairs to provide:

> opportunities for Māori to contribute to and benefit from a thriving New Zealand economy. It seeks to enhance Māori entrepreneurship and innovation to position Māori for future strategic economic opportunities and promote kaupapa Māori and Māori structures as drivers of prosperity (Te Puni Kōkiri 2010).

The Taskforce contracted Business and Economic Research Ltd (BERL) to conduct a number of reports around the Māori economy, and, in the more general media, BERL promoted and marked the change in the way that the Māori economy was being described in New Zealand. One article in 2010 described the Māori economy as a 'sleeping giant' and argued that 'the Māori economy is an integral part of the New Zealand economy and spans several industries' (BERL 2010).

Most importantly, the 2010 BERL article highlighted the recognition of the Māori *economy*, and suggested that Māori people were adding *economic* value to the New Zealand economy. Clearly there are many ways Māori had been contributing to New Zealand earlier alongside the economic contribution—but the fact that the economic contribution aroused so much interest is indicative of the level to which neoliberal policies and practices have permeated the New Zealand Government and government-related research.

Te Puni Kōkiri has also partnered with the Federation of Māori Authorities, which represents *iwi* and Māori landowners and regional councils to commission 'Māori economy' reports for their regions (Te Puni Kōkiri 2013, 2014). In Auckland, the Independent Māori Statutory Board commissioned research from the New Zealand Institute of Economic Research (NZIER) for a similar report for the Auckland region (NZIER 2015). These commissioned reports have a dual function. For the *iwi* organisations, they provide statistics to support their own awareness of the nature of their business and to communicate that position to their people. The second function of these reports is for the *iwi* to use in communication with external entities to raise awareness in the broader non-Māori community of the existence of the Māori economy. In this latter regard, *iwi* are seeking recognition from local government, local businesses, central government and national businesses of the contribution that Māori make to economies, and to encourage them to therefore be more attentive to Māori concerns and rights.

Alongside an increasing recognition and quantification of the Māori economy asset base has been a parallel Māori conversation about the need for Māori to balance the articulation of their *economic* nature and success with their *Māori* nature and success *for* Māori. The idea of bringing together Māori ways of doing things with those of non-Māori, whether it be in the areas of, for example, business or research, is not a new phenomenon and has been regularly discussed by Māori since non-Māori arrived in New Zealand. Māori leader and politician of the early 19th century Apirana Ngata instructed Māori to maintain a balance between acquiring the tools of Europeans (Pākehā) and protecting the treasures of Māori, and is commonly quoted by Māori scholars (Mahuika 2008). The combining of dual cultural and legal values and practices has been used by many Māori in an attempt to retain land and maintain levels of self-determination in response to colonisation (Durie 1999).

This combining of dual cultural and legal values and practices in response to colonisation has resonance with Māori strategies in the context of a 'neoliberal age'. When some Māori began using phrases such as 'corporate warriors' in the 1980s, it was reflecting the sense of a need to link Māori values with the increasingly common neoliberal policies and practices that the government was encouraging, including in their interactions with Māori (Bargh 2007). As O'Sullivan also noted in Chapter 13 of this volume, some Māori also saw potential in the neoliberal rhetoric of 'empowerment' to support their self-determination aspirations (Bargh 2007). Some Māori continue to see potential in connecting neoliberal policies that value particular forms of economic entrepreneurship and Māori political and economic aspirations (Keelan & Woods 2006).

Political recognition

The greater recognition of Māori economic entities has been accompanied by forms of greater political recognition, much of which has been channelled by the Māori Party. After the 2008 general election, the National Party entered a Relationship Accord and Confidence and Supply Agreement with the Māori Party. This agreement has enabled a number of channels for political conversations between not just the two political parties, but also some of their key supporters. In the case of the Māori party, some of those key supporters are economically larger *iwi* enterprises, which have a clear agenda for the return of particular natural resources and most of which want to advance their cultural, environmental, political and economic aspirations.[3] In their chapters of this volume, O'Sullivan (Chapter 13) and Humpage (Chapter 14) detail examples of some of the social policy aspirations. To a certain extent, therefore, forms of economic recognition are helping to produce some forms of political recognition for *iwi*. One way of interpreting this is that economically powerful Māori are seen to have acquired the necessary skills to be more capable of governing their own affairs (Bargh 2011).

It is worth noting that those *iwi* that do receive political recognition constitute a small group of the total number of *iwi* and are primarily those that attend the Iwi Chairs' Forum. The Iwi Chairs' Forum was first convened in 2005 with around five established *iwi*. The numbers of *iwi* attending has increased substantially, and subcommittees work

---

3   For more information, see the Iwi Chairs' Forum website: iwichairs.maori.nz/.

between meetings on select issues of importance (Te Aho 2014). Those *iwi* representatives working on select issues have access to government ministers and officials. For some issues, such as freshwater management, for example, the Iwi Chairs' Forum also has 'technicians' and '*iwi* leaders' on Ministry for the Environment internal water allocation policy groups, and on the government-established Land and Water Forum to advise government officials (Te Aho 2014).

The challenge that accompanies this dynamic—a small group with influence—is that the lines of transparency and accountability are not always clear. Lawyer Annette Sykes spoke on this topic in her 2011 Bruce Jesson lecture, where she criticised the Iwi Chairs' Forum and requested greater transparency regarding the mandate of particular officials and decision-making processes within the forum. Sykes' broader concern was that these forms of decision-making were neoliberal in nature and practice. She argued that, seen in this context, 'the newly constructed layer of Māori leadership seems to be a quango which the Crown then resources as part of its specific consultation requirements in the expectation it will generate an acceptable Māori view' (Sykes 2011).

She argued further that the Iwi Chairs' Forum was using achievements by Māori in the areas of education, language and the political and legal struggle regarding ownership of the foreshore and seabed for narrow neoliberal aims.

> The NICF [National Iwi Chairs' Forum] has capitalised on that momentum for change. Surfing on the tide of discontent they have assumed the space that grass roots activists created, and promoted neo liberal goals, such as the right to exploit the vast natural resources under the sea, that are more in keeping with capitalism than with the tino rangatiratanga that was being called for (Sykes 2011: n.p.).

Sykes provided the example of government consultation on the Emissions Trading Scheme to illustrate her point that a small group of Māori who alone have access to information, without broader Māori or public discussion and scrutiny, is prone to being captured by advocates of neoliberal policies.

Similar processes have been evident in 2015 and 2016, with consultation between the government and the Iwi Chairs' Forum on water ownership and allocation models. The options being proposed by the government and now considered by the Iwi Chairs' Forum are primarily options for the marketisation of the water allocation regime (Ministry for the Environment 2016). Non-neoliberal options that involve water being cooperatively managed by guardians, who might also manage, say, plant restoration projects, are considered and advocated by *iwi* at regional meetings but do not result in a change in government policies (Te Aho 2014).

Multiple roles in a diverse economy

There is plenty to be concerned about when it comes to the persuasive and pervasive nature of neoliberal policies and practices. The extension of the market mechanism to govern areas previously governed in other ways has resulted in breaches of Māori rights in the areas of water management, Māori land management and resource exploitation (Bargh 2016). Sykes' perspective on the interaction between the Iwi Chairs' Forum and the Crown suggests a Māori elite co-opted by neoliberal policies and practices. However, it would be counter-productive to assume that all Māori actions can be reduced to sit within a neoliberal framework. Māori, like other peoples, inhabit multiple roles in the economy and are employing multiple strategies simultaneously. Māori are 'economic actors with multiple roles' (Gibson-Graham et al. 2013: xx).

The continued prevalence of neoliberal policies in many countries has led some scholars within groups on the left to analyse the way leftist analysis tends to operate. In her article 'Resisting Left Melancholy', for example, Wendy Brown argues that traditional leftist analyses and politics are too rigid and no longer provide a compelling vision or strategy for another 'order of things' (Brown 1999: 25). Similarly, JK Gibson-Graham (2006) has written extensively on the role that emotions play in leftist critique and has argued that negativity and pessimism within leftist thinkers has often produced paralysis. The relevance of their argument here is their insistence that, instead of being fixated on a particular form of power from which leftists are excluded, a more productive orientation is to look for the places where people and communities are already engaged in multiple roles with multiple possibilities for political and economic transformation (Gibson-Graham 2006). Scholars like JK Gibson-Graham argue that when scholars and communities focus on the diverse nature of the economy and the multiple roles people have, it extends a vision of where change can occur: 'small actions can initiate major changes' (Gibson-Graham et al. 2013: xxiii).

If the Iwi Chair's Forum is taken as a focus point from which to consider the diverse economy framework, a wide range of activities become apparent that are not simply neoliberal but that promote labour, enterprises, transactions, property and finance that are non-capitalist or alternative capitalist. For example, if the Waikato River Settlement and associated *iwi* enterprises are taken as an illustration, there are numerous associated activities that are other than just neoliberal practices. Representatives from the Waikato *iwi* participate in the Iwi Chairs' Forum and were responsible for negotiating the Waikato River Settlement that created five River Trusts for *iwi*, with tributaries flowing into the Waikato River.[4] One of these is the Te Arawa River Iwi Trust, which has funded projects for riparian planting of waterways, investigating and building a micro-hydroelectric dam and the restoration of native freshwater species (George 2016). Within each of those projects, *iwi* members have been involved in paid labour, voluntary work and other forms of labour. The micro-hydroelectric project has led to the building of a native nursery, for which seeds have been eco-sourced from the tribe's forest and research (paid and voluntary) into the feasibility of a glasshouse for restoration of native fresh water species has begun. It has generated non-market transactions: gift and cultural exchanges.

Another example of an enterprise that is involved with the Iwi Chairs' Forum and a multiplicity of other activities is the Te Arawa Lakes Trust. Formed after the 2006 Te Arawa Lakes Settlement between the Crown and Te Arawa tribe, it returns ownership of the beds of a number of lakes in the Bay of Plenty area to Te Arawa, along with a dedicated role in the management of the lakes.[5] The Trust aims to increase the financial asset base of the organisation alongside supporting people into training and promoting a cultural values framework about the lakes. In 2015, the Trust provided its membership list to enable the Rotorua District Council to establish a Te Arawa Partnership Board for the *iwi* to contribute directly to local government decision-making (Te Arawa Lakes Trust 2015). Therefore, while there is limited transparency about the exact nature of the discussions that Te Arawa Lake Trust representatives participate in at the Iwi Chairs' Forum and with government ministers, it would be far too simplistic to label the organisation as just promoters of neoliberal policies (see Table 16.1).

---

4   For the full text of the *Waikato-Tainui Raupatu Claims (Waikato River) Settlement Act 2010*, see www.legislation.govt.nz/act/public/2010/0024/latest/DLM1630002.html.

5   For the full text of the *Te Arawa Lakes Settlement Act 2006*, see www.legislation.govt.nz/act/public/2006/0043/latest/DLM381398.html.

Table 16.1: Elements of a Te Arawa Lakes Trust diverse economy

Labour	Enterprise	Transactions	Property	Finance
Wage Chief Executive (CE) salary. Elected Trustees paid stipend. Chair and CE attend Iwi Chairs' Forum.	**Capitalist** Companies may be set up as subsidiaries of Trust to generate a profit.	**Market** Sells trout fishing licences. Contracts for training services.	**Private** The Trust has owned commercial property on the lakefront in Rotorua.	**Mainstream market** A bank loan may be taken out to finance development of commercial property.
Alternative paid Self-employed fixed-term tutors for private training. Establishment run by the Trust.	**Alternative capitalist** The Trust has been created by a Treaty Settlement between the Crown and Māori and governed by tribally elected Trustees and managed by a CE.	**Alternative market** Joint ventures considered with other *iwi* on technological projects relating to fresh water.	**Alternative private** Te Arawa owns the lake beds. Crown owns the 'Crown Stratum'. *Marae* (meeting place) lands are reserves governed by the *Māori Land Act 1993*.	**Alternative market** The NZ Qualifications Authority provides funding for the Private Training Establishment.
Unpaid *Kaumātua* (elders) perform cultural duties on the *marae* for the AGM. Chair of Trust attends *tangi* (funerals) in the Bay of Plenty area. Te Arawa members volunteer time to help monitor freshwater species in streams. Grandmother looks after grandchildren so Trustee can attend meetings.	**Non-capitalist** *Marae* and *hapū* enterprises of Te Arawa engage with Trust regarding fisheries and water issues.	**Non-market** Allow membership register to be used by the Te Arawa Partnership Board for local government elections. University-funded researchers providing analysis of Te Arawa Lakes Trust elections.	**Non-market** Water is owned by *hapū* according to *tikanga Māori* (Māori law).	**Non-market** Donations are given to *marae*.

Source: Author's summary.

When Julie Graham and Katherine Gibson began creating the diverse economies framework, one of the challenges that emerged came from other leftist thinkers who argued that simply creating inventories of diverse practices was at best not going to work and at worst going to result in complicity with global capitalism (Gibson-Graham 2006). To consider that challenge in the context of Māori enterprises, one way of clarifying that highlighting new possibilities and activities aims to support the proliferation of 'another possible world' is to also highlight those entities that are comprised more of non-capitalist and non-market elements. Due to limitations on space in this chapter, I would like to mention two examples with different forms to give a sense of the range that exist for Māori. The first example comes from Ngāi Tūhoe, who in their settlement with the Crown in the *Te Urewera Act 2014* insisted on creating legal personhood for their traditional mountain Te Urewera. Tūhoe have also built Te Kura Whare, a living building, at Taneatua that utilises renewable energy and other sustainable practices.[6] The second example is the Tuaropaki Power company, which is owned by the Tuaropaki Trust, a Māori Land Trust that generates electricity with a geothermal power station and has established a milk-processing factory, temperature-controlled horticulture and worm farm to support sustainable environmental practices.[7]

Maliha Safri and Julie Graham argue that if you change the way you identify and speak about the economy, you create a new imagining of possibilities. In their article about the global household, they argue that household production can 'account for as much as half of world economic activity (depending on the accounting system being employed)' (Safri & Graham 2010: 104). That kind of image redefines who would be considered the most significant actors. Similarly, creating an inventory of who is involved in the diverse economy of Māori rights and recognition creates a much more complex picture of alternative and non-capitalist aspects. Using a language of economy that includes these multiple activities assists in making them more visible and bring them further into reality.

---

6   For more information, see the Ngāi Tūhoe website: www.ngaituhoe.iwi.nz/sustainability-and-the-living-building-challenge.

7   For more information, see the Tuaropaki website: tuaropaki.com/.

Conclusion

Many aspects of the relationship between Māori and the Crown have changed markedly in New Zealand. In large part, this has been influenced by neoliberal policies that value economic relationships. Many *iwi* have engaged in the Crown's Treaty of Waitangi settlement process for recognition and compensation for breaches of Te Tiriti o Waitangi and have established new governance entities as a result. Post-settlement governance entities generally fit within the parameters of forms of organisation the Crown finds acceptable, arguably reflecting more longstanding traditions of imperial recognition of cultural difference that it finds appropriate (Buchan 2008). Many of those post-settlement governance entities seek solidarity, cooperation and political leverage through the Iwi Chairs' Forum. The operations and decision-making processes of the Iwi Chairs' Forum are not particularly transparent and have led to criticism that the forum functions to support neoliberal policies and practices.

However, that is not all post-settlement governance entities or *iwi* enterprises are. Closer examination suggests that many of the activities of the *iwi* entities that participate in the forum contain non-neoliberal and alternative neoliberal aspects, and a much more diverse economy becomes apparent. In order to sustain hope that there are possibilities outside a 'neoliberal age', an identification and critique of neoliberal policies and practices must be accompanied by an elaboration of the multiple roles that enterprises and peoples also play in a diverse economy.

References

Bargh M (2007). Māori development. In Bargh M (ed.), *Resistance: An indigenous response to neoliberalism*, Huia, Wellington.

Bargh M (2011). Moving on from a developmental view of humanity. *Alternatives* 36(1):79–85, doi.org/10.1177/0304375411402022

Bargh M (2016). Alternative energy and economics. Paper presented at In the Eye of the Storm: Pacific Climate Change Conference, Victoria University of Wellington, 17 February.

BERL (Business and Economic Research Limited) (2010). *The Māori economy—A sleeping giant about to awaken?* 22 December, berl.co.nz.

Brown W (1999). Resisting left melancholy. *Boundary 2* 26(3):19–27.

Buchan B (2008). Asia and the moral geography of European enlightenment political thought 1600–1800. In Nederman C and Shogimen T (eds), *Western political thought in dialogue with Asia*, Lexington Books, Lanham.

Cowie D (2012). The Treaty settlement process. In Wheen N and Hayward J (eds), *Treaty of Waitangi settlements*, Bridget Williams Books, Wellington, doi.org/10.7810/9781927131381_3.

Durie M (1999). *Te mana te kawanatanga: The politics of Māori self-determination*, Oxford University Press, Oxford.

George K (2016). *Iwi environmental management plan, Te Rūnanga o Ngāti Kea/ Ngāti Tuara*, Rotorua.

Gibson-Graham JK (2006). *A post capitalist politics*, University of Minnesota Press, Minnesota.

Gibson-Graham JK, Cameron J & Healy S (2013). *Take back the economy*, University of Minnesota Press, Minneapolis, doi.org/10.5749/minnesota/ 9780816676064.001.0001.

Graham D (1998). *Whakatohea Deed of Settlement to be terminated*, media release, Wellington, 13 March, www.beehive.govt.nz/release/whakatohea-deed-settlement-be-terminated.

Hudson JT (2014). Te Paewai o te Rangi: A framework for measuring iwi outcomes. PhD thesis. Massey University, Albany.

James C (2003). Revising stereotypes of Māori economy. *New Zealand Herald*, 3 February, www.nzherald.co.nz/business/news/article.cfm?c_id=3&objectid =3099282.

Keelan J & Woods C (2006). Mauipreneur: Understanding Māori entrepreneurship, *International Indigenous Entrepreneurship, Advancement, Strategy and Education*, www.indigenousjournal.com/IIJEASVolIIIss1 Woods.pdf.

Mahuika R (2008). Kaupapa Māori theory is critical and anti-colonial. *MAI Review* 3.

Mataira JP (2000). Ngā kai arahi tuitui Māori: Māori entrepreneurship: The articulation of leadership and the dual constituency arrangements associated with Māori enterprise in a capitalist economy. PhD thesis. Massey University Albany, Auckland.

Ministry for the Environment (2016). *Fresh water: Allocation work programme*, Cabinet paper, Wellington, www.mfe.govt.nz/sites/default/files/media/Fresh%20water/Freshwater%20Allocation%20Work%20Programme%20%20Terms%20of%20Reference%20and%20Appointmen....pdf.

Mutu, M (2010). Constitutional intentions: The Treaty of Waitangi texts. In Mulholland M and Tawhai V (eds), *Weeping waters: The Treaty of Waitangi and constitutional change*, Huia Publishers, Wellington.

NZIER (New Zealand Institute of Economic Research) (2003). *Māori economic development: Te ōhanga whanaketanga Māori*, NZIER, Wellington.

NZIER (2015). *The Auckland Māori economy report: Sizes, issues and opportunities*, nzier.org.nz/publication/the-auckland-m%C4%81ori-economy.

OTS (Office of Treaty Settlement) (2015). *Healing the past: Building a future*, www.govt.nz/assets/Documents/Red-Book-Healing-the-past-building-a-future.pdf.

Petrie H (2006). *Chiefs of industry*. Auckland University Press, Auckland.

Prendergast-Tarena ER (2015). Indigenising the corporation: Indigenous organisation design: An analysis of their design, features, and the influence of indigenous cultural values. PhD thesis. University of Canterbury, Christchurch.

Safri M & Graham J (2010). The global household: Toward a feminist postcapitalist international political economy. *Signs* 36(1):99–125, doi.org/10.1086/652913.

Spiller C, Barclay-Kerr H & Panoho J (2015). *Wayfinding leadership: Groundbreaking wisdom for developing leaders*, Huia, Wellington.

Sykes A (2011). *Bruce Jesson memorial lecture*, 5 July, Auckland, www.brucejesson.com/annette-sykes-2010-bruce-jesson-memorial-lecture/.

Te Aho L (2014). *Report to the* Iwi *Advisory Group from the Freshwater* Iwi *Leadership Regional Hui*, iwichairs.maori.nz/wp-content/uploads/2015/06/Waimaori-Report-IAG-Hui-2014-revised-5.12.14.pdf.

Te Arawa Lakes Trust (2015). *Te Arawa Lakes Trust annual report 2014/2015*, www.tearawa.iwi.nz/files/te_arawa_iwi/keydocuments/TALT%20Annual%20Report%202014-2015.pdf.

Te Ohu Kaimoana (n.d.). *Mandating process*, teohu.maori.nz/iwi/mandate_process/flowchartFLASH.swf.

Te Puni Kōkiri (2010). *Annual report for the year ended 30 June 2010*, www.tpk. govt.nz/mi/a-matou-mohiotanga/corporate-documents/annual-report-for-the-year-ended-30-june-2010/online/13.

Te Puni Kōkiri (2013). *Māori economic development strategy*, www.bayof connections.com/downloads/BOC%20MAORI%20ECONOMIC%20 Strategy%202013.pdf.

Te Puni Kōkiri (2014). *Māori economy in the Waikato Region,* www.tpk.govt.nz/ en/a-matou-mohiotanga/business-and-economics/maori-economy-in-the-waikato-region.

Vertongen B (2012). Legal challenges to the Treaty Settlement process. In Wheen N and Hayward J (eds), *Treaty of Waitangi Settlements*, Bridget Williams Books, Wellington, doi.org/10.7810/9781927131381_4.

Waitangi Tribunal (2007). *Final report on the impacts of the Crown Treaty Settlement policies on Te Arawa Waka and other tribes*, Legislation Direct, Wellington.

Waitangi Tribunal (2014). *Te Paparahi o Te Raki: Northland inquiry part one*, Legislation Direct, Wellington.

Warriner V (2009). Internationalisation of Māori businesses in the creative industry sector. PhD thesis, Massey University, Auckland.

Index

Note: Footnotes are indicated by page numbers in the form '125n3', this example meaning footnote 3 on page 125.

CAEPR Research Monograph Series

1. *Aborigines in the economy: a select annotated bibliography of policy relevant research 1985–90*, LM Allen, JC Altman and E Owen (with assistance from WS Arthur), 1991.

2. *Aboriginal employment equity by the year 2000*, JC Altman (ed.), published for the Academy of Social Sciences in Australia, 1991.

3. *A national survey of Indigenous Australians: options and implications*, JC Altman (ed.), 1992.

4. *Indigenous Australians in the economy: abstracts of research, 1991–92*, LM Roach and KA Probst, 1993.

5. *The relative economic status of Indigenous Australians, 1986–91*, J Taylor, 1993.

6. *Regional change in the economic status of Indigenous Australians, 1986–91*, J Taylor, 1993.

7. *Mabo and native title: origins and institutional implications*, W Sanders (ed.), 1994.

8. *The housing need of Indigenous Australians, 1991*, R Jones, 1994.

9. *Indigenous Australians in the economy: abstracts of research, 1993–94*, LM Roach and HJ Bek, 1995.

10. *The native title era: emerging issues for research, policy, and practice*, J Finlayson and DE Smith (eds), 1995.

11. *The 1994 National Aboriginal and Torres Strait Islander Survey: findings and future prospects*, JC Altman and J Taylor (eds), 1996.

12. *Fighting over country: anthropological perspectives*, DE Smith and J Finlayson (eds), 1997.

13. *Connections in native title: genealogies, kinship, and groups*, JD Finlayson, B Rigsby and HJ Bek (eds), 1999.

14. *Land rights at risk? Evaluations of the Reeves Report*, JC Altman, F Morphy and T Rowse (eds), 1999.

15. *Unemployment payments, the activity test, and Indigenous Australians: understanding breach rates*, W Sanders, 1999.

16. *Why only one in three? The complex reasons for low Indigenous school retention*, RG Schwab, 1999.

17. *Indigenous families and the welfare system: two community case studies*, DE Smith (ed.), 2000.

18. *Ngukurr at the millennium: a baseline profile for social impact planning in south-east Arnhem Land*, J Taylor, J Bern and KA Senior, 2000.

19. *Aboriginal nutrition and the Nyirranggulung Health Strategy in Jawoyn country*, J Taylor and N Westbury, 2000.

20. *The Indigenous welfare economy and the CDEP scheme*, F Morphy and W Sanders (eds), 2001.

21. *Health expenditure, income and health status among Indigenous and other Australians*, MC Gray, BH Hunter and J Taylor, 2002.

22. *Making sense of the census: observations of the 2001 enumeration in remote Aboriginal Australia*, DF Martin, F Morphy, WG Sanders and J Taylor, 2002.

23. *Aboriginal population profiles for development planning in the northern East Kimberley*, J Taylor, 2003.

24. *Social indicators for Aboriginal governance: insights from the Thamarrurr region, Northern Territory*, J Taylor, 2004.

25. *Indigenous people and the Pilbara mining boom: a baseline for regional participation*, J Taylor and B Scambary, 2005.

26. *Assessing the evidence on Indigenous socioeconomic outcomes: a focus on the 2002 NATSISS*, BH Hunter (ed.), 2006.

27. *The social effects of native title: recognition, translation, coexistence*, BR Smith and F Morphy (eds), 2007.

28. *Agency, contingency and census process: observations of the 2006 Indigenous Enumeration Strategy in remote Aboriginal Australia*, F Morphy (ed.), 2008.

29. *Contested governance: culture, power and institutions in Indigenous Australia*, J Hunt, D Smith, S Garling and W Sanders (eds), 2008.

30. *Power, culture, economy: Indigenous Australians and mining*, J Altman and D Martin (eds), 2009.

31. *Demographic and socioeconomic outcomes across the Indigenous Australian lifecourse*, N Biddle and M Yap, 2010.

32. *Survey analysis for Indigenous policy in Australia: social science perspectives*, B Hunter and N Biddle (eds), 2012.

33. *My Country, mine country: Indigenous people, mining and development contestation in remote Australia*, B Scambary, 2013.

34. *Indigenous Australians and the National Disability Insurance Scheme*, N Biddle, F Al-Yaman, M Gourley, M Gray, JR Bray, B Brady, LA Pham, E Williams and M Montaigne, 2014.

35. *Engaging Indigenous economy: debating diverse approaches*, W Sanders (ed.), 2016.

36. *Better than welfare? Work and livelihoods for Indigenous Australians after CDEP*, K Jordan (ed.), 2016.

37. *Reluctant representatives: blackfella bureaucrats speak in Australia's north*, E Ganter, 2016.

38. *Indigenous data sovereignty: toward an agenda*, T Kukutai and J Taylor (eds), 2016.

39. *Teaching 'proper' drinking? Clubs and pubs in Indigenous Australia*, M Brady, 2017.

Centre for Aboriginal Economic Policy Research,
College of Arts and Social Sciences,
The Australian National University, Canberra, ACT, 2601

Information on CAEPR Discussion Papers, Working Papers and Research Monographs (Nos 1–19) and abstracts and summaries of all CAEPR print publications and those published electronically can be found at the following website: caepr.anu.edu.au.